German Army Uniforms & Insignia, 1933—45

German Army Uniforms and Insignia 1933-1945

by Brian L. Davis

Military Book Society

Frontispiece (plate 1) : the German soldier in peace and war. Top left, Army NCOs taking part in a parade held in honour of the Führer's birthday, Berlin, 20th April 1937. Top right, Grenadiers pause for rest during the heavy fighting for the city of Rostov. Centre, presentation of the Knights Cross to the Iron Cross to Feldwebel Mose, 9th April 1943. Below left, in the ring around Sebastopol infantry await the moment for the attack upon the Crimean city. Below right, high ranking officers in Berlin during the early years of the Third Reich. In the foreground, from left to right, are Reichswehrminister Freiherr von Blomberg, Generalfeldmarschall von Mackensen and General der Artillerie von Fritsch.

This edition published by
The Military Book Society,
St. Giles House,
49/50 Poland Street,
London W1A 2LG,
by arrangement with
Arms and Armour Press

This book is respectfully dedicated to Eberhard Hettler, Herbert Knötel, Paul Pietsch and Egon Jantke

Second, revised edition, 1973

Printed in Great Britain

Contents

Preface 6
Introduction 8
The National Emblem of Germany and the
Reich Cockade 10
1: Ranks and Rank Insignia **11**
1.1. German Army ranks: the Active List 11
1.2. The German Army Reserve and Retired
Lists 11
1.3. German Army Ranks, 1933–45.
Introductory notes 12
1.4. German Army Ranks, 1933–45.
Active ranks 13
1.5. German Army Waffenfarbe; its purpose,
origins and use 16
1.6. Basic German Army Waffenfarben, with
details of colour and arm of service 18
1.7. The expansion of the basic German Army
Waffenfarbe system, with details of colours,
formations and designated shoulder strap
insignia 21
1.8. Wehrmachtbeamten Nebenfarbe
(secondary colours) with appropriate branches 22
1.9. Colour section 24
1.10. Shoulder straps 29
1.11. Shoulder strap buttons 31
1.12. Army shoulder strap insignia 31
1.13. Army shoulder strap 'tradition badges'
and élite unit shoulder strap insignia 31
1.14. 'Anwärter' shoulder strap braiding and
regimental shoulder strap colour bars 33
1.15. Slip-on shoulder strap titles and shoulder
strap camouflage covers 34
1.16. Collar and cuff-facing patches 34
1.17. Army collar and cuff rank braiding 35
1.18. Rank chevrons, 1921–45 38
1.19. Rank insignia worn on the jacket of the
Denim Uniform 43
1.20. Insignia of rank used on camouflage and
special combat clothing 43
2: Badges and Insignia **47**
2.1. Army trade and specialist badges 47
2.2. Army proficiency badges 52
2.3. Military Field Police eagle arm badge 54
2.4. Army marksmanship lanyards 54

2.5. Military decorations (badges) awarded to
troops for individual skill at arms under battle
conditions 57
2.6. Army sports vest emblems 59
2.7. Officers' aiguillettes, and those worn by
army adjutants 59
2.8. Gorgets 60
2.9. The Army standard bearer's arm-shield 66
2.10. The Army standard bearer's carrying sash 67
2.11. 'Swallows' nests' 67
2.12. Troddel, Faustriemen and Portepee 70
2.13. German Army cuff-titles 76
2.14. Arm-bands 83
2.15. Red-and-yellow Battle Practice Helmet
Band 86
2.16. Military umpires' white cap band 87
2.17. Tradition badges worn on German Army
head-dress 87
2.18. Official and semi-official Army cap
emblems 90
3: Uniforms—Tunics, Military clothing,
Head-dress and Footwear **93**
3.1. German Army head-dress 93
3.2. Helmet colourings 107
3.3. Helmet coverings 109
3.4. Footwear 114
3.5. The Army Denim Fatigue Uniform 121
3.6. Army issue sports kit 121
3.7. Service Tunic Model 1936 121
3.8. Service Uniform Model 1936, as worn by
non-commissioned officers 123
3.9. Service Uniform for officers 124
3.10. Service Uniform as worn by generals
and above 126
3.11. Field Service Uniform for mountain
troops 126
3.12. Service Tunic Model 1943 127
3.13. The Model 1944 Field Blouse 128
3.14. The M44 Field Blouse worn by generals 131
3.15. The reed-green Denim Field Service
Uniform 131
3.16. Army Bandsmen's Service Uniform with
'Swallows' nests' 132
3.17. Service Uniform for Military Field Police 132

3.18. Service Uniform for Army Field Post personnel   133
3.19. Army Sonderführer Field Service Uniform and insignia   134
3.20. Officers' Old Style 'Reichsheer' Service Tunic   135
3.21. Officers' Old Style White Summer Tunic   135
3.22. Officers' New Style White Summer Tunic   136
3.23. Officers' Piped Field Service Tunic   137
3.24. Field Service Uniform as worn by army clergy   137
3.25. Field-grey Frock Coat as worn by army clergy   138
3.26. Greatcoat for German Army chaplains and field bishops   140
3.27. The German Army Greatcoat, basic styles and variations   140
3.28. The Army Officers' Cloak   148
3.29. Motorcyclist's Waterproof Coat   148
3.30. The Uniform Tunic for other ranks   150
3.31. Special uniform for Infantry Regiment 'Grossdeutschland'   153
3.32. Special greatcoat for the Infantry Regiment 'Grossdeutschland'   153
3.33. Utilisation of the basic German Army Uniform for various forms of dress   153
3.34. The Special Black Panzer Uniform   160
3.35. The reed-green two-piece Panzer Denims   166
3.36. Special field-grey uniform worn by crews of tank destroyer and self-propelled assault gun units   166
3.37. Army Tropical Field Service Uniform   168
3.38. The German Army Shirt   170
3.39. Mountain Troops' sage-green Windjacket   172
3.40. German Army Anoraks   172
3.41. The four-pocket Army Camouflage Field Service Jacket   175
3.42. The lightweight Army Camouflage Smock   175
3.43. The Camouflage Body-Apron   175
3.44. Army Red Cross Medical Attendant's Vests   175
3.45. Camouflage 'string-vests'   176
3.46. Reversible Winter Uniforms   176
3.47. German Army snow camouflage: single and double garments   181
3.48. White and camouflaged face masks   182
3.49. 'Zeltbahn' waterproof shelter triangle   185
4: Personal Equipment   **189**
5: Select Chronology—significant dates relevant to the German military period 1933–1945   **211**
6: Glossary   **213**
6.1. Glossary of Uniforms and Equipment   213
6.2. General Glossary: German/English   214
6.3. General Glossary: English/German   218
7: Bibliography   **223**
7.1. Primary sources   223
7.2. Secondary sources   224

Preface

This book presents the uniforms, insignia and accoutrements of the German army during the period of the Third Reich. It is based on original research and on contemporary records and, it is hoped, provides for the first time a logical basis and system for the study of this important subject in military uniform history.

In the many years which have passed since the end of World War II, and especially during the last ten years, there has been an increasing interest in the technical aspects of the war—both Allied and Axis. The emphasis over the years has shifted from, in general terms, books telling of individual exploits and personal reminiscences to campaign histories and, in the last five years or so, works have commenced to be published dealing with uniforms, equipment and weapons in considerable detail.

There have been two books of note published on German Army uniforms of this period but both appeared before the outbreak of war. In Germany— probably in 1938—Hauptmann Eberhard Hettler, serving in the Reichsluftfahrtsministerium as it was then known, compiled *Uniformen der Deutschen Wermacht: Heer, Kriegsmarine, Luftwaffe* which in collaboration with Herbert Knötel, Paul Pietsch and Egon Jantke set out to illustrate every important aspect of the military uniforms worn in the new German Wehrmacht. However, despite the 1939–40 *Nachtrag* (supplement) the contents covered the subject no further than the uniforms worn during the first year of the war in Europe.

The second work is the well-known *Ranks and Uniforms of the German Army, Navy and Airforce* by Denys Erlam which was based on Hettler's book and published in London in 1939. This book was the only contemporary English language source and has therefore gained a considerable reputation although being long out of print in its original edition. It can, however, now be seen to contain too many translation and printing errors to make it an accurate reference work and, of course, only dealt with the uniform up to the date of publication as well as ignoring several sections of the original Hettler.

Serious students of uniform history may also have studied the contemporary Allied intelligence manuals and handbooks. Although these served an important and necessary wartime function they have considerable drawbacks when taken as sources for accurate data. Such manuals suffered disadvantages in so far as they were based on the gleanings of intelligence work, interrogation of prisoners of war, reports from resistance networks and the scrutiny of neutral and Axis publications. These sources were often inaccurate or in conflict in essential detail, and were naturally always to varying degrees behind in the recognition of new developments. Very few attempts have been made since the war to produce serious studies on German army uniforms and those that have appeared are almost without exception of West German origin. Worthy of particular note are *Feldgrau*, under the original editorship of Friedrich Schirmer and Dr. Fritz Wiener and presently edited by Dr. Kurt-Gerhard Klietmann, and also Dr. Klietmann's own series *Die Deutsche Wehrmacht: Uniform und Ausrüstung 1934–1945*.

German Army Uniforms and Insignia, 1933–1945 is the first postwar attempt of its kind in the English language. It is the first detailed reference supported by full photographic evidence in any language. The text concentrates on the official, or in some cases the accepted, versions of the army uniform together with the related insignia, but it will be apparent from the photographs that the official rules were very often modified to a wide variety of the requirements of individual soldiers or to sometimes meet the special requirements of battle conditions. This book deals only with the regular German Army. It does not cover or include direct reference to any of the special politically motivated para-military units created by the National Socialist régime, and amongst the branches excluded are the Waffen-SS, foreign volunteer and non-German army units, women's auxiliary army formations, German forces engaged in the Spanish Civil War (1936–9), or Volkssturm units raised late in the war.

Many years of interest and research have gone into the preparation of this book. I have had important help and assistance from various archives and institutions. My thanks are due to the Directors and staff of the following for the access I have had to their records and upon which this work is largely based.

British Museum, London
Bundesarchiv, Koblenz
Freiburg Archiv, Freiburg-im-Breslau
Imperial War Museum, London
Institute of Contemporary History, London
La Musée de l'Armée, Bruxelles

My thanks are also offered to the following individuals who kindly gave of their time and knowledge: Christopher Beadle, Rose Coombs, Howard Davies, Winifred Christine Davis, Richard E. Deeter, Tony Froom, Bryan Hunt, William and Ursula Jean Lazard, John and Catherine Lazard, David Littlejohn, Jim Lucas, Dennis Mayne, David Nash, Hans Joachim Nietsch, Hubert Walter and Jensen Winters; figure drawings are by Malcolm McGregor.

Those photographs which are not from the author's collection were kindly supplied by Christopher Beadle, Bundesarchiv, P. Christiansen, Howard Davies, Deutscher Verlag, Euro Foto, Imperial War Museum, Press-Bild-Zentrale, Presse Illustrationen Hoffmann, G. Scherl and United States Army Photos.

Brian L. Davis,
Meadvale, 1971

Introduction

Armies for the preparation of peace do not exist. They exist for triumphant exertion in war. Adolf Hitler

Prewar uniform development:

When Adolf Hitler came to power as Chancellor of the German Nation on 30th January 1933 the National Army of Germany was the Reichsheer, a 'limited' Army of 100,000 troops allowed to Germany by the Treaty of Versailles. The uniform these troops wore was field-grey in colour and was an extension of the first Feld-uniform issued to the Imperial German Army on 15th September 1915.

With the addition of the 'new' National Emblem on the tunic and caps, and the Wehrmachtadler with the black, white and red tricolour on the steel helmet, the uniform of the Reichsheer continued to be used by the German Army for the next three or so years.

In 1936, however, a year after the reintroduction of military conscription, new uniforms were introduced. The army in peacetime provided all its personnel with both a Dress Uniform (Waffenrock) and a Service Uniform (Dienstanzug) which, with the addition of field equipment, also served as a Field Uniform (Feldanzug).

Both these uniform styles were well designed, expertly manufactured with a remarkable degree of standardization and were universally issued and worn throughout the army. There was a very marked emphasis on the retention of traditional features incorporated into these uniforms as well as the accoutrements that were worn with them.

1936 was the year when the first of a number of important orders were set out which introduced new uniform features and—more important still—reintroduced earlier Imperial German Army accoutrements, many of which dated back to before World War I, and which, redesigned, were once again worn on the Army uniform. During the period of the Weimar Republic (1920–1933) various features of the German uniform were discontinued, the intention being to deliberately suppress the glorification of the armed forces, closely linked with the standing army permitted by the Treaty of Versailles. After 1933, however, under the National Socialist régime, the military authorities were responsible for the reintroduction of many Imperial and pre-Imperial features on the uniforms of the 'new' Wehrmacht thus emphasizing that the German soldier was bearing arms in a traditional role and for the

honour of the German people.

Special uniforms were provided for armoured and mountain troops while suitable clothing items were furnished for wear by personnel engaged in various other specialized tasks or on duty in unusual weather conditions.

Economic factors had a great influence on these uniforms owing to anticipated strategic and production conditions. In particular the necessity of stockpiling wool and cotton in anticipation of adverse wartime conditions and shortages caused the Germans to mix about 20% of rayon with the wool of the uniform cloth. So carefully was this material prepared that the resultant clothing suffered little actual loss of thermal efficiency and wearing quality.

With the event of the Anchluss, Austrian troops were absorbed into the German Army. The Austrian Army field-grey uniforms, which dated back to World War I, were modified and, with the use of the German National Emblem and rank insignia, continued to be worn for some time until they were finally replaced with the standard pattern German Army uniforms.

Wartime uniform development:

The prolongation of the war into 1942 and the effective economic blockade brought to bear upon the German Reich resulted in a need for simplification of the field uniform and in the use of poorer quality cloth. By the winter of 1943–4 the average wool content of the field uniform cloth had sunk to approximately 50% with some uniforms dropping as low as 35%; the wool itself was of low quality because it had been reworked.

By 1943 the press of economic conditions resulted in the introduction of a simplified uniform, the Model 1943 Service Uniform and in September 1944 of an entirely new field uniform called the M44 Felduniform. These uniforms were to replace the pattern introduced in 1936 as stocks of the latter became exhausted. They were designed to conserve resources and to permit production by relatively unskilled labour.

Canvas web equipment first used in North Africa gradually began to replace the traditional leather equipment throughout the Army in all theatres of operation, although leather did not by any means disappear altogether.

The Dress Uniform no longer continued to be issued to Army personnel. Its suspension was intended to last for the duration of the war after which, Germany being victorious, it was to have been reissued. No doubt in the light of future developments, manufacturing techniques and new materials it would probably have been redesigned. Use of the Waffenrock during the war was confined to those army officers already owning Dress Uniforms, officer candidate battalions, higher staffs in rear areas, permanent staffs of service schools and similar personnel.

Although it was not generally issued throughout the army, camouflage clothing first introduced in 1942 was worn in increasing numbers and in a variety of forms. Two basic patterns of Army camouflage colouring were used, and towards the last years of the war these were supplemented by the use of camouflage clothing made from stocks of unused Italian Army camouflage material.

Special winter clothing was introduced during the winter of 1942—3 designed specifically to combat the severe sub-zero weather conditions encountered by the German Forces serving on the Eastern Front. For cleaning and repair purposes, as well as replacement with fresh stocks, this winter clothing was collected from the troops in the spring and returned to the east for redistribution during the following autumn.

The Special Field Grey Uniform originally intended for wear by crews of assault gun units and by tank destroyer formations, and first introduced for wear in 1940, quickly became a widespread form of Army clothing. By the end of the war many varied types of German Army formations had been issued with this uniform.

The erroneous statement often quoted implying that there was a deliberate increase in the number and variety of awards, badges and decorations specifically instituted and issued to German troops to compensate for the decrease in the quality of the military uniform is not only misleading and inaccurate but does not stand up to close inspection. The majority of German Army decorations had been designed and instituted before the end of 1942, whereas the severe decline in the quality of the material used in the production of the Army uniforms did not begin until 1943. By 1942 the number of troops serving in the German Army had increased rapidly, the greatest extent of land conquests had been achieved and, until El Alemein and Stalingrad, the army had suffered no major reverses. As the war progressed the number of troops eligible for these established awards also increased, especially as the fighting became more bitter. This in turn led to the need to recognize those troops that had distinguished themselves in continuous combat with the enemy which resulted in the upgrading of certain awards. Seen in this light it would be more correct to say that the apparent relationship between the increase in the number of awards and the decrease in the quality of the uniform material was pure coincidence. With the advantage of hindsight it becomes increasingly apparent that the German Army's uniforms and equipment during the National Socialist period were much in advance of other contemporary nations both in design and manufacture. The German uniforms were of excellent manufacture but with the constant shortage of raw materials in the latter stages of the war new designs of inferior quality had to be produced: the poor material, however, was no reflection on the skill that was used to design these clothes and to also overcome the considerable production obstacles.

Allied propaganda labelled the German uniforms as gaudy and overdecorated when, in fact, they were well designed with inbuilt smartness and practicality. Many of the features introduced during World War II have since influenced the uniforms, head-dress and equipment adopted by other nations.

The National Emblem of Germany and the Reich Cockade

Two important items of insignia appeared on almost all German Army uniforms. These were the National Emblem (das Hoheitszeichen) and the cap cockade (die deutsche Reichskokarde).

The National Emblem was by law worn on the right breast of (most) army jackets and in a smaller version on all army cloth head-dress. The emblem consisted of an eagle, by tradition the National Emblem of Germany, with outstretched wings clutching in its claws a wreath containing a swastika (Hakenkreuz), the emblem of the National Socialist Workers' Party of Germany (NSDAP) which in combination constituted the official emblem of the Third Reich.

The other insignia was the Reich Cockade which was made up of the national colours of Germany— red centre, white (or silver) and black outer. This national cockade was surrounded by a wreath of oakleaves (symbolizing strength) when worn on the Uniform Cap, the black Panzer Beret and on the old style Officers' Field Service Cap. On all other cloth head-dress only the cockade was used.

Many styles and variations in design and colouring of the National Emblem, the Reich Cockade and the oakleaf surround existed and these will be noted in the various plates where they are clearly shown being worn.

The National Socialist style and new colours laid down for the Reichskokarde and steel helmet transfers were introduced by order dated 15th March 1933 and instructions for the wearing of all forms of the new National Emblem on military uniforms were issued on 30th October 1935.

2. *Although wide variations in quality and colour existed in these insignia, those illustrated here are the metal-type National Emblem (i) and Oakleaf wreath with Cockade (ii) normally worn on the Army Schirmmütze and the cloth version of the National Emblem (iii) worn over the right breast of the Army tunic.*

1. Ranks and Rank Insignia

1.1. German Army ranks: the Active List

1.1(1). *Non-commissioned officers and men.* The men on the German Army Active List comprising 'the ranks' were of two distinct types: those who were conscripted into the Army for the purpose of performing their military service, and enlisted men who had voluntarily signed on for a given period of years.

Non-commissioned officers known from the rank of Obergefreiter to Unterfeldwebel as Unteroffiziere ohne Portepee, and from Feldwebel onwards as Unteroffiziere mit Portepee were appointed to their ranks in the accepted way both in peacetime and during the war, but with strong emphasis laid on the amount of service fulfilled by any applicant for promotion.

1.1(2). *The German Army rank of 'Fähnrich'.* Persons holding the rank title of Fähnrich served in the ranks of the German Army first as a junior NCO and then in the subsequent grades equivalent to Unterfeldwebel, Feldwebel and Oberfeldwebel. An officer in the making, the German rank of Fähnrich had—and still has—no equivalent rank in the British Army, although the French forces had a parallel rank known as 'Aspirant'.

An Oberfähnrich was afforded the special distinction of being allowed to wear officers' silver cap cords to his NCO Uniform cap and to wear the silver Portepee which was normally only granted to officers and Hauptfeldwebel or Stabsfeldwebel.

The word Fähnrich was derived from the old German military title of Fahnenträger, and only became a distinct military rank by the Allerhöchsste Kabinetts-Ordre (A.K.O.) of 1st January 1899.

1.1(3). *Officers.* German Army officers were divided into two main groups: regular serving officers, and officers who had been recalled for service, who were known as Ergänzungs officers. An Ergänzungs officer, although a regular commissioned officer, had been retired and subsequently recalled for further military service. There was no difference in the uniform or uniform detail worn by this class of officer except when they were attached to the High Command when as Ergänzungs officers they did not wear the special High Command distinctions to their military uniforms. They were not subject to the general regulations relating to promotion.

1.1(4). *Administrative officials or 'Wehrmachtbeamten' of the German Army.* Officials employed in the various German ministries and government departments connected with the armed services were uniformed and given special Beamten ranks.

A Wehrmachtbeamter in the army was not necessarily a regular officer or non-commissioned officer of the army but could be a person who, because of a specialist knowledge, was employed as an official within the structure of the army. As complete a list as possible of the multitude of German Army Beamten ranks with the corresponding English equivalent ministerial positions can be found on page 14.

So definite a distinction was drawn between these officials, who although included in the Wehrmacht were regarded as separate from the army proper, that when a soldier was appointed to a position as a Wehrmachtbeamter he was obliged to resign from the active list first—although he was permitted to remain on the reserve.

1.2. The German Army Reserve and Retired Lists

1.2(1). *Officers listed as 'a.D.', 'z.V' and 'z.D'.* With the exception of regimental 'Chef', army officers who retired from the regular Active-Duty Roster were either declared unavailable for further duty, in which case they were listed as 'a.D.' (ausser Dienst—out of service), or, if subject to recall to duty as 'z.V.' (zur Verfügung—available for duty or at disposal). When 'z.V.' officers were detailed for duty they became 'z.D.' (for Disposition) and they were then subject to the same rules relating to uniforms as Ergänzungs officers were.

1.2(2). *Charakterisiet rank.* Occasionally, but not always, on retirement from active duty or to meet some special situation army generals and senior army officers were given a form of 'brevet' rank in which case their titles of rank were preceded by the word Charakterisiert (literally 'in the character of') commonly abbreviated as 'Char'. These officers wore the insignia of their Charakterisiert rank but remained junior on the rank list to all those who held the same rank without this prefix.

Von Kleist was promoted from Oberst to Char.

Generalmajor on 1st January 1932 when he was promoted over several senior Obersten and given command of the 2.Kavallerie-Division stationed at Breslau. Generals Beck, Chief of the General Staff, and Adam, of the Armed Forces Academy were both given the Charakterisiert rank of Generaloberst when they retired at the end of 1938.

1.2(3). *Beurlaubenstand. Officers of 'd.R.' and 'd.L.' status.* German Army officers and men of the Beurlaubtenstand (of reserve status) corresponded to some extent to the British Army reserve. They were indistinguishable from regular army personnel but on official correspondence were permitted to use the prefix 'd.R.' (der Reserve) or 'd.L.' (der Landwehr).

1.2(4). *The honorary rank of regimental 'Chef'.* The army rank of regimental 'Chef' was first introduced by the Führer when in April 1936 he bestowed the title of Chef der 67.Infanterie-Regiment on the ageing von Seeckt. Although it was an honorary rank persons on whom this title was conferred were listed as if on active duty. Altogether there were six German general officers holding this rank of regimental Chef in the German Army.

The uniform worn by these Chefs of regiments was that of a regular officer of his own rank. Generalfeldmarschall von Rundstedt favoured wearing infantry officer's parade quality collar patches on his Service Uniform with, at the same time, his shoulder straps for the rank of Generalfeldmarshall with their crossed batons plus the number '18' indicating his connexion with the 18.Infanterie-Regiment (plate 3).

In the table of ranks on pages 13-14 will be found all active military ranks that could be held in the German Army; not all of these ranks have an exact English equivalent and in some cases an approximation has been made.

1.3. German Army Ranks, 1933-45.
Introductory notes

1.3(1). *The army rank of Grenadier.* By a special order of November 1942, in which Hitler revived the tradition of Frederick the Great, all German infantry regiments, with the exception of mountain regiments (Gebirgsjäger-Regimenter) and rifle troop battalions (Jäger-Bataillonen) were in future to be known as 'Grenadier-Regimenter' Hitler had previously decreed that infantry regiments of armoured divisions should be called 'Panzer-Grenadier'.

These changes meant that a private soldier—a Schütze—was in future called a Grenadier, and that a Panzerschütze was to be called a Panzer-Grenadier.

1.3(2). *Comparison of certain infantry and cavalry ranks.* It should also be noted that certain rank designations used in the German cavalry and artillery differed from the equivalent rank used by other arms of the German Army. The rank of Feldwebel in the infantry was replaced by Wachtmeister for the cavalry and artillery (this was also the case for police units). Again a Hauptmann in the signals, for instance, would have been a Rittmeister in the cavalry.

3. *Generalfeldmarschall Gerd von Rundstedt, 'Chef' of Infanterie-Regiment 18. This photo shows the dress uniform style collar patches normally used by army officers below the rank of General being worn in combination with shoulder straps for a General Field Marshal. The shoulder straps show the wearer's rank as well as the number of the regiment (18) to which the wearer was honorary 'Chef'. The collar patches, on a backing of appropriate Waffenfarbe cloth, emphasized the wearer's honorary rank of Regimental 'Chef'.*

1.3(3). *The correct form of address for an Army General.* The rank of General was formally given with the bearer's branch of service as, for example, General der Artillerie or General der Pioniere, etc.

1.3(4). *The rank of Generalfeldmarschall.* The rank of Generalfeldmarschall was first used in the new Wehrmacht when Hitler reintroduced the title and conferred the rank on Generaloberst von Blomberg on 20th April 1936. However owing to the scandal created 21 months later which erupted over his marriage, Blomberg's name was stricken from the Army Rolls in January 1938 and was never again carried in the rank lists. This meant that, at the beginning of World War II and up to August 1940, there was no German officer holding the rank of Generalfeldmarschall; after August 1940 nine Generalfeldmarschälle were newly promoted.

1.4. German Army Ranks, 1933-45.
Active ranks
1.4(1). *German Army rank terms with British Army equivalent ranks*

German Army rank term/British Army equivalent rank[1]

MANNSCHAFTEN: MEN
Schütze   Private, infantry
Grenadier[2]   Private, infantry
Fusilier[3]   Private, infantry
Musketier[4]   Private, infantry
Jäger   Private in a rifle battalion or mountain regiment

Reiter   Trooper, cavalry
Kanonier   Gunner
Panzerschütze   Tank crew member
Panzergrenadier   Infantry private, armoured unit
Pionier   Sapper
Funker   Signaller
Fahrer   Driver, horse-drawn vehicles
Kraftsfahrer   Driver, mechanized
Musikerschütze   Musician
Trompeterreiter   Cavalry trumpeter
Sanitätssoldat   Medical orderly
Beschlagschmiedschütze   Farrier
Beschlagschmiedreiter   Cavalry farrier
Oberschütze   Senior private
Oberreiter   Senior trooper
Oberkanonier   Senior gunner
Panzeroberschütze   Senior tank crew member
Oberpanzergrenadier   Senior infantry soldier with armoured unit

4. *Generalfeldmarschall Wilhelm Keitel, Chief of the German High Command. Clearly shown here are the standard pattern collar patches for a Generalfeldmarschall worn together with the normal shoulder straps for the rank.*

German Army rank term/British Army equivalent rank[1]

Oberpionier Senior sapper
Oberfunker Senior signaller
Oberkraftfahrer Senior driver, mechanized units
Oberfahrer Senior driver, horse drawn vehicles
Musikoberschütze Senior musician
Trompeteroberreiter Senior cavalry trumpeter
Sanitätsobersoldat Senior medical attendant
Beschlagschmiedoberschütze Senior farrier
Beschlagschmiedoberreiter Senior cavalry farrier
Gefreiter Lance-corporal
Fahnenjunker-Gefreiter Cadet lance-corporal[1]
Sanitätsgefreiter Lance-corporal, medical troops
Beschlagschmiedgefreiter Farrier lance-corporal
Obergefreiter Corporal
Beschlagschmiedobergefreiter Farrier corporal
Sanitätsobergefreiter Corporal, medical troops
Stabsgefreiter Senior staff corporal[1]

UNTEROFFIZIER OHNE PORTEPEE: JUNIOR NCOs
Unteroffizier Lance-sergeant
Fahnenjunker-Unteroffizier Cadet lance-sergeant
Sanitätsunteroffizier Medical lance-sergeant
Beschlagschmiedunteroffizier Farrier lance-sergeant
Unterfeldwebel Sergeant, in the infantry, sappers, armoured units, mechanized supply units, and smoke troops
Unterwachtmeister Sergeant, in the cavalry, artillery, signals and horse-drawn supply troops
Sanitätsunterfeldwebel Medical segeant
Beschlagschmiedunterwachtmeister Farrier sergeant, cavalry
Fähnrich Ensign

UNTEROFFIZIER MIT PORTEPEE: SENIOR NCOs
Feldwebel Company sergeant-major
Wachtmeister Sergeant-major, cavalry
Sanitätsfeldwebel Medical segeant-major
Beschlagmeister Farrier sergeant-major
Feuerwerker Ordnance segeant-major
Wallfeldwebel Fortifications sergeant-major
Festungspionierfeldwebel Fortress engineer sergeant-major
Funkmeister Signals sergeant-major
Brieftaubenmeister Sergeant-major, carrier pigeons
Schirrmeister Saddler sergeant-major
Oberfeldwebel Battalion sergeant-major
Oberwachtmeister Squadron sergeant-major
Oberfähnrich Senior ensign
Sanitätsoberfeldwebel Battalion sergeant-major, medical troops
Oberbeschlagmeister Battalion farrier sergeant-major
Oberfeuerwerker Battalion ordnance sergeant-major
Walloberfeldwebel Fortifications battalion sergeant-major
Festungspioniereroberfeldwebel Fortress engineer battalion sergeant-major
Oberfunkmeister Battalion sergeant-major, signals
Oberbrieftaubenmeister Battalion sergeant-major, messenger pigeons
Oberschirrmeister Battalion saddler sergeant-major
Hauptfeldwebel Regimental sergeant-major
Hauptwachtmeister Regimental sergeant-major, cavalry
Stabsfeldwebel Staff sergeant-major
Stabswachtmeister Staff sergeant-major, cavalry
Sanitätsstabsfeldwebel Staff sergeant-major, medical troops
Stabsbeschlagmeister Farrier staff sergeant-major
Stabsfeuerwerker Ordnance staff sergeant-major
Wallstabsfeldwebel Fortifications staff sergeant-major
Festungspionierstabfeldwebel Fortress engineer staff sergeant-major
Stabsfunkmeister Staff master wireless operator
Stabsbrieftaubenmeister Staff master carrier pigeon handler
Stabschirrmeister Staff master saddler

Hufbeschlaglehrmeister Farrier instruction master
Festungswerkmeister Fortress construction master
Oberhufbeschlaglehrmeister Senior farrier instruction master
Festungsoberwerkmeister Senior fortress construction master

LEUTNANTE: LIEUTENANTS
Leutnant Second lieutenant
Assistenzarzt Second lieutenant, Medical Corps
Veterinär Veterinary second lieutenant
Musikmeister Director of Music, second lieutenant[5]
Oberleutnant Lieutenant
Oberarzt Medical lieutenant
Oberveterinär Veterinary lieutenant
Obermusikmeister Director of Music, lieutenant[5]

HAPTLEUTE: CAPTAINS
Hauptmann Captain, infantry
Rittmeister Captain in the cavalry and horse-drawn supply units
Stabsarzt Captain, Medical Corps
Stabsveterinär Captain, Veterinary Corps
Stabsmusikmeister Director of Music, captain[5]

STABSOFFIZIERE: FIELD OFFICERS
Major Major
Oberstabsarzt Major, Medical Corps
Musikinspizient Inspector of Music[5]
Oberstabsveterinär Major, Veterinary Corps
Oberstleutnant Lieutenant-colonel
Oberfeldarzt Lieutenant-colonel, medical troops
Oberfeldveterinär Veterinary lieutenant-colonel
Obermusikinspizient Senior Inspector of Music[5]
Oberst Colonel
Oberstarzt Medical colonel
Oberstveterinär Veterinary colonel

GENERÄLE: GENERALS
Generalmajor Major-general
Generalarzt Medical general
Generalveterinär Veterinary general
Generalleutnant Lieutenant-general
Generalstabsarzt Deputy-general, medical services
Generalstabsveterinär Deputy-general, Army Veterinary Department
General der Infanterie General of infantry
General der Kavallerie General of cavalry
General der Artillerie General of artillery
General der Pioniere General of engineers (sappers)
General der Panzertruppen General of Armoured troops
General der Gebirgstruppen General of mountain troops
Generaloberstabsarzt Colonel-general, head of the medical services
Generaloberstabsveterinär Colonel-general, head of the veterinary services
Generaloberst Colonel-general
Generalfeldmarschall General field-marshal

---

[1] As a basic point of reference, English rank equivalents are used here; however, certain equivalents do not exist in the British Army, e.g. ranks from Oberfeldwebel to Oberschirrmeister where the British Army equivalents are given as 'Battalion sergeants major' etc. There is no such rank in the British Army—but if there were this would be the nearest possible translation.
[2] For information on the rank of 'Grenadier' see the passage headed German Army Ranks—1933 to 1945, which deals with the introduction of this 'new' title in November 1942.
[3] An infantry private from an army unit designated as or honoured with the title of 'Fusilier'.
[4] Another 'new' title introduced for use by certain infantry personnel within the Panzer Korps 'Grossdeutschland'.
[5] Personnel holding these ranks Musikmeister to Obermusikinspizient were not officers but were specialist soldiers with officers' rank. They wore the uniforms of an army officer with special insignia.

1.4(2). *German Army Wehrmachtbeamten ranks, 1933–1945*

Wehrmachtbeamten rank term[1]/English equivalent Ministerial position

ARMY ADMINISTRATION OFFICIALS HOLDING POSITIONS EQUIVALENT TO GENERAL CLASS ARMY OFFICER RANKS

Generalstabintendant General Staff commissariat commander
Generalintendant General commissariat commander
Heeresintendant Army commissary
Ministerialdirektor A minister, head of a ministry
Oberreichskriegsanwalt Judge Advocate General
Senatspräsident President of a court martial
Ministerialdirigent Administrative official, usually of lieutenant-general rank
Gruppenintendant Army Group commissariat commander
Korpsintendant Army Corps commissariat commander
Ministerialrat (mit den Dienstgradeabzeichen des Generales) Ministerial advisor with the rank of general
Oberreichskriegsanwalt Senior attorney in the War Office
Senatspräsident beim Reichskriegsgericht President of a court martial
Reichskriegsgerichtsrat Army court martial councillor
Präsident des Heeresarchivs Wien President of the Army Archives at Vienna
Feldbischof Chaplain-General to the Forces
Präsident President
Vorstand der Heeres-Plankammer Head of the Army Chamber of Planning

ADMINISTRATION OFFICIALS HOLDING POSITIONS EQUIVALENT TO 'STABSOFFIZIERE' (FIELD OFFICER) CLASS ARMY OFFICER RANKS

Abteilungschef im Reichskriegs-Ministerium Departmental head in the War Office
Ministerialrat Ministry advisor
Intendant Commissary
Direktor Director
Oberintendanturrat Lieutenant-colonel in commissariat
Intendanturrat Major in commissariat
Obermusikinspizient Senior Director of Music
Heeresmusikinspizient Director of Army Music
Ministerialbürodirektor Ministerial administration official, with the rank of lieutenant-colonel
Amtsrat Senior administration official, with the rank of major
Oberfeldzahlmeister Senior paymaster
Intendanturamtmann Member of an army commissary department
Oberstabzahlmeister Senior paymaster, with the rank of lieutenant-colonel or major
Oberstkriegsgerichtsrat Colonel on court martial committee
Oberkriegsgerichtsrat Lieutenant-colonel on court martial committee
Kriegsgerichtsrat Major on court martial committee
Heeresjustizamtmann Major in the army judicial service
Bibliothekar Librarian
Oberregierungsrat Senior administration official, with rank of lieutenant-colonel
Regierungsrat Administration official with the rank of major
Vermessungsamtmann Survey official with the rank of major
Oberregierungsbaurat Construction or building administration official with the rank of lieutenant-colonel
Regierungsbaurat Construction or building administration official with the rank of major
Technischer Oberamtsmann Technical administration official with the rank of major
Verwaltungsamtmann Administration official with the rank of major
Oberregierungschemiker Chemistry administration official,
with the rank of lieutenant-colonel
Regierungschemiker Chemistry administration official, with the rank of major
Oberstapotheker Apothecary colonel
Oberfeldapotheker Apothecary lieutenant-colonel
Oberstabsapotheker Apothecary major
Direktor bei der Heeresplan-kammer Director of the Army Chamber of Planning
Direktor des Heerestechnischen Büros Director of the Army Technical Bureau
Heeresarchivdirektor Army Archive Director
Direktor bei der Heeresfeuerwerker und Panzertruppenschule Director of the Army Ordnance and Panzer (Armoured) Troop Schools
Heeresmaschinenbaudirektor Director of Army Construction Machinery
Heeresbaudirektor Director of Army Building or Construction
Direktor beim Heeresarchiv Wien Director of Army Archives at Vienna
Direktor beim Heeresmuseum Berlin-Zeughaus Director of the Army Museum at Berlin-Zeughaus
Regierungsdirektor (Museum Wien) Administration Director of Vienna Museum
Wehrmachtdekan Senior chaplain to the forces, Army dean
Wehrmachtoberpfarrer Senior chaplain to the forces
Wehrmachtpfarrer Chaplain to the forces
Heeresoberpfarrer Senior army chaplain
Heerespfarrer Army chaplain
Heeresoberforstmeister Senior army forestry commissioner
Heeresforstmeister Army forestry commissioner
Heeresforstamtsmann Administration official in Army Forestry Commission
Oberstudiendirektor Army education official with the rank of colonel
Studiendirektor Army education official with the rank of lieutenant-colonel
Studienrat Army education official with the rank of captain
Oberfachschulrat Principal in a technical school with the rank of lieutenant-colonel
Fachschulrektor Assistant principal in a technical school with the rank of captain
Oberfachstudiendirektor Director of Technical Studies with the rank of colonel
Fachstudiendirektor Deputy Director of Technical Studies with the rank of lieutenant-colonel
Fachstudienrat Instructor in Technical Studies with the rank of major
Oberlandwirtschaftsrat Agricultural advisor with the rank of lieutenant-colonel
Heereslandwirtschaftrat Councillor in the Army Agricultural Department
Heeressportlehrer Army sports instructor
Oberheeresarchivrat Army archival advisor holding the rank of lieutenant-colonel
Heeresarchivrat Army archival advisor holding the rank of major

ADMINISTRATION OFFICIALS HOLDING POSITIONS EQUIVALENT TO THE REMAINING ARMY OFFICER RANKS CLASSED AS 'HAUPTLEUTE' AND 'LEUTNANTE'

Kriegsrichter Judge Advocate General Branch holding the rank of captain
Stabsapotheker Chemist with the rank of captain
Intendanturassessor Officer in the commissary department, with the rank of captain
Assessor (technische und nichttechnische) Official on probation with the rank of captain
Stabzahlmeister Paymaster with the rank of captain
Oberzahlmeister Paymaster with the rank of lieutenant
Zahlmeister Paymaster with the rank of second-lieutenant
Oberinspektor und Inspektor der verschiedenen Laufbahnen (technische und nichttechnische) Officials graded as lieutenants and second-lieutenants with various technical and non-technical trades

Wehrmachtbeamten rank term/English equivalent
Ministerial position [1]

Ministerialkanzleivorsteher Administration official; head
clerk with the rank of captain
Kanzleivorsteher Orderly Room: head clerk holding the
rank of lieutenant
Ministerialregistrator Ministry registrar
Obertrigonometer Senior trigonometric official
Trigonometer Trigonometric official
Waffenoberrevisor Senior armament official
Waffenrevisor Armament official
Oberwaffenmeister Senior armourer
Waffenmeister Armourer
Betriebsmeister Managerial works supervisor
Betriebsleiter Works managerial leader
Oberwerkmeister Senior workshop supervisor
Heeresoberförster Army forester of senior rank
Heeresrevierförster Army forestry official
Heeresförster Army forester
Fachschulrektor Headmaster of a technical school
Oberfachschullehrer Teacher in an advanced technical
school
Gewerbeoberlehrer Senior teacher in trade subjects
Handelsoberlehrer Senior teacher in commercial subjects
Lehrer Teacher
Fachlehrer Instructor official of professional studies
*Obersekretär und Sekretär der verschiedenen Laufbahnen
(technische und nichttechnische)* Senior secretary and
secretary of various grades, both technical and non-
technical
Heeresschneidermeister Army master tailor
Heeresschuhmachermeister Army master shoemaker/
cobbler
Heeresmaschinenmeister Army master machinist/
mechanic
Heeressattlermeister Army master saddler
Korpssattlermeister Army corps master saddler
Heereshauptwerkmeister Army workshop superintendent,
holding the rank of captain
Heeresoberwerkmeister Army workshop superintendent,
holding the rank of lieutenant
Werkstättenvorsteher A commissioned rank in charge of a
workshop
Wallmeister Fortification official with the rank of lieutenant
Oberkartograph Senior cartographer with the rank of
captain
Kartograph Cartographer with the rank of lieutenant
Lithograph Lithographer with the rank of lieutenant
Photograph Photographer with the rank of lieutenant

ADMINISTRATION OFFICIALS HOLDING POSITIONS EQUIVALENT TO THOSE ARMY RANKS CLASSED AS 'UNTEROFFIZIER MIT PORTEPEE' AND 'UNTEROFFIZIER OHNE PORTEPEE'

Werkführer Foreman
Mühlenmeister Master miller
Bäckermeister Master baker
Regimentssattlermeister Regimental master saddler
Oberfuttermeister Senior fodder sergeant
Futtermeister Fodder sergeant
Festungsoberwerkmeister Fortifications NCO in charge of
a workshop
Festungswerkmeister Fortifications NCO in a workshop
Heereswerkmeister NCO in charge of an army workshop
Präparator Candidate
Magazinmeister NCO in charge of a depot
Oberbotenmeister Senior messenger
Botenmeister Messenger
Oberlagermeister Senior sergeant in a store
Lagermeister Sergeant in a store
Ministerialoberamtsgehilfe Senior administration clerical
official in a ministry
Ministerialamtsgehilfe Administration clerical official in a
ministry

Amtsobergehilfe Senior Administration clerical official in a
department
Amtsgehilfe Administration clerical official in a department
Heeresunterförster Army forester
Obermaschinist Senior fitter
Drucker Printer
Laborant Laboratory technician
Reichskriegsgerichtswachtmeister State judicial service
orderly sergeant
Heeresjustizwachtmeister Army court martial orderly
sergeant
Heizer Fireman
Hauswarte Caretaker
Lagerwarte Storeman
Wächter Watchman
Arbeiter Labourer

---

[1] Wehrmachtbeamten ranks or titles were normally preceded by a
noun indicating the importance of the post; thus:
Stadt Baurat: member of a town building council.
Kreis Baurat: member of a rural area building council.
Landes Baurat: member of a state or county building council.
Staats Baurat: member of a national building council.
Regierungs Baurat: member of a governmental building council.
The use of the word Ober where it precedes Stab indicated someone
with a rank higher than a major, so that 'Stab' = major, 'Oberst' =
lieutenant-colonel and 'Hauptstab' = colonel.
'Heeres' indicated the highest rank before the rank of 'Ministerial',
and the title 'Assessor' was used for an applicant on probation for
higher service after having passed the required professional
examinations.

1.5. German Army Waffenfarbe; its purpose, origins and use

The word Waffenfarbe, literally translated means 'arm
(of service) colour'; 'Waffen' being short for Waffengattung which is 'arm of service' and 'Farbe' meaning
'colour'.

Under the Third Reich military system certain
selected colours were employed in the design of
German military uniforms (such as uniform and cap
piping) and military accoutrements (such as background colouring to certain regalia) by all arms of the
army as a methodical, if colourful, means of identification.

This was not an innovation peculiar to this period.
Colours used for identification purposes had been
incorporated into the design of German military
uniforms since 1870, the Prussians having adopted a
system of piped shoulder-straps as far back as 1835
However these early colours cannot be strictly considered as Waffenfarbe as they did not indicate any
arms of service but instead tended to represent various
other types of classification.

At the outbreak of World War I, with the exception
of Cavalry and certain technical troops, a system of
coloured piping which included shoulder strap piping
was used by the Imperial German Army to distinguish
various German army corps.

It was not until 15th September 1915 that Waffenfarbe in the accepted sense was first introduced when
new dress regulations were issued throughout the
Imperial Army which for the first time laid down certain
basic colours for use by definite arms. It should be
noted, however, that the Imperial authorities of the
time were aware that certain colours had been histori-
cally associated with particular formations and they
acknowledged this by perpetuating these colours in

5. *A Schütze from the 3rd Machine-gun unit.*

6. *Army Musikmeister.*

7. *A member of an Army Engineer Instruction unit.*

8. *A Kanonier from Artillerie-Regiment 59.*

the newly introduced Waffenfarben.

This logical identification practice was continued throughout the remainder of World War I, carried over into the Reichsheer and continued to be used in the army of the Third Reich. During this later period it was perfected into a highly complex colour identification system which combined with the use of shoulder strap insignia covered every arm of service, military organization, formation and unit possessed by Germany during that period.

Since September 1915 the conception of Waffenfarbe as identification colouring for definite arms of service had remained constant. What changed and altered over the years to varying degrees were the colours employed for this purpose and, to a lesser extent, where they were to be found or displayed on military uniforms and military accoutrements.

On page 18 will be found a list of 'basic' German Army Waffenfarben. As the expansion and development of the German Army took place new colours were introduced for new arms, existing colours were extended to new types of formations, certain colours were dropped when some types of units ceased to

exist and, in a number of instances, certain formations and organizations were given completely new colours.

The German military shoulder-strap of the Third Reich period was the main and most important means of displaying this colour system.[1] Waffenfarbe incorporated into the design of the Army uniform varied from the type of uniform to the period when the uniform was manufactured. No matter how desperate the position was with the amount of material available for the manufacture of uniforms, and even when all unnecessary additions were being dropped to conserve material and skilled labour, the German shoulder strap constantly showed Waffenfarben.

1.6. Basic German Army Waffenfarbe, with details of colours and arms of service

Generally the 'basic' German Army Waffenfarben allotted to arms of service or groups of military personnel, as opposed to specific military units was as follows:

[1] See footnote on page 29 concerning early pattern unpiped shoulder straps.

9. *A Wachtmeister from the 667th Assault Gun unit.*

10. *German Army Sonderführer.*

Colour/Arm of service

Carmine (Karmesin)   General staff officers of the German High Command, Veterinary Corps other than veterinary generals

Bright red (Hochrot)   Personnel of artillery units, generals of all arms including medical and veterinary generals

White (Weiss)   Infantry

Gold yellow (Goldgelb)   Cavalry

Lemon yellow (Zitronengelb)   Signals

Light brown (Hellbraun)   Also signals, used at different times

Rose pink (Rosa)   Armoured troops

Light green (Hellgrün)   Rifle battalions and Mountain Rifle regiments

Bordeaux red (Bordorot)   Smoke troops[1]

Cornflower blue (Kornblumenblau)[2]   Medical personnel other than medical generals

Light blue (Hellblau)   Mechanized supply troops

Black (Schwarz)   Engineers

Orange (Orangerot)   Personnel of recruiting offices

Dark green (Dunkelgrün)   Administrative officials (Wehrmachtbeamten) plus a secondary colour; for the full range of these secondary colours (nebenfarbe) see page 22

These basic colours were utilised by many new, and in some cases subdivided old, military formations, organizations and units. The increase in the number of specified units appointed to wear these and new colours grew rapidly from *c.* 1936 and only declined after 1943. However each unit, formation or organization thus appointed was almost always instructed to wear their Waffenfarbe in conjunction with a distinctive shoulder strap insignia. This took the form either of a letter, a number or a device—or even a combination of two or all of these. A comprehensive list of those specified units allotted particular colours plus the designated shoulder strap insignia is given later. The reader's attention is also drawn to the section dealing with shoulder strap insignia.

---

[1] The designation 'Smoke Troops' was a camouflage name first used during the Reichswehr period when under the Versailles Treaty Germany was forbidden to have armour and armour-piercing weapons but was allowed non-toxic smoke screen equipment. This led to the development of a large calibre smokescreen projector with a rapid rate of fire. During World War II these smokescreen weapons were developed as mortar and rocket weapons firing highly destructive missiles and the 'smoke troops' were employed in manning these Nebelwerfer regiments. The old name of 'Smoke Troops' survived throughout the war and its use was encouraged for reasons of security.

[2] Cornflower blue is dark blue. The Cornflower is the National Flower of Prussia.

German Army shoulder straps and shoulder strap insignia.
11. Oberstleutnant, Gebirgsjäger 4 Divisional Staff. Light green Waffenfarbe. 12. Major, Ordnance Technician School (circa 1938). Bright red Waffenfarbe. 13. Major, Military Justice. Bordeaux red Waffenfarbe. 14. Hauptmann, Supply officer. Cornflower blue Waffenfarbe. 15. Oberleutnant, Panzer-Regiment 4. Rose pink Waffenfarbe. 16. Leutnant, Smoke Troop School. Bordeaux red Waffenfarbe. 17. Leutnant, 3rd Army Group Command. White Waffenfarbe. 18. Leutnant, Medical officer. Cornflower blue Waffenfarbe.

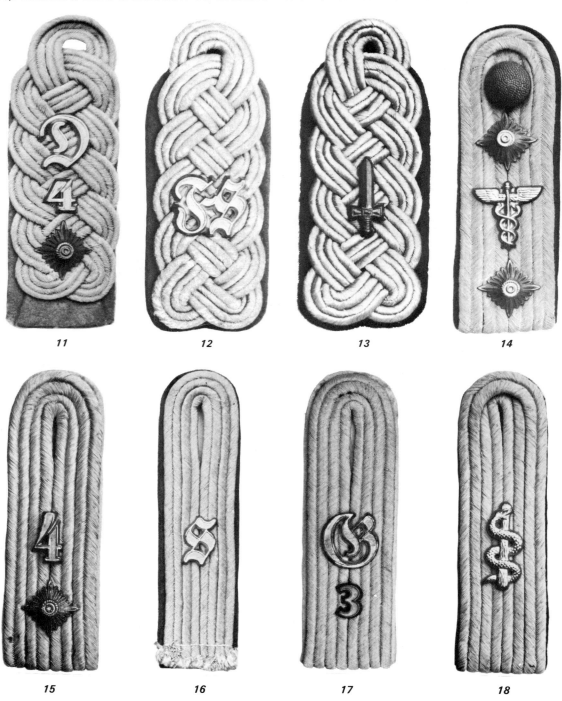

11   12   13   14

15   16   17   18

1.7. The expansion of the basic German Army Waffenfarbe system, with details of colours, formations and designated shoulder strap insignia[1]

[1]This list is intended primarily to show the full 'expanded' range of Waffenfarbe whilst giving some idea of the complexity of the units appointed to use these colours with (in order to be separately identifiable) the type of shoulder strap insignia used by these units.

Colour	Arm of Service	Shoulder strap insignia
Carmine	Officers of the O.K.W. and O.K.H.	None
(Karmesin)	War Academy	'KA'
	Veterinary officers and NCOs	Snake
	Veterinary troops	Number of unit
	Veterinary research and inspection department	Wehrkreis number in Roman style
	Army Veterinary Academy	Gothic 'A'
	Veterinary training and research	Gothic 'L'
Bright Red	Generals	None
(Hochrot)	Artillery regiments	Number of unit
	Mounted artillery units	'R' with unit number below
	Artillery observation units	'B' with unit number below
	Artillery School	Gothic 'S'
	Artillery NCOs School	'US' plus initial letter of the school
	Artillery training regiments	'L'
	Artillery observation training regiments	'BL' entwined
	Ordnance Technician School	'FS' and Arabic numeral I or II
	School for Artificers	'WS' and Arabic numeral I or II
	Experimental command Hillesleben	'VH'
	Experimental command Kummersdorf	'VK'
	Individual officers (W)	2 crossed cannon
	Army Ordnance Director	None
Colour of unit	Bandmasters	Lyre with unit number below
White	Army map and military survey personnel	'V'
(Weiss)	Recruiting office personnel	'W' plus Roman Wehrkreis no below (1942–)
	Army group command	'G' with Group number below
	General command	Roman number of command
	Infantry divisional staff	'D' and divisional number below
	Infantry regiments	Number of unit
	Infantry regiment 'Grossdeutschland'	'GD'
	Garrison Battalion Vienna	Roman 'W'
	Machine-gun battalions	'M' with unit number below
	Motorcycle units	'K' with unit number below
	Mortar battalions	'GW'
	Army antiaircraft units	'Fl'
	Infantry training regiments	'L'
	NCOs and men of the Staff of the Military Authority of the Reichsprotektor	'WB'
	War College	'KS' plus letter of school
	NCOs' Preparatory School	Roman Wehrkreis number
	NCOs' schools	'US' with initial letter of school
	Infantry School	Gothic 'S'
	Army Sports School	Gothic 'SS'
	Army School of Music	Lyre plus Arabic number of the school[1]
Gold yellow	Cavalry units	Number of unit
(Goldgelb)	Reconnaissance, mounted	'A' with unit number below
	Motorcycle units	'R' with unit number below
	Army Cavalry School	'RS'
	Cavalry Schools	Gothic 'S'
	Military District Cavalry Schools	Roman number of Wehrkreis
	Light division staff	'D' and divisional number below
Lemon yellow	Signals units	Number of unit
(Zitronengelb)	Fortress signals	'Fp' with unit number below
	Signals training regiments	'L'
	Signals Schools	Gothic 'S' with Arabic number
	Signals NCOs' School	'US' plus initial letter of the school
	Army School of Dog and Carrier Pigeon Services	Gothic 'S' with 'HB' below
Copper brown	Reconnaissance, motorized	'A' with unit number below
(Kupferbraun)	Motorcycle units	Number of unit
Rose pink	General armoured commands	Roman number of command
(Rosa)	Armoured division staff	'D' and divisional number below
	Rifle brigade staff	Number of unit
	Armoured units	Number of unit
	Anti-tank units	'P' with unit number below
	Armoured trains	'E' with unit number below
	Motorcycle units	'K' with unit number below
	Armoured training regiments	'L'
	Armour Schools	Gothic 'S'

Colour	Arm of Service	Shoulder strap insignia
	Army School of Motoring	'MS'
	Motor maintenance troops	'J'
Light green (*Hellgrün*)	Mountain troop divisional staff	'D' with divisional number below
	Rifle and mountaineering units	Number of unit
	Alpine and Mountain Troops' School	Gothic 'S'
Grass green (*Wiesengrün*)	Motorcycle units	'K' with unit number below
	Armoured infantry regiments	Number of unit
Bordeaux red (*Bordorot*)	Smoke units	Number of unit
	Smoke training units	'L'
	Army Gas School	Gothic 'S'
	Smoke Troop School	Gothic 'S'
	Army Gas Defence School	'GS' with I or II below
	Military justice	A short sword
Cornflower blue (*Kornblumen Blau*)	Military Medical Academy	'A'
	Medical officers and NCOs	Staff and serpent
	Medical troops	Number of unit
	Medical training units	'L'
	Supply officer	Mercury's staff
Light blue (*Hellblau*)	Transport units	Number of unit
	Transport training units	'L'
	Transport Supply School	Gothic 'S'
Black (*Schwarz*)	Pioneer battalions	Number of unit
	Fortress pioneer units	'Fp' with unit number below
	Railway pioneers	'E' with unit number below
	Pioneer training battalions	'L' with I or II
	Pioneer NCOs' School	'US' plus initial letter of the school
	Pioneer School	Gothic 'S' with Arabic number
	Railway Pioneer School	Gothic 'S' outlined in white
	Railway pioneer training companies	'L' in waffenfarbe outlined in white
	Technical officers	'T'
Black and white (*Schwarzweiss*)	Armoured engineer companies	
Orange (*Orangerot*)	Engineer Officers' Academy	Cog wheel
	Recruiting personnel	Roman Wehrkreis number (pre-1942)
	Military field police	
Grey-blue (*Grau blau*)	Specialist officers	
Light grey (*Hellgrau*)	Army propaganda troops	

[1] No Waffenfarbe piping was used on shoulder straps for N.C.O.s and other ranks.

In addition to the Waffenfarbe appointed to active military units, all Wehrmachtbeamten (with the exception of the army clergy) wore the dark-green Waffenfarbe. In order that they could be distinguished from each other, each administrative branch was given a second colour which was worn together with the dark green. It was used as piping around the dark green collar and cuff patches and as a second underlay above the dark green on the shoulder straps.

A list of colours covering the period 1933 to 1945 with their appropriate branches is given below.

1.8. Wehrmachtbeamten Nebenfarbe (secondary colours) with appropriate branches

Colour/Administrative branch

Carmine (Karmesin)   All permanent officials of the High Command
All education officials
Army surveyors
Army librarians
Army archivists
Army officials of the War Research Institute
Army museum officials
Army meteorologists
Army sports instructor officials
Record officials attached to various commands
Army psychiatrists
Bright red (Hochrot)   District administration officials
White (Weiss)   Army paymaster officials, other than those serving a Wehrkreis administration
Other garrison and victualling officials
Gold yellow (Goldgelb)   Remount officials
Light brown (Hellbraun)   Non-technical instruction personnel in army schools
Rose pink (Rosa)   Army clothing officials
Light green (Hellgrün)   Pharmaceutical officials
Bordeaux red (Bordorot)   Military Supreme Court officials
Cornflower blue (Kornblumen blau)   Hospital officials
Light blue (Hellblau)   Military law officials
Black (Schwarz)   Technical officials (building, engineering, armoury)
Regimental saddle and harness officials
Fortress pioneer officials
Orange (Orangerot)   Recruiting office officials
Violet (Violetten)   German Army clergy (note: no shoulder straps used by military clergy and no dark-green Beamten Waffenfarbe either)

As well as using a double underlay of colour on the shoulder straps these Wehrmachtbeamten (except, of course, the army clergy) were further distinguished by the wearing of a small metal shoulder strap 'emblem' consisting of the ornately styled letters 'HV'; the 'V' was superimposed on the 'H' and the whole design stood for Heeresverwaltung (Army Administration) (plate 24).

German Army shoulder straps and shoulder strap insignia.
19. Leutnant, Individual Officer (W). Bright red Waffenfarbe. 20. Leutnant, Horse Artillery unit. Bright red Waffenfarbe. 21. Leutnant, Officer on the Staff of the School for NCOs at Sigmaringen. White Waffenfarbe. 22. Leutnant, 42nd Machine-gun unit. White Waffenfarbe. 23. Leutnant, Artillery Observation Training Regiment. Bright red Waffenfarbe. 24. Zahlmeister, Army Paymaster Official. White on dark-green Waffenfarbe. 25. Sonderführer, Specialist Officer. Grey-blue Waffenfarbe. 26. Oberfeldwebel, Army anti-aircraft unit. White Waffenfarbe.

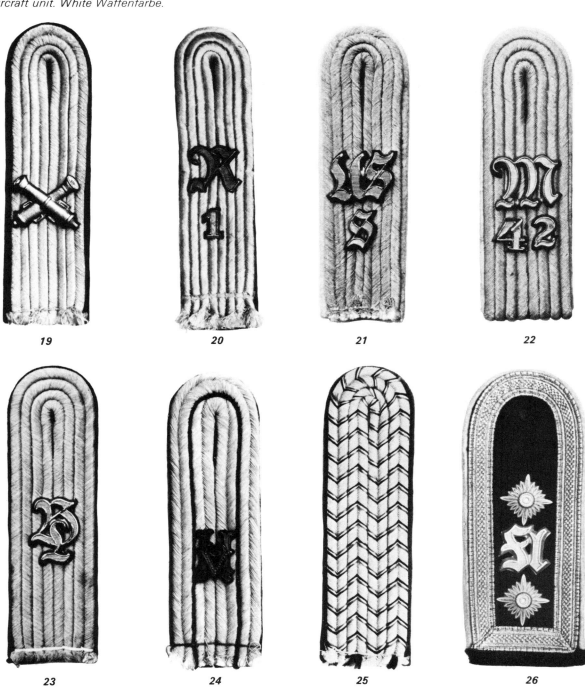

19   20   21   22

23   24   25   26

Shoulder straps and insignia

27. Oberfeldwebel, Infanterie-Regiment 10. White Waffenfarbe. 28. Unteroffizier, Recruiting office, Wehrkreis VII, München. White Waffenfarbe. 29. Unteroffizier, Infanterie-Regiment 16. White Waffenfarbe. 30. Musician, Army School of Music. No Waffenfarbe piping.

27   *28*

29   *30*

1.9. Colour section

Side-Arm Knots (page 25):

Arabic numbers refer to company/battery/squadron of
a. infantry regiments
b. artillery regiments
c. horse artillery and artillery instruction regiments
d. rifle regiments
e. cavalry and rifle regiments
f. horse artillery, motorised and armoured troops

Roman numbers refer to battalion staff (thus, III means III Battalion Staff) Asterisks refer to Regimental Staff. Troddeln marked † are Honorary Knots (Erinnerungstroddeln) worn by the 3rd Bttn, 67th Infantry Regiment. E indicates a supplementary company for both infantry and artillery regiments.

Note also that infantry companies 15, 16, 17, 18, 19, 20 and battalion staffs IV and V were reserve and replacement companies. Company 13 (heavy machine-gun company) and company 14 (anti-tank company) were introduced just prior to the outbreak of the war, being added to the full complement of an infantry regiment. Before the war, c. 1936, V battalion staff and companies shown as 18, 19, and 20 had light brown stems to their side-arm knots (at that time the numbering sequence of these companies was slightly different, being V battalion staff, companies 15, 16, 17, and 18). These stems were later changed to light green.

Shoulder straps and Collar patches (pages 26, 27, 28):

1. **Kanonier, IV Battery, 2nd Artillery Regiment.** Early pattern unpiped 'Feldbluse' strap and first pattern field service patch. Bright red Waffenfarbe.
2. **Schütze, 9th Company, 10th Infantry Regiment.** 'Waffenrock' quality insignia. White Waffenfarbe.
3. **Kanonier, II Battery, Self-propelled Artillery Unit.** Field service insignia, late pattern patch, red piping.
4. **Pionier, 2nd Company, 6th Pioneer Battalion.** Black Waffenfarbe.
5. **Panzerschütze, 4th Company, Panzer-Regiment.24** (formerly 1st Cavalry Regiment). Service insignia as worn on the Black Panzer Uniform. Gold-yellow Waffenfarbe.
6. **Schütze, Recruiting office in VI Military District (Münster)** Service insignia. This form of strap insignia, and the orange Waffenfarbe, was superseded during 1942 by the type of strap and Waffenfarbe shown in 26.
7. **Unteroffizier Anwärter, Staff Section of the OKH.** Service insignia, first pattern patch. Carmine Waffenfarbe.
8. **Panzerschütze, 7th Company Panzer Instruction and Demonstration unit.** Service insignia as worn on the Black Panzer Uniform, patch worn by all ranks of Panzer units. Rose pink Waffenfarbe.
9. **Reiter, 1st Squadron, 17th Cavalry Regiment.**
10. **Kanonier, 186th Artillery Regiment.** Field service insignia, third pattern patch strap with slip-on title.
11. **Grenadier, Führer-Begleitbataillon.** Service uniform insignia, second pattern patch. White Waffenfarbe.
12. **Kraftfahrer.** Tropical field service insignia. Patch colour variations were sometimes found on tropical clothing. Light blue Waffenfarbe.
13. **Jäger.** Field service insignia. regimental coloured identification loop shown worn on strap. Third pattern collar patch. Light green Waffenfarbe.
14. **Sanitätsunteroffizier, 1st Company, 8th Medical unit.** Early pattern unpiped 'Feldbluse' strap and first pattern field service patch. Cornflower blue Waffenfarbe.
15. **Unteroffizier, 101st Landesschützen Regiment.** Field service insignia with slip-on strap title.
16. **Unteroffizier 3rd Signal Regiment.** Lemon-yellow Waffenfarbe.
17. **Unteroffizier, 6th Antitank Battery.** Tropical service uniform insignia.
18. **Unteroffizier, armoured pioneer company.** Service insignia as worn on the Black Panzer uniform. The black and white Waffenfarbe piping was used for a limited period during 1940.
19. **Unteroffizier, signals regiment.** Pre-war Waffenfarbe of copper-brown for Army signals units was superseded by lemon-yellow. Early type field service insignia shown here with coloured regimental identification loop worn on shoulder strap. Copper-brown Waffenfarbe.
20. **Unteroffizier, 6th Company, Horse and Motor vehicle supply unit.** Strap that of an Offizieranwärter.
21. **Unterfeldwebel, 5th Smoke projector Regiment.** Field Service insignia, second pattern patch. Bordeaux red Waffenfarbe.
22. **Unterfeldwebel, pioneer battalion.** Tropical service.
23. **Fähnrich, 11th Self-propelled Assault Artillery Regiment.** Insignia as worn on the Special field-grey uniform. The patch shown here is the early 'Totenkopf' pattern, dark green edged with Artillery red piping. This pattern was superseded by the type of collar patch shown in 3. White metal insignia.
24. **Feldwebel, 5th Company mountain troop regiment.**
25. **Sanitätsoberfeldwebel.** White metal strap insignia.
26. **Oberfeldwebel.** Military recruiting office in the Military District

Side-arm Knots

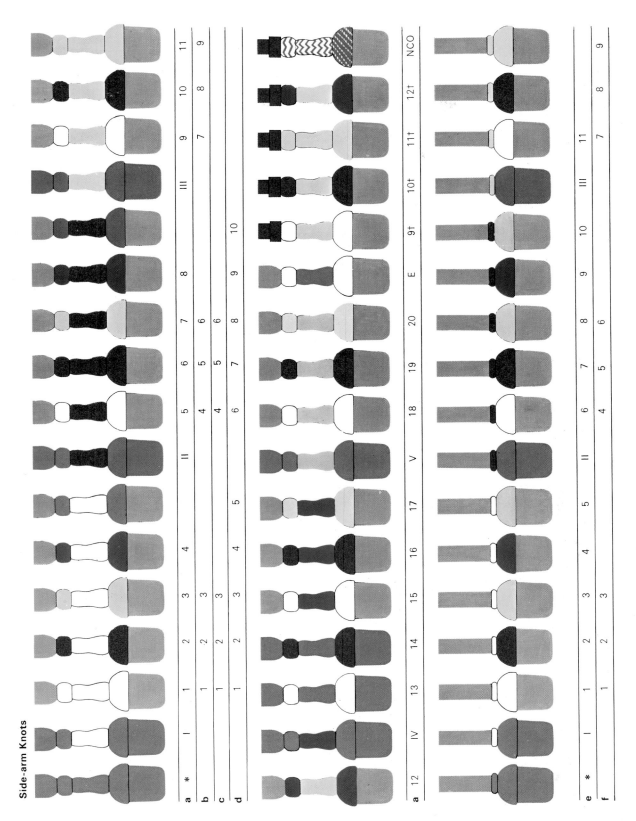

*	I	1	2	3	4		5	II	6	7	8	III	9	10	11
a															
b	1	1	2	3		4	5	6		7	8	9		8	9
c	1	1	2	3		4	5	6			6				
d	1	1	2	3	4	5	6	7		8	9	10			

12	IV	13	14	15	16	17	V	18	19	20	E	9†	10†	11†	12†	NCO

*	I	1	2	3	4	5	II	6	7	8	III	9	10	11
e	1	1	2	3		4	5	6		7	8		9		
f	1	1	2	3		4	5	6		7					

25

Shoulder straps and Collar patches: Officers

31 32 33 34 35 36 37 38 39

40 41 42 43 44 45 46 47 48

49 50 51 52 53 54 55 56 57 58

Shoulder straps and Collar patches: Generals

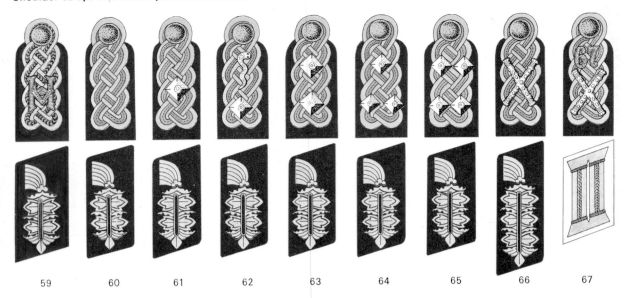

| 59 | 60 | 61 | 62 | 63 | 64 | 65 | 66 | 67 |

German Army camouflage patterns and colourings (¼ life size)

Green splinter pattern camouflage material.

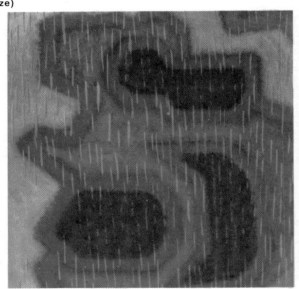

Tan water pattern camouflage material.

Mouse-grey coloured material, a colour used in the manufacture of certain forms of camouflage clothing.

of Nurnberg, c. 1942. See also 6. Service insignia with first pattern patch. White metal strap insignia.

27. Oberfeldwebel, armoured infantry regiment. Field Service insignia with late pattern 'Doppellitzen' patches with grass green piping.

28. Stabsfeldwebel. 12th Armoured Train Unit. Field service insignia with early pattern patch. White metal strap insignia.

29. Feldpostbote. Army Field Post rank equivalent to the army Beamte rank of Lagermeister. Service insignia. White metal strap insignia. Lemon on dark green Waffenfarbe.

30. Ministerialoberamtsgehilfe. A senior administration clerical official in a ministry. White metal 'HV' insignia with gilt metal pips. Red on dark green Waffenfarbe.

31. Assistenzarzt. Gilt metal strap insignia.

32. Leutnant. Artillery. Field service insignia.

33. Veterinär. 'Waffenrock' quality insignia. Gilt metal serpent insignia.

34. Leutnant. Individual officer concerned with weapons systems. These officers wore the uniform of an artillery officer, with gilt metal 'crossed cannons' strap insignia.

35. Leutnant der Reserve, 1st Pioneer Battalion. Numeral in white metal. Black on light grey.

36. Feldpostsekretär, Army Field Post rank equivalent to the Beamte rank of a.P.Zahlmeister. Service insignia. Gilt metal 'FP'.

37. Verwaltungssekretar. Service insignia.

38. Sonderführer (Z), with the rank of Leutnant. Blue-grey Waffenfarbe.

39. Polizeisekretar, Geheime Feldpolizei. Service insignia.

40. Oberleutnant, Feldgendarmerie unit. Field Service insignia. Orange-red Waffenfarbe.

41. Musikmeister, pioneer battalion. Army Band officers used the Waffenfarbe of the unit to which they were attached.

42. Oberleutnant der Landwehr, Mountain troop regiment from IV Military District (Dresden). Roman numeral in white metal. Gilt metal pip.

43. Obermusikmeister, Panzer-Regiment.33.

44. Oberleutnant, Infantry Regiment. Field service insignia showing cover camouflaging strap insignia.

45. Hauptmann on the staff of the OKW or OKH. 'Waffenrock' quality insignia. (Officers on the staff of the German Army General Staff wore the same design of collar patches but in silver wire embroidery in place of the gilt shown here.)

46. Hauptmann on the staff of a pioneer school. Field Service insignia.

47. Hauptmann, 27th Smoke Projector Regiment.

48. Stabszahlmeister. Service insignia.

49. Major, signals troops.

50. Major, motor-cycle unit.

51. Major, pioneer battalion.

52. Oberleutnant. 2nd Motorised Reconnaissance Unit.

53. Oberst, 131st Infantry Regiment. Field service insignia.

54. Oberst. Officer on the Staff of Army Engineer Officers' Academy.

55. Kriegsgerichtsrat, with the rank of major. Service quality insignia.

56. Oberintendanturrat.

57. Army Chaplain. Silver embroidery on violet patch. Field service use only. No shoulder straps worn by Army Clergy.

58. Army Field Bishop. Gilt embroidery on violet patch. Field service use only. No shoulder straps worn by Army Clergy.

59. Wehrmachtbeamte im Generalrang. The insignia shown here is for an official serving on the staff of the OKW or OKH. White metal 'HV', gilt metal strap buttons.

60. Generalmajor.

61. Generalleutnant. White metal insignia and pips.

62. Generalstab Veterinär. Gilt metal strap buttons, white metal insignia.

63. General der Infanterie, Kavallerie, Artillerie. etc. Gilt metal strap buttons, white metal strap insignia and pips.

64. Generaloberst. Gilt metal strap buttons, white metal strap insignia and pips.

65. Generaloberst with the rank of Generalfeldmarschall. This was a prewar rank discontinued before the outbreak of hostilities.

66. Generalfeldmarschall. The 'crossed batons' shoulder strap insignia was introduced in 1940. At that time the patches were those used by the rank of Generaloberst. The 'special' patch design shown here was introduced for use by General Field Marshals during 1942 and continued in use until 1945.

67. Generalfeldmarschall with the honorary rank of Regimental 'Chef' of Infantrie-Regiment.67. Officers' 'Waffenrock' quality collar patches worn with shoulder straps for Generalfeldmarschall. White metal strap insignia. Gilt metal strap buttons.

German Army camouflage patterns and colourings:
It should be noted that the actual shapes of the camouflage patterns varied as did the exact shades of the colouring used. The colours and patterns shown here are as accurate a representation of the original mint condition materials as is possible to obtain.

1.10. Shoulder straps[1]
Schulterklappen und Schulterstücke

Shoulder straps on the German Army military uniform served a dual purpose. They were a means of displaying the wearer's rank as well as his branch of service and, in some cases, a special function; at the same time, and when required, they could be used to help hold the wearer's military equipment in place on the shoulders.

Shoulder straps worn by Army personnel classed as Mannschaften wore plain cloth straps showing only coloured piping (Waffenfarbe) (plate 31).

For the ranks of Unteroffizieren the straps had the addition of flat 0·9cm wide cloth braiding stitched on to the strap around the inner edge of the Waffenfarbe piping (plates 32, 33).[2]

Officers classified as Leutnante and Hauptleute used shoulder straps slimmer in width than the above mentioned cloth straps and constructed of two strands of flat silver braid, each strand woven to appear as two thinner strands—known as 'Russia Braid'—all of which were stitched on to the Waffenfarbe underlay of the strap, the braiding laying flat on the strap and passing around the button hole in the strap in a 'U' fashion. There appeared to be eight separate strands of braid when in fact there were only two (plate 34).

Officers classified as Stabsoffizieren had shoulder straps constructed of two strands of silver Russia Braid plaited to show a series of five loops on each side of the strap not including the single loop around the button at the top of the strap (plate 35).

General class officers, including Generalfeldmarschälle wore a similar style of shoulder strap with the important exception that the braiding used was constructed from two strands of finely woven gold cording braid on either side of a single strand of silver Russia Braid. This triple braiding was plaited on the strap to show only four loops of braid on each side of the strap, not including the single loop around the button at the top of the strap (plate 36).

In the main shoulder straps worn by all ranks of Wehrmachtbeamten followed a similar style of construction to the shoulder straps worn by the active Army ranks.[3] They did, however, differ slightly with the introduction of dark green incorporated into the design of the shoulder strap braiding as well as the use of a distinctive shoulder strap emblem.

---

[1] In all cases concerning shoulder straps, collar patches, shoulder strap buttons, shoulder strap insignia, shoulder strap braiding, etc, the reader's attention is drawn to the colour plates on pages 26–28.

[2] Prior to 1938 a particular form of Army shoulder strap was issued for use on the army Feldbluse (the field service tunic) and worn by all ranks below officer. These were of a special pattern and were made entirely from dark blue-green material; they were slightly pointed at the button end and had no Waffenfarbe piping. The wearer's appropriate Waffenfarbe was only shown on those shoulder straps that displayed the shoulder strap insignia (numbers, letters, emblems) in an embroidered form (plates 37–39).

[3] Other styles of shoulder straps (and collar patches) existed for Army Officials which differed considerably in design of construction and colouring from these Wehrmachtbeamten styles dealt with here. An example of this difference can be seen in the shoulder straps (and collar patches) worn by army Sonderführer, see page 134 and page 158.

Basic types of German Army shoulder straps and early pattern 'Feldbluse' shoulder straps
31. Shoulder strap for Army Soldat. 32. Shoulder strap for Army Unteroffizier. 33. Shoulder strap for Army Feldwebel. 34. Shoulder strap for Army Leutnant. 35. Shoulder strap for Army Major. 36. Shoulder strap for Army Generalmajor. 37. Early pattern 'Feldbluse' shoulder strap for a Soldat on the Staff of the Army Ordnance Technicians' School

(c. 1937–8). No piping, but letters FS stitched in bright red silk. 38. Early pattern 'Feldbluse' shoulder strap for an Unteroffizier on the Staff of the 3rd Army Group Command. No piping, but insignia G 3 stitched in white cotton. 39. Early pattern 'Feldbluse' shoulder strap for an Oberfeldwebel from Infanterie-Regiment 7. No piping, but shoulder strap insignia in white metal.

31   *32*   *33*   *34*   *35*

36   *37*   *38*   *39*

Army Administrative personnel below officer's rank wore shoulder straps constructed from dark green silk or woollen cording worked on either side of a single silver cord. This appeared plaited down the centre of the strap with a line of dark green and silver braid running around the edge. The whole of this braiding was mounted on the double underlay of Wehrmachtbeamten Waffenfarbe—dark green—superimposed with the appropriate secondary colour.

Officials of officer rank below General had a slightly less elaborate design to their straps. Both the 'Leutnante' and 'Hauptleute' as well as the 'Stabsoffizier' type of shoulder strap had the addition of a very thin strand of dark green piping which for the former two followed the shape of the flat silver braid, and for the latter was plaited with the silver braid.

Administrative officials holding the rank equivalent to army general and above wore shoulder straps constructed in exactly the same way but had the distinctive introduction of fine dark green chevrons set 1 cm apart worked into the single silver Russia Braid used on these general's type straps.

The shoulder straps for all these officials holding administrative ranks equivalent to army officers and generals also had double underlays of Waffenfarbe and nebenfarbe.

1.11. Shoulder strap buttons
Schulterknöpfe

Shoulder straps were attached to the uniform tunic at their base, usually by being stitched into the seam at the shoulder or by having the 'tongue' of the strap threaded through a thin strip of cloth stitched on to the tunic shoulder. The other end of the shoulder strap nearest the wearer's collar was held in position by a button. This button allowed the strap to be undone.

In prewar Germany and, to a lesser extent, in wartime Germany full use was made of the shoulder strap button to show yet another method of displaying a subdivision of the position held by the wearer (NCOs and men only) within his military unit. These buttons featured a number raised out from the dimpled metal surface; there were two types of numerals shown on shoulder strap buttons, Roman and Arabic. Roman numerals indicated the wearer's battalion or battery number while Arabic numerals on shoulder strap buttons indicated the number of the wearer's Company.

Metal buttons used on the uniform, including shoulder strap buttons, came in three main colour finishes—silver white, yellow gilt (for generals and other officers in that class) and field-grey. Two other colours existed; white (overpainted field-grey buttons) used on the white side of camouflage clothing and dark grey used on late model army uniforms.

All buttons were manufactured in silver white metal and, for use on service and field uniforms, were sprayed in bulk with a field-grey paint before leaving the factory. Because of the dimpled finish given to the untreated metal buttons this paint adhered to the buttons longer than would normally be the case with buttons of a smooth finish.

1.12. Army shoulder strap insignia
Abzeichen für Heeres Schulterklappen

With very few exceptions—such as certain 'tradition badges' and reserve officers' insignia—the rule for the display of shoulder strap insignia was as follows: for all those ranks classed as Mannschaften and Unteroffizier ohne Portepee, the insignia was worked on the shoulder strap in silk or wool thread in the same colour as the wearer's shoulder strap Waffenfarbe piping.[1]

For the group of ranks known as Unteroffizier mit Portepee the insignia was manufactured from white metal alloy and mounted on the shoulder strap.

For all officer ranks up to, but not including generals, the shoulder strap insignia was of gilt coloured metal alloy.

Generals and above had shoulder strap insignia finely cast in quality white metal or frosted silver metal.

The actual appearance and design of the shoulder strap insignia used in the German Army fell into three types:
1. Numerals; in both Roman and Arabic style
2. Letters; in both Gothic and Script, single and entwined
3. Emblems; which were of various forms

The reader's attention is drawn to the list of shoulder strap emblems and insignia shown on page 21 under the heading of 'The Expansion of the Basic German Army Waffenfarbe System'.

1.13. Army shoulder strap 'tradition' badges
and elite unit shoulder strap insignia
Errinerungsabzeichen und Elite-Truppen
Abzeichen auf Heeres Schulterklappen

Certain élite German Army formations, some of whom had proud military traditions stretching back over many centuries and others who were comparatively new, were distinguished by the wearing of special symbols on their shoulder straps.

The insignia appointed to these selected units usually took the form either of an emblem peculiar to the unit or its historical role, or of a single or double letter indicative of the initial letters of the unit's name or title.

Those German Army units known to be thus honoured were as follows.

Name of Unit or Title/Appointed emblem and details

5. Kavallerie Regiment   A 'Totenkopf', derived from the headdress emblem worn by the Preussische 1 und 2 Leib-Husaren Regiment. A metal emblem worn by all ranks of the 5th Cavalry Regiment on the shoulder straps and head-dress (plate 40)

Grenadier-Regiment 134 replacement unit and Divisional Staff of the Reichsgrenadier-Division 'Hoch und Deutschmeister'   The 'Hoch und Deutschmeister Kreuz', an old traditional German emblem adapted with the addition of

---

[1] See footnote on page 29 concerning early pattern unpiped shoulder straps.

German Army shoulder strap 'Tradition Badges' and Elite Unit shoulder strap insignia.
40. Oberwachtmeister, 5th Cavalry Regiment. Gold yellow Waffenfarbe. 41. Leutnant, Grenadier-Regiment 134. White Waffenfarbe. 42. Leutnant, Panzer-Grenadier-Regiment 60, 'Feldherrnhalle'. Grass green Waffenfarbe. 43. Grenadier, Panzer-Grenadier-Regiment 60, 'Feldherrnhalle'. White Waffenfarbe. 44. Oberstleutnant, Infantry Regiment 'Grossdeutschland'. White Waffenfarbe. *45. Unter-offizier, Infantry Regiment 'Grossdeutschland'. White Waffenfarbe. 46. Major, Artillery Regiment, Führer-Grenadier-Division. Red Waffenfarbe. 47. Ober-leutnant, Guard Regiment Berlin. White Waffenfarbe. 48. Oberfeldwebel, Guard Troop Berlin. White Waffenfarbe. 49. Leutnant, Guard Battalion Wien. White Waffenfarbe.*

40   41   42   43   44

45   46   47   48   49

an Eagle and Swastika emblem to be worn on the shoulder straps of all ranks of those units shown above from 23rd March 1944 onwards. It was a blue-grey metal emblem (plate 41)

60. *Panzergrenadier-Division 'Feldherrnhalle'* The 'Feldherrnhall Kampfrunen'. An emblem used by the élite S.A. unit 'Feldherrnhalle' consisting of Kampfrunen and the S.A. symbol. It was appointed to be worn by all ranks in this army unit from the spring of 1943. It commemorated the fact that the main body of men forming this unit were drawn largely from personnel who had been members of the Sturm Abteilung. The wearing of this emblem followed the normal rank precedence in shoulder strap insignia—embroidered insignia, white metal and gilt metal emblems (plates 42, 43)

All army formations bearing the title 'Grossdeutschland' The entwined letter 'GD' (in script) standing for 'Gross Deutschland'. This élite unit originally started life as an infantry regiment and, by the end of the war, had expanded to become a Panzer-Korps. The 'GD' emblem was introduced by an order dated 20th July 1939 (plates 44, 45)

Führer-Grenadier-Bataillon The entwined letters 'FG' (in script) standing for 'Führer-Grenadier'. This emblem was first introduced to be worn by all ranks of this élite battalion on the 16th September 1943 (plate 46)

Wachttruppe Berlin A gothic letter 'W' standing for 'Wache' (guard). This emblem was worn by all ranks of this unit from its early origins in the summer of 1934 (plates 47, 48)

Wachtbatallion Wien A roman letter 'W' standing for both 'Wache' and Wien (Vienna). This emblem was worn by all ranks of this élite Guard battalion serving in the Austrian capital of Vienna and was introduced by an order dated 7th September 1938 (plate 49)

1.14. 'Anwärter' shoulder strap braiding and regimental shoulder strap colour bars

Single bars of 0·9cm rank braiding were used worn across the Army shoulder straps for those ranks from Schütze/Grenadier to Obergefreiter. They indicated that the wearer was an aspiring non-commissioned officer (Unteroffizieranwärter) (plate 50).

Double bars of 0·9cm rank braiding were also worn across the shoulder straps for those ranks from Unteroffizier to Stabsfeldwebel. They indicated that the wearer was an aspirant officer (Offizieranwärter) (plates 51, 52).

Certain German Army formations fighting on the Eastern Front adopted a system of coloured cloth loops which were worn on the shoulder straps of all regimental personnel within these formations. This use of different basic colours served to identify different battalions within these Army regiments. An example of this form of colour identification was used by the 29.Panzer-Grenadier-Regiment from the 3.Panzer-Grenadier-Division. The colours were used as follows: 1.Bataillon wore white shoulder strap bars, the 2.Bataillon wore red shoulder strap bars, and the

51. Infantry Oberfeldwebel Offizieranwärter, Italy 1944.

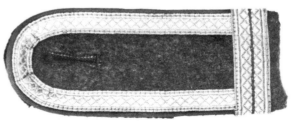

52. Shoulder strap for an Artillery Unteroffizier with special double bar shoulder strap insignia indicating the wearer to be an aspirant officer.

50. A newly appointed Unteroffizieranwärter from Infantry Regiment 'Grossdeutschland' receiving a field promotion.

3. Bataillon wore yellow shoulder strap bars.

It is not known how widespread this practice was nor why it was necessary to distinguish between battalion troops in this manner.

1.15. Slip-on shoulder strap titles and shoulder strap camouflage covers
Überziehbare Inschriften für Schulterklappen und Tarn Uberzüge für Schulterklappen

In peacetime, and during the early stages of the war, shoulder straps worn by troops below the rank of officer were normally either embroidered in coloured silk or wool with the wearer's regimental number or insignia or alternatively they displayed white metal numerals or insignia depending on the wearer's rank.

For wartime security reasons alone this was impractical. It also proved to be uneconomical. When a soldier was transferred to a new unit he had to discard all his old straps and had to be issued with new shoulder straps bearing his new regimental number or insignia.

From the point of view of labour time and costs it was far more expensive to manufacture a properly constructed shoulder strap than it was to produce the simple band of field-grey cloth that made up the slip-on title. With these three considerations of security, economy and labour cost in mind the German Army began to introduce the slip-on shoulder strap title. It was extensively used and could be worn on the shoulder straps of all ranks below officer (plate 53).

The slip-on shoulder strap title was a loop of cloth made from a single piece of field-grey material 3cm deep and wide enough (5cm) to slip over the normal Army cloth shoulder strap. Numbers, letters or a combination of both were stitched or embroidered on to these titles in the same colour as that of the wearer's waffenfarbe (plate 54).

Camouflage covers were used on officers' shoulder straps. They were either a band of field-grey cloth large enough when worn on the shoulder strap to cover up any metal insignia mounted on the strap, or they were a complete cover worn over the entire strap.

One other interesting form of camouflage was adopted by individual German NCOs during the early Polish and French campaigns which is worth mentioning. In order to disguise their rank displayed on their shoulder straps they simply wore the straps on the tunic upside down. The underside of the shoulder strap did not show any noticeable rank details and thus denied the enemy any information that they might normally have obtained with the use of binoculars.

1.16. Collar and cuff-facing patches
Kragenpatten und Ärmelpatten

Collar patches worn on the army uniform were almost as important a means of displaying rank and branch of service as the shoulder strap. Cuff-facing patches only fulfilled this function on the Uniform Tunic.

1.16(1). *Collar patches.* There were two basic styles of collar patch worn by all ranks up to, but not including,

53. *The use of slip-on shoulder strap titles. This soldier pauses for refreshment during bomb damage clearance and rescue work after an air raid on Berlin during August 1943.*

54. *Three examples of German Army slip-on shoulder strap titles.*

the rank of general. These were the patches worn on the Service and Field Service Uniforms, and the collar patches worn on the Uniform Tunic. Generals and above wore the same design and quality collar patches on all forms of uniform tunics. Collar patches were worn in matching pairs.

The main difference between the Service Uniform quality collar patches and those used on the Uniform Tunic was in the colour of the collar patch background cloth, the design and the quality.

Bright, flat, fine silver wire was embroidered on to a patch of cloth in the Waffenfarbe required for the patches used on the Uniform Tunic. Dull aluminium thread or grey cotton yarn was used for the Service Tunic collar patches backed with a patch of dark blue-green material. Waffenfarbe was shown on certain types of these Service Uniform patches as thin bars of colour forming part of the dull aluminium/cotton yarn embroidery.

Following the normal precedence in all cases of rank differentiation the embroidery employed in the making of collar patches of the lower ranks from Soldat to Feldwebel was fairly simple. From Leutnant to Oberst the embroidery work was more elaborate and for Generäle and above, as well as those officers of the General Staff, they were by comparison very elaborate.

1.16(2). *Cuff-facing patches.* As has been mentioned these were only worn on the Uniform Tunic with its dark blue-green 'Swedish' cuffs. The embroidery used on these cuff-facing patches was of the same quality, and in the same style, as that used on the corresponding Uniform Tunic collar patches. The embroidery work was backed with a section of coloured material which represented the wearer's waffenfarbe and matched the backing cloth to the collar patches. As part of the design to these cuff-facing patches there was a 'dummy' button which served no purpose other than to act as a form of decoration and as a reminder of styles

of military uniforms long since vanished.

It should be noted that Wehrmachtbeamten of all ranks wore both collar and cuff-facing patches edged, in the case of collar patches on three sides and for cuff-facing patches on all four sides, in their secondary waffenfarbe piping 0·2cm thick.

As the basic Waffenfarbe allotted to German Army Wehrmachtbeamten was dark green, it was found necessary to emphasize the collar and cuff-facing patches with a secondary colour in order to distinguish them against the dark blue-green of the collar and cuff material (plates 55–66 inclusive).

1.17. Army collar and cuff rank braiding Dienstgradabzeichen für Unteroffizier- dienstgrade Besatz auf Heeres Kragen und Ärmel

Collar and cuff rank braiding was a very distinctive feature of uniform detail worn by those army personnel classified as Unteroffizier ohne Portepee and Unter-

55. *(left) German Army other ranks' field service collar patches seen here stitched directly onto the field-grey collar without the customary backing cloth of dark blue-green material.* *56.* *(right) Field service quality collar patches worn by Army NCOs on the Service Tunic and the special Field-grey Panzerjäger Uniform. The holder of the Knight's Cross is Oberwachtmeister Kessel, member of the Grossdeutschland Panzerjäger Abteilung*

57. *Officers' field service quality collar patches worn on the special Field-grey Panzerjäger Uniform. The name of this Knight's Cross holder is not known*

59. *Panzer Totenkopf collar patches, worn by all ranks of the German Panzer arm. Leutnant Leidermann, taken prisoner when Fort Driant — the German stronghold near Metz — finally fell to the 3rd U.S. Army on 8th December 1944.*

58. *The use of metal Totenkopf collar patch insignia worn together with normal tropical field service collar patches was a feature of the tropical field service uniforms worn by German Panzer troops serving in North Africa and Italy.*

60. *Collar patches for a Generalfeldmarschall. Generalmajor Kreipe, commanding officer of the 22nd (Luftlande) Panzer-Grenadier-Division and holder of the Knight's Cross.*

61. Collar patches for an Army General. General-leutnant Ferdinant Heim, commander of the German garrison at Boulogne, September 1944.

63. Collar patches for an Army Official of the German Higher Staff.

62. Collar patches for a German Army Beamten General. Gold embroidery on dark green backing material piped in the appropriate bright red waffen-farbe. Shown here is General Mantell.

64. Collar patches for an Army Sonderführer.

65. *Collar patches for an Army Official with the rank of Amtsgehilfe.*

66. *Collar patches for an Army Official with the rank of Oberinspektor.*

offizier mit Portepee.

The braiding was, in the case of the Uniform Tunic, in 0·9cm wide bright aluminium silver and, for the Service and Field Service Tunics, 0·9cm wide dull grey cotton yarn.[1] This distinction did not always hold good as individual NCOs often used the bright silver braiding (incorrectly) on the Service Tunic.

The rank braiding used by the army was manufactured in such a way as to show a fine pattern of lines criss-crossing throughout the design. This braiding was the same as that used on shoulder straps (plates 27, 28, 29, 32, 33, 39, 45, 48). some arm rank 'winkeln', and was also used as the double sleeve stripes on the cuffs of the tunics worn by 'der Spiess' (plate 292).

When used on the tunic collar it was worn down the front of, and around the lower edge to, the collar on the Service Tunic and around the upper edge to, and again down the front of, the collar to the Uniform Jacket. When used on the cuffs, braiding of this sort was used only on the dark blue-green 'Swedish' cuffs of the Uniform Tunic. It was worn right round the upper edge of the cuff facings directly below the waffenfarbe piping and down the outer edge of the

cuff join at the rear of the sleeve. In the case of the German Army non-commissioned officer holding the rank of Hauptfeldwebel or Stabsfeldwebel and referred to as 'der Spiess' an additional band of braiding was worn on the Uniform Tunic sleeves 0·5cm above the upper edge of the cuff-facings with their coloured piping. On the Service and Field Service Tunics of the 'Spiess' two bands of 0·9cm wide braiding were worn approximately 13cm up both the sleeves and positioned 0·5cm apart. On the Greatcoat the lowest edge of the two bands would have been just 1cm above the upper edge of both the turn-back cuffs. With the exception of the 'Spiess' rank braiding was not used on the cuffs of the Service and Field Service Tunic by any other ranks of non-commissioned officers.

1.18. Rank chevrons, 1921-45
Dienstgradabzeichen für Mannschaften

A system of arm rank chevrons—'Winkeln'—was first introduced in 1921; there were three major changes in design and rank titles to these arm chevrons between 1921 and 1945. These are shown in the chart on page 41.

In the main these chevrons and stars were embroidered or stitched on to a backing cloth of dark blue-green material (Panzer troops used black cloth and for tropical wear a tan coloured backing cloth was

---

[1] The 0·9cm wide rank braiding used on the shoulder straps, the collars and the sleeves of Tropical Uniforms was normally of a dull copper brown or copper-gold colouring. The design was the same as that stated above.

67. *German Army Collar and Cuff-facing Patches and rank braiding as worn on the 'Waffenrock'.*

1. Schütze/Grenadier, etc
2. Unteroffizier
3. Hauptfeldwebel/Hauptwacht-
  meister (Der Spiess)
4. Leutnant
5. Generalmajor

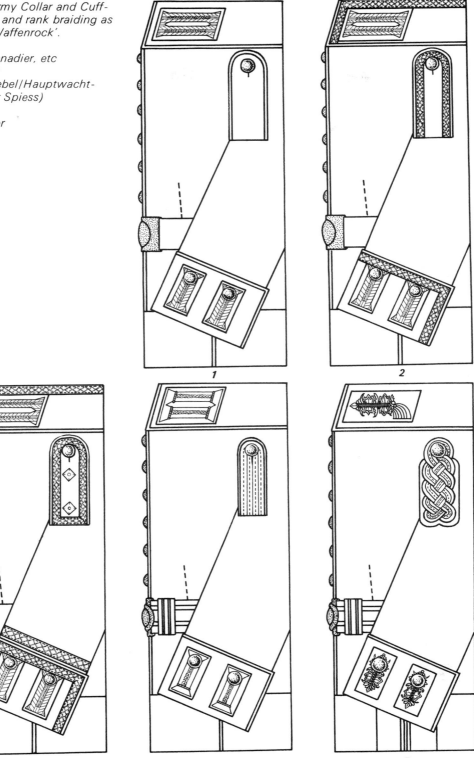

68. *German Army Collar Patches and rank braiding as worn on the 'Feldbluse'.*

1. *Schütze/Grenadier, etc*
2. *Unteroffizier. (Service tunic shown here worn open at the neck)*
3. *Hauptfeldwebel/Hauptwachtmeister (Der Spiess)*
4. *Leutnant*
5. *Generalmajor*

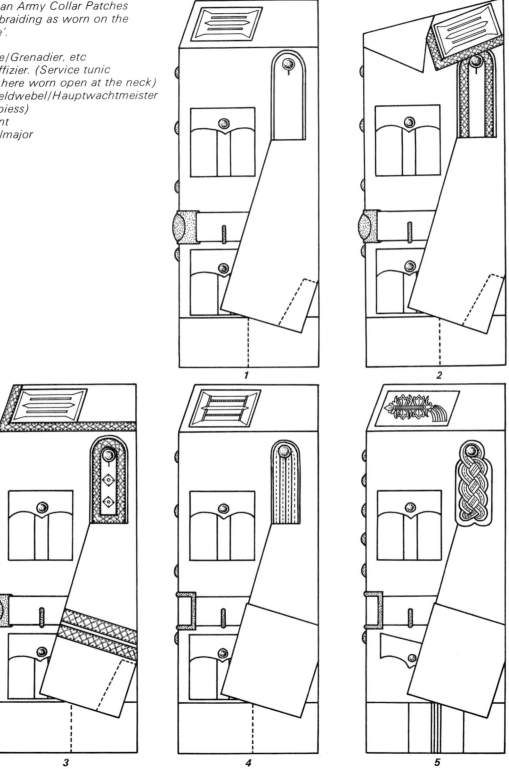

1921

1936

1942/3–1945

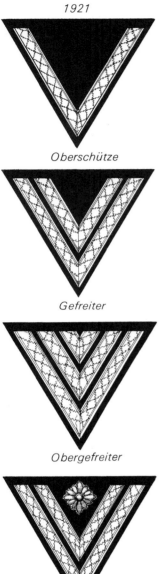

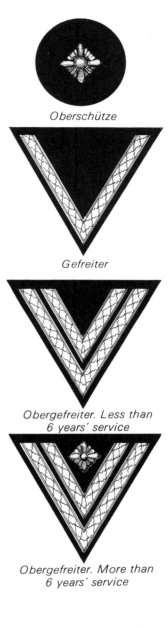

Oberschütze

Oberschütze

Oberschütze

Gefreiter

Gefreiter

Gefreiter

Obergefreiter

Obergefreiter with less than
6 years' service

Obergefreiter. Less than
6 years' service

Stabsgefreiter

Obergefreiter with more than
6 years' service

Obergefreiter. More than
6 years' service

Stabs Gefreiter

69. German Army
Rank Chevrons, 1921–1945

70. The 'Oberschütze' rank star, here being worn by an Oberkanonier.

71. The rank chevrons for an Obergefreiter.

72. The rank chevron for a Gefreiter.

73. The rank chevrons for an Obergefreiter, of a slightly different design to the ones shown in plate 71. Fashioned in the same manner as the normal pattern of arm rank chevrons, these have the additional feature of a thin black thread line running along the length of each side of the chevrons.

used). However field-grey backing cloth was also used as well as the off-white denim material. In addition to this the 0·9cm wide rank chevrons were sometimes stitched directly on to the sleeve of the Field Service tunic without any backing cloth.

Stars were square in shape or square with the four corners slightly protruding. These were usually embroidered on to a circular backing cloth.

The chevrons were constructed from 0·9cm wide braiding dull grey or bright silver depending on the type of uniform they were worn on. The braiding and embroidered stars used by troops of the Deutsches Afrika Korps (D.A.K.) was coloured a dull gold or copper-brown, usually backed with lightweight tan material.

All types, colours and 'editions' of these arm rank chevrons and stars were worn on the upper left arm of the Uniform Tunic, the Service and Field Service tunics as well as the Greatcoat (plates 70–73).

1.19. Rank insignia worn on the jacket of the Denim Uniform
Abzeichen am Drillichrock

Certain insignia of rank were introduced during the winter of 1938–9 designed to show the wearer's rank when dressed in the Denim Uniform. Those German Army ranks with their designated insignia are listed as follows:

1.19(1). *For the rank of Oberschütze:* a single star in dull grey cotton embroidered on to a circular backing of denim material. Worn on the left upper arm.

1.19(2). *For the rank of Gefreiter:* a single 'winkel' in dull grey cotton braid stitched on to a triangular piece of denim material. Worn on the left upper arm.

1.19(3). *For the rank of Unteroffizier:* 0·9cm wide dull grey cotton braid worn down the front and around the lower edge to the Denim Jacket collar.

1.19(4). *For the rank of Feldwebel (Wachtmeister):* a single band of 0·9cm braid worn on both cuffs 10cm from the bottom of the sleeve.

1.19(5). *For the rank of Oberfeldwebel (Oberwachtmeister):* a single band of 0·9cm braid positioned just below a single inverted chevron also constructed of the same braid and set at an angle of 120° and 7cm long. As before worn on both cuffs 10cm from the bottom edge of the sleeve.

1.19(6). *For the rank of Stabsfeldwebel (Stabswachtmeister):* a single band of 0·9cm braid with two 7cm long chevrons both set at a 120° angle one above the other and 0·5cm apart. This insignia was also worn on both cuffs 10cm from the bottom edge of the tunic sleeve.

1.19(7). *For the rank of Hauptfeldwebel (Hauptwachtmeister) and acting Hauptfeldwebel (Hauptwachtmeister):* two bands of 0·9cm wide rank braid set 0·5cm apart and worn on both cuffs 10cm from the bottom edge of the tunic sleeve.

The design of the braiding used was that described in the section on German Army collar and cuff rank braiding. On page 44 will be found a chart of these

rank insignia (plate 74).

1.20. Insignia of rank used on camouflage and special combat clothing
Dienstgradabzeichen an Bekleidungsstücken ohne Schulterklappen (Schulterstücken)

With the introduction in the late summer of 1942 of regulation issue camouflage, heavy winter and new forms of denim clothing which did not normally display rank by means of shoulder straps (or collar patches), it was found necessary to design a distinctive system of rank insignia which could be used on all varieties of military dress not using the normal system of displaying rank.

The German Military Authorities introduced by an order dated 22nd August 1942 a new and complete system of rank insignia to cover all ranks from Unteroffizier to Generalfeldmarschall. Simple in design and colour, they were to be worn on the left upper arm 10cm below the shoulder seam and at the corresponding height on those jackets with no shoulder seams.

The forms of military dress that these badges were intended to be worn on were as follows:

1. The new Winter Uniform (Winteranzügen) (plate 75)
2. The Snow Uniform (Schneeanzügen)
3. The Snow Shirt (Schneehemden)
4. The Wind Blouse (Windblusen)
5. The animal skin uniforms (Nachtpelzen (plate 76)
6. The Denim Overalls for Panzer Troops (Drillichschutzanzügen für Panzertruppen) (plate 77)
7. The Reed-green Overalls for Gun Crews of Batteries and Operators of 2cm anti-aircraft guns (Schilfgrünen Schutzanzügen für Geschützbedienungen der Batterien [E] und Bedienungen der 2cm Flak)
8. The Denim Overalls for the Crews of Armoured Reconnaissance Vehicles (Drillichschutzanzügen für die Besatzungen der Panzerspähwagen)
9. The Protective Flight Overalls for Balloon Service (Fliegerschutzenanzügen für Ballondienst)
10. The Tropical Shirt (Tropenhemden)
11. Denim Jackets (Drillichjacken)
12. Training Uniforms (Trainingsanzügen)
13. Jackets of Work Uniforms (Jacken zum Arbeitsanzug)

The colours of these badges are as indicated on the chart showing the ranks (plate 78). The width of the badge was approximately 10cm, the height varied according to the rank.

Those badges for Unteroffizier to Oberst were normally printed on thin cotton cloth; from Generalmajor to Generalfeldmarschall they were worked in yellow and in yellow and white thread on black woollen material.

These rank badges were also issued to all members of the Waffen-SS on items of uniform similar to those listed above. However the rank titles were those as used in the Waffen-SS.

74. *German Army rank insignia worn on the jacket of the Denim Uniform.*

1. Oberschütze
2. Gefreiter
3. Unteroffizier
4. Feldwebel/Wachtmeister
5. Oberfeldwebel/ Oberwachtmeister
6. Stabsfeldwebel/ Stabswachtmeister
7. Hauptfeldwebel/ Hauptwachtmeister and acting Hauptfeldwebel and acting Hauptwachtmeister

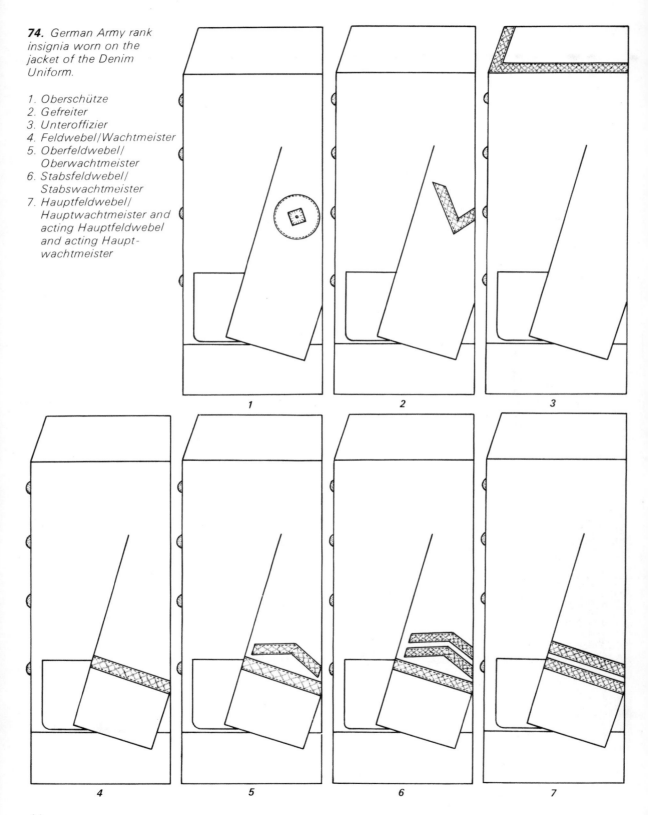

75. Knight's Cross holder Major Jähde with his crew members on the Eastern Front, May 1944. Note the special rank insignia worn on the Winter Uniform.

76. General der Gebirgstruppen Weisenberger in North Finland. Special rank insignia worn on animal skin coats.

77. German Panzer crew members relaxing. Special rank insignia is shown being worn on the reed-green denim Panzer suit.

78. *Rank Insignia used on German Army camouflage and special combat clothing.*

Unteroffizier

Unterfeldwebel

Feldwebel

Oberfeldwebel

Stabsfeldwebel

Leutnant

Oberleutnant

Hauptmann

Major

Oberstleutnant

Oberst

Generalmajor

Generalleutnant

General der Inf. etc.

Generaloberst

Generalfeldmarschall

Black

White

Green

Yellow

2. Badges and Insignia

2.1. Army trade and specialist badges
Heeres Laufbahn und Sonder Dienstellungen Abzeichen

In order to distinguish those German troops that performed a specific military function and that had achieved proficiency in a specialist trade a system of Trade and Specialist badges were introduced at varying times and were worn by all qualifying ranks below the rank of Leutnant.

A chart of line drawings will be found on pages 48—9 showing these badges as well as an explanation of the colours, on which arm they were worn and the position on the arm as well as the title of the badge and what it represented.

German Army trade and specialist badges were normally worked in yellow cotton or silk thread on to a circular or oval backing of dark blue-green material. However other colour variations existed. Field-grey and tan-brown materials were used as backing cloth and certain insignia, which are noted in the chart, were embroidered in white cotton or silver wire and even produced in white metal.

Only one sample trade badge has been illustrated with silver edging. Other trade and specialist badges which were known to have been edged with silver piping are indicated in the chart by an asterisk (*).

2.1(1). *German Army Trade and Specialist Badges: a descriptive listing*

German title	Worn by	Description	Arm and position
Brieftaubenmeister	Pigeon-post master	Gothic 'B' in yellow on dark blue-green circular background	Lower right sleeve
Feuerwerker	NCO artificer or ordnance technician	Gothic 'F' in yellow on dark blue-green circular background	Lower right sleeve (plate 80)
Festungsbaufeldwebel	Fortress construction sergeant-major	Gothic 'Fb' in yellow on dark blue-green circular background	
Festungspionierfeldwebel	Fortress engineer sergeant-major	Gothic 'Fp' in yellow on dark blue-green circular background	Lower right sleeve
Gerätverwaltungsunteroffizier	Supply administration NCO	Gothic 'G' in yellow on dark blue-green circular background	
Gasschutzunteroffizier	Gas defence NCO	Gothic 'Gu' in yellow on dark blue-green circular background	
Nachrichtenmechaniker	Signals mechanic	Gothic 'M' in yellow above a horizontal yellow lightning 'blitz' all on a dark blue-green circular background	
Regimentsuntersattlermeister	Regimental NCO saddler	Gothic 'Rs' in yellow on dark blue-green circular background	
Schirrmeister	Motor Transport NCO	Gothic 'S' in yellow on dark blue-green circular background	Lower right sleeve (plate 81)
Truppensattlermeister	Troop NCO saddler	Gothic 'Ts' in yellow on dark blue-green circular background	Lower right sleeve
Zahlmeisteranwärter	Paymaster Trainee	Gothic 'V' in yellow on dark blue-green circular background	Lower right sleeve
Wallfeldwebel	Fortifications sergeant-major	Gothic 'W' in yellow on dark blue-green circular background	Lower right sleeve
Zeugmeister	Clothing stores NCO	Gothic 'Zg' in yellow on dark blue-green circular background	
Hufbeschlagmeister, Geprüfte Anwärter	Farrier candidate	Yellow horseshoe on dark blue-green circular background; silver bar to bottom edge of background	
Geprüftes-Hufbeschlagpersonal	Qualified farrier	Yellow horseshoe on dark blue-green circular background	Lower right sleeve
Hufbeschlag Lehrmeister	Farrier instructor	Yellow horseshoe and star on dark blue-green circular background	

79. *German Army Trade and Specialist badges.*

Brieftaubenmeister	*Feuerweker*	*Festungsbaufeldwebel*	*Festungspionierfeldwebel*
*Gerätverwaltungs Unteroffizier**	*Gasschutzunteroffizier*	*Nachrichten Mechaniker**	*Regimentsuntersattler-meister*
*Schirrmeister**	*Truppensattlermeister*	*Zahlmeisteranwärter*	*Wallfeldwebel*

Zeugmeister

*Hufbeschlagmeister,
Geprüfte Anwärter*

*Geprüftes-
Hufbeschlagpersonal**

*Hufbeschlag-
Lehrmeister*

Veterinärpersonal

Sanitätsunterpersonal*

Waffenfeldwebel*

Funkmeister*

*Kraftzeug, Panzer
warte II*

Handwerker

*Kraftzeug, Panzer
warte I*

Vorhandwerker

Nachrichten personal

*Richtabzeichen für
Artillerie (Richtkanonier)*

*Richtabzeichen für
Nebeltruppen*

Steuermann

49

80. *Feuerwerker Feldwebel.*

81. *Schirrmeister Oberfeldwebel.*

82. *Sanitätsunteroffizier.*

83. *Waffenfeldwebel.*

German title	Worn by	Description	Arm and position
Veterinärpersonal	Veterinary personnel	Yellow snake on dark blue-green circular background	
Sanitätsunterpersonal	Medical personnel	Yellow serpent and staff (Askulapstab) on dark blue-green circular background	Lower right sleeve (plate 82)
Waffenfeldwebel	Ordnance NCO	Two crossed rifles in yellow on dark blue-green circular background	Lower right sleeve (plate 83)
Nachrichtenpersonal	Signals-operators	A lightning 'Blitz' in any one of the waffenfarben listed below[1] on a dark blue-green oval background	Upper left sleeve (plate 84)
Funkmeister	Radio operator	A yellow 'Blitzbundel' on a dark blue-green circular background	Lower right sleeve
Kraftzeug, Panzer Warte II	Motor or armoured mechanic 2nd class	A pink cogwheel 'Zahnrad' on a field-grey circular background	Lower right sleeve
Handwerker	Technical artisan	A pink 'Zahnrad' on a field-grey circular background edged with silver-grey piping	Lower right sleeve
Kraftzeug oder Panzer Warte I	Motor or armoured mechanic 1st class	A pink 'Zahnrad' on a field-grey circular background edged with pink piping	Lower right sleeve
Vorhandwerker	Master technical artisan	A pink 'Zahnrad' on a field-grey circular background edged with yellow piping	Lower right sleeve
Richtabzeichen für Artillerie (Richtkanonier)	Gun layer, artillery	An upright 'flaming shell' in yellow, surrounded by a wreath of yellow oakleaves all on a dark blue-green oval background	Lower left sleeve
Richtabzeichen für Nebeltruppen	Smoke-projector (Nebelwerfer) operator	An upright mortar projectile in white surrounded by a wreath of white leaves all on a dark blue-green oval background	Lower left sleeve
Steuermann	Qualified helmsman for engineer assault boats	A silver anchor superimposed with a silver steering wheel on a dark blue-green oval background	Upper left sleeve (plate 85)

[1]The lightning 'blitz' appeared in the following colours: white, gold yellow, bright red, rose pink, Bordeaux red, light blue, light green, grass green, and black picked out with white edging.

84. *Nachrichten Gefreiter.*

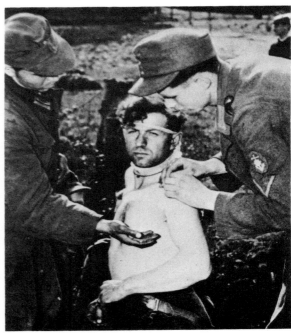

85. *Gefreiter Steuermann.*

2.2. Army proficiency badges
Heeres Leistungs Abzeichen

Certain military insignia was worn on the German Army uniform which, although representing a qualification, distinguished the wearer as possessing a special skill directly related to the type of military unit in which he was serving. These badges therefore tended to be regarded with more esteem by the recipient than was the case with the trade badges and specialist insignia.

These proficiency badges were:
1. The Gebirgsjäger Edelweiss arm badge in cloth (plate 86)
2. The Jäger oakleaves arm badge in cloth (plate 87)
3. The Ski-Jäger arm badge in cloth
4. The Bergführer breast badge in enamelled metal (plate 88)

2.2(1). *The Gebirgsjäger arm badge* was first introduced for wear on 2nd May 1939. It was to be worn on the right upper arm 16cm from the shoulder seam on the Field Blouse, the Uniform Tunic and the Greatcoat by all qualified members of army mountain troop units. The badge consisted of an embroidered Edelweiss flower with white petals and yellow stamens, and with a pale green stem and leaves. Surrounding the flower was a twisted mountaineering rope in matt grey thread with a silver-white piton (spike and ring).

The entire design was worked on a dark green oval background. Two forms of this badge exist; the superior quality silk machine-woven type and the felt embroidered version (plate 89). Reference has been seen to an all pale green machine-woven example of this badge as well as a copper-brown Afrika Korps version also silk-woven.

2.2(2). *The Jäger arm badge.* As with the Gebirgsjäger arm badge, the Jäger oakleaves arm badge was issued to be worn on the right upper arm of the Greatcoat, the Service Tunic and the Uniform Tunic by those personnel of Jäger divisions and Jäger battalions. The badge was first introduced by an order dated 2nd October 1942. It had three green oakleaves and one green acorn attached to a small brown twig all of which was embroidered on to a dark green oval background edged with a pale green rope.

Again this emblem exists in two qualities, the felt embroidered version and the quality silk machine-woven example (plate 90).

2.2(3). *The Ski-Jäger arm badge* was an emblem much rarer than either of the preceding two. Similar in design and colour to the Jäger emblem, it had the addition of a pair of copper-brown coloured skis entwined with the green oakleaves. This emblem was also worn on the right upper arm of the military uniform by those personnel from rifle units qualified in the use of snow skis (plate 91).

2.2(4). *The Bergführer breast badge* was a coveted award as well as being a mark of proficiency, worn only by those Army mountain troops who acted as a mountain guide, and had had one year's qualifying experience in this active role. It was a small metal and

86. *The Gebirgsjäger arm badge. A young German taken prisoner at Bayeux, France, June 1944.*

87. *The Jäger arm badge. A Major from the 49th Assault Artillery Regiment, holder of the Knight's Cross.*

88. *The Bergführer breast badge. General der Gebirgstruppen Ringel presenting the Iron Cross to members of the German Mountain units which took part in the battle for Crete, June 1941.*

89. *Felt embroidered Gebirgsjäger arm badge.*

90. *BeVo quality silk version of the Jäger arm badge.*

91. *The Ski-Jäger arm badge.*

93. *The Feldgendarmerie eagle arm badge.*

enamelled pin-backed badge worn on the left breast pocket of the Service Tunic and on the lower left breast of the Uniform Tunic. It had a silver (with gilt centred) metal Edelweiss flower, without stem, set in a small white enamelled oval rim bearing the words *HEERESBERGFÜHRER* in gothic lettering on the lower portion of the rim (plate 92). This badge was first introduced for wear by an order dated 10th August 1936.

It should be noted that worn with the Gebirgsjäger, the Jäger and the Ski-Jäger arm badges were cap badges of a similar design. Information and details regarding these cap badges can be found in the section dealing with the subject of head-dress insignia.

2.3. The Military Field Police eagle arm badge
Das Feldgendarmerie Polizei Adler Ärmel Abzeichen

Worn on the upper left arm of the army Service Tunic this badge showed the Police-style Eagle and Swastika set against an oval wreath of oakleaves.

Officer's arm badges were worked in fine silver wire on a background of field-grey cloth. All other junior ranks wore the badge embroidered in orange coloured thread with the swastika worked in black thread (plate 93).

For additional information on the Feldgendarmerie see the section on cuff-titles and Part III, Uniforms and Tunics, Head-dress and Footwear dealing with the Feldgendarmerie Uniform.

2.4. Army marksmanship lanyards
Schützen Abzeichen des deutschen Heeres

In order to stimulate the soldiers' interest in marksmanship and, at the same time, to recognize the ability of skilled marksmen a series of marksmanship lanyards were awarded in varying grades for skill with a variety

92. *Metal and enamelled version of the Bergführer breast badge.*

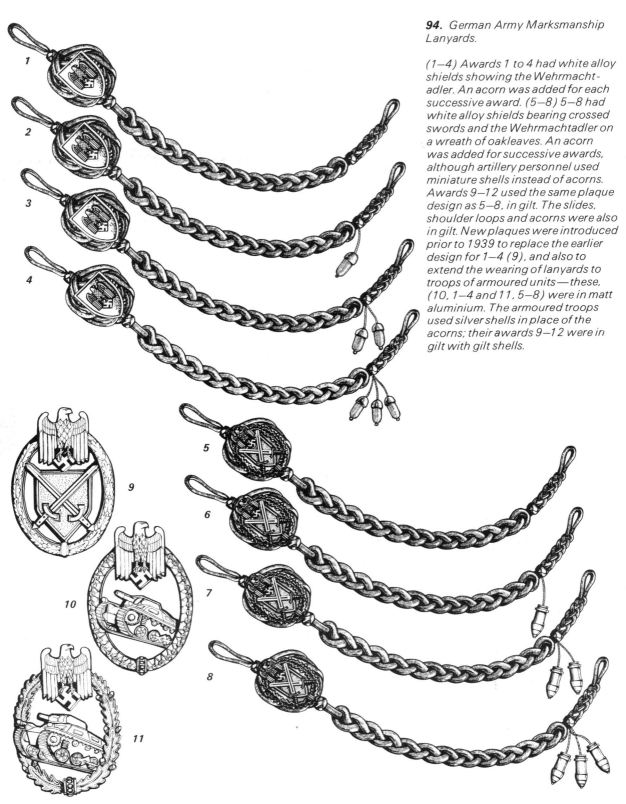

94. German Army Marksmanship Lanyards.

(1–4) Awards 1 to 4 had white alloy shields showing the Wehrmacht-adler. An acorn was added for each successive award. (5–8) 5–8 had white alloy shields bearing crossed swords and the Wehrmachtadler on a wreath of oakleaves. An acorn was added for successive awards, although artillery personnel used miniature shells instead of acorns. Awards 9–12 used the same plaque design as 5–8, in gilt. The slides, shoulder loops and acorns were also in gilt. New plaques were introduced prior to 1939 to replace the earlier design for 1–4 (9), and also to extend the wearing of lanyards to troops of armoured units — these, (10, 1–4 and 11, 5–8) were in matt aluminium. The armoured troops used silver shells in place of the acorns; their awards 9–12 were in gilt with gilt shells.

55

95. Examples of three Army marksmanship lanyard plaques, (i) Basic award for marksmanship groups 1 to 4 (early pattern plaque). (ii) Basic award for marksmanship groups 1 to 4 (new pattern plaque). (iii) Basic award for Panzer marksmanship groups 5 to 8 (new pattern plaque).

96. The method of wear for the German Army Marksmanship Lanyard. 5th class award with the new pattern lanyard plaque being worn for parade.

97. Collecting for winter relief. The Feldwebel is wearing the lowest grade marksmanship lanyard with the early pattern plaque worn for walking out.

of weapons. These Lanyards, a list of which can be found on page 55, were constructed in semi-bright aluminium cords plaited with a flat portion bearing an alloy metal plaque of varying design (plate 95) worn nearest the right shoulder held in position under the right shoulder strap by a small grey horn button. The other end to the lanyard was extended across the chest and attached inside the tunic flap to the second button down from the neck of the tunic (plate 96).

Marksmanship lanyards for the army were originally introduced by an order dated 29th June 1936 and were to be worn by all qualifying ranks below that of officer. They could be worn with the Parade, Reporting, Walking-out and Guard Uniform but not on the Greatcoat (plate 97).

2.5. Military decorations (badges) awarded to troops for individual skill at arms under battle conditions

Three separate types of decorations were awarded by the Germans at different times during the war. Each of them can be considered as different from the many other awards and decorations[1] in so far as they were each awarded to an individual person in recognition of that person's particular skill and destruction of the enemy with a hand-held weapon under battle conditions. It could almost be said that these awards were a wartime extension of the early shooting insignia and marksmanship lanyards which themselves were awarded for individual skill at arms. The badges in question were:
1. The Special Badge for single-handed destruction of a Tank (plate 98)
2. The Badge for shooting down Low-Flying Aircraft (plate 99)
3. The Sniper's Badge in three grades (plates 100, 101, 102)

2.5(1). *The Special Badge for the single-handed destruction of a Tank (Sonderabzeichen für das niederkämpfen von Panzerkampfwagen durch Einzelkämpfer).* This badge was instituted on 9th March 1942 but was backdated to 22nd June 1941 to cover the Russian Campaign. It was in two classes, silver and gold. Each silver award represented one enemy

tank destroyed by the recipient single-handed and without the use of an anti-tank weapon. Five such awards could be bestowed on any one man, any further awards being in gold; e.g., for 2 enemy tanks destroyed the recipient received 2 silver emblems, for 5 tanks destroyed 1 gilt emblem, for 8 tanks destroyed 1 gilt and 3 silver emblems.

The badges were a rectangular *Ärmelstreife* 8·5cm long by 3cm deep. They were constructed from silver aluminium corded cloth edged top and bottom with a band 0·3cm wide of black woven thread. In the centre of the badge was a bronze coloured metal representation of a tank, the design of which was based on a mixture of the Pz.Kpfw.III and Pz.Kpfw.IV tanks, facing to the left. The gold class to this award was of the same design as the silver but the corded cloth used was of a gold colour. It was worn by all qualifying ranks of the Army on the right upper sleeve on the Service, Field Service and Uniform Tunic but not the Greatcoat (plate 103).

2.5(2). *The Badge for shooting down Low-Flying Aircraft (Tieffliegervernichtungsabzeichen).* This badge was instituted on 12th January 1945. It was in two classes, silver and gilt. Each silver award represented the shooting down of an enemy aircraft by the recipient with a hand-held weapon, such as a rifle, machine-pistol or machine-gun of 1·2cm calibre or smaller. For every extra aircraft destroyed in this way an additional silver badge was awarded. After five such awards a gold version of the badge was given. The system of awarding this type of badge corresponded to the awards of the 'tank destruction badge'.

The badges were a rectangular Armelstreife 9cm long and 3·2cm deep made of silver or gold (depending on the class) corded cloth both with top and bottom edged in black, 0·3cm thick. On the silver class of this award there appeared a black metal representation of an aircraft as seen from above set at an angle across the background cloth. The gold class used the same design of aircraft but this appeared in gold.

It was intended to be worn by all qualifying personnel on the right upper arm of the Service, Field Service and Uniform Tunic but not on the Greatcoat. However it is not known if this award was ever made or issued, being instituted so late in the war.

2.5(3). *The Snipers' Badge (Scharfschützenabzeichen).* The Snipers' Badge was instituted by an order dated 20th August 1944. It was awarded in one of three classes depending on the recipient's qualifi-

[1] Further research into the subject of German military awards and decorations may be aided by the excellent publication written by Colonel C. M. Dodkins, *D.S.O., O.B.E.* and David Littlejohn, *M.A., A.L.A.* entitled *Orders, Decorations, Medals and Badges of the Third Reich—including the Free City of Danzig,* published by Roger James Bender publications of California, U.S.A.

98. *The silver class of the Tank Destruction Badge.*

99. *The Low Flying Aircraft Destruction Badge.*

100. *Sniper's Badge, 3rd class*

101. *Sniper's Badge, 2nd class.*

102. *Sniper's Badge, 1st class*

103. *An Obergefreiter awarded four Panzervernichtungsabzeichen for his single handed destruction of four Soviet tanks.*

104. *The Reichsheer sports vest emblem, seen here being worn during the Reichswehr sports festival held at Berlin Moabit, 1934.*

105. The German Army Officers' aiguillettes.

106. The aiguillettes worn by Adjutants.

cations and only those marksmen employed in the capacity of a sniper were eligible. The badge was worn on the right cuff above all other insignia on the Field Service, the Service and the Uniform Tunic but not on the Greatcoat.

The design of the badge was as follows: a black eagle's head rising out of three green oakleaves and a small brown acorn all of which were embroidered on to an oval background of grey cloth. The eagle's beak and eye were worked in yellow thread with the details of the feathers emphasized in white cotton.

The three classes to this award were as follows. The 3rd class award of the snipers' badge was as described above and to be eligible the recipient had to have made 20 kills. The 2nd class award had the addition of a silver border to the oval badge and to be awarded this class meant a total of 40 kills. The 1st, and highest class, of the award had a gold border to the badge and its award required the recipient to have made 60 kills.

2.6. Army sports vest emblems
Heeres Sport Hemd Abzeichen

White vests were worn as part of the sports kit issued to the German soldier and, in common with most military, para-military and political formations of the German Third Reich, an emblem was displayed on the front of the vest which identified either by design or by colour the wearer's branch of service, para-military or political formation.

The German Army were issued a large (25cm × 12cm) machine-woven National Emblem in black cotton on a white cloth background. This was sewn on to the vest and worn in a position across the chest front (plate 236).

Prior to the introduction of the Eagle and Swastika National Emblem badge an earlier emblem was used during the Reichsheer and early National Socialist period, consisting of a red shield with a black short sword, point downwards. Again this emblem was worn on the vest on the front of the chest (plate 104).

2.7. Officers' aiguillettes, and those worn by army adjutants
Die Achselbänder und Adjutantschnüre

German Army aiguillettes were possibly the one item of uniform accoutrement that was worn purely for display purposes. Worn only by Army officers, officials and Generals on certain ceremonial occasions and on certain forms of uniform dress it represented no trade, skill or speciality and, although the origins of the aiguillette can be traced back beyond the Franco-Prussian War,[1] the 1935 model aiguillette had no function other than that of pure decoration.

The German Army officers' aiguillette was first introduced on 29th June 1935 at the same time as the

[1] The 'modern' German aiguillette originated prior to the War of Liberation and was in use in Prussia after the reforms of 1808. Aiguillettes of a type were, however, in use in the Prussian Army as early as 1730.

introduction of the new German Army Waffenrock or Uniform Tunic. It was manufactured from silver cording and was worn by all army officers, including Panzer officers wearing the black Panzer Uniform, army administrative officials—Wehrmachtbeamten, but not military clergy—with the Parade, Full Dress and Walking-out uniforms. It was also to be worn on parades for the Führer, and parades held on the Führer's birthday (plate 105).

The aiguillettes worn by directors of music and music inspectors were of the same design and colour but had the addition of a red silk thread decoration running through the silver cords.

Army Generäle and Generalfeldmarschälle, as well as administrative officials of equivalent rank, wore aiguillettes made from gilt cord.

The parade aiguillette was worn around the right shoulder and across the right side of the tunic chest. It was held in position under the right shoulder strap by a small horn button, the other end being fastened in place by the second and third button from the neck of the tunic under the tunic flap. It was not worn on the Greatcoat.

The aiguillettes worn by army adjutants, however, were a mark of office. They were also worn by staff officers; these aiguillettes were constructed from dull silver cord and were of a more simple design than the parade aiguillettes. In keeping with the latter, the adjutants' aiguillettes were also worn suspended from the right shoulder, carried across the right breast of the uniform and held in position under the tunic flap by the second button down from the tunic collar (plate 106). These were intended to be worn on the officers' Service, Field Service, and Reporting Uniform as well as the Greatcoat.

2.8. Gorgets
Ringkragen

Ringkragen were worn as a distinguishing mark, indicating to an observer that the wearer held a special position within the military framework of his particular unit.

The known varieties of gorgets worn by army personnel during the period from 1933 to 1945 were as follows:
1. The Fahnenträger Ringkragen, both Imperial and National Socialist design (plate 107)
2. The Feldgendarmerie Ringkragen (plate 108)
3. The Bahnhofswache Ringkragen (plate 109)
4. **The Kommandantur Ringkragen (plate 110)**
5. The Feldjägerkorps Ringkragen (plate 111)
6. The Feldherrnhalle Ringkragen (plate 112)

107. *The German Army Regimental Standard Bearers' Gorget, National Socialist design. The shield is of 'new silver', a dull silver finish with a bronzed coloured 'chain'. The bosses, oakleaves and design are also of a bronzed coloured finish.*

108. *The German Army Feldgendarmerie duty Gorget. The shield and chain are of a dull matt silver finish, the bosses and eagle and swastika emblem have a luminous paint finish, and the scroll is coloured a dark field-grey with lettering picked out in luminous paint.*

109. *The Bahnhofswache duty gorget. The shield and chain are of a dull matt silver finish. The scroll is painted field-grey with the lettering picked out in luminous paint. The 'Wehrmachtadler' bosses are also finished with a yellow/green luminous paint.*

110. The Kommandanture duty gorget. The shield and chain are in dull matt silver finished metal and the field-grey scroll has lettering picked out in luminous paint. The bosses are also finished with luminous paint.
111. The Feldjägerkorps gorget. Almost identical in design and finish to the Feldgendarmerie duty gorget this Ringkragen is coloured in exactly the same way as the Field Police gorget.

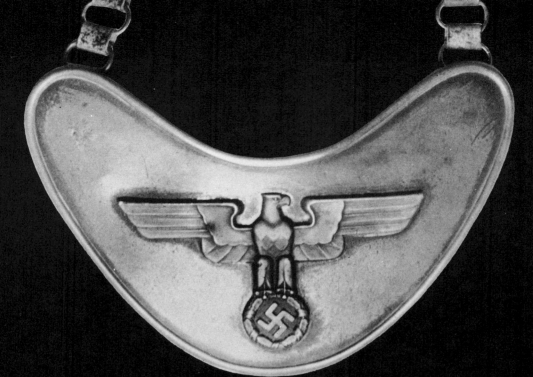

112. *The Feldherrnhalle gorget. The shield and chain is finished in 'new silver'. The raised outer rim to the shield and the eagle and swastika emblem are in a polished gilt finish.*

113. *An Oberwachtmeister from an Army Feldgendarmerie unit questioning a soldier of the 'Russian Army of Liberation', the R.O.A.*

114. *German Field Police accompanied by native police patrolling through a bazaar in the Arab quarter of Derna.*

2.8(1). *Fahnenträger Ringkragen* were only worn by army NCOs appointed as colour bearers and only used while they were parading their regimental Standarten or Fahnen. During the period 1933–45 both the old Imperial standard bearer's gorget (plate 115) and the Wehrmacht pattern gorgets were used (plate 116). The latter superseded the former when it was introduced on 4th August 1936. They were intended to be worn on the Service, Field Service and Uniform Tunic as well as the Greatcoat.

2.8(2). *The Feldgendarmerie Ringkragen* were worn by all field police personnel when on duty (plate 113). For details describing the duties performed by the Feldgendarmerie see page 132. The Feldgendarmerie Ringkragen was intended to be worn with the Service, the Field Service, the Uniform Tunic, the Winter Tunic,

the Tropical Uniform (plate 114) and the Greatcoat as well as with the Motorcycle Coat.

2.8(3). *The Bahnhofswache Ringkragen.* Certain German Army troops were selected to act as a form of military police and advisers to military personnel at main line passenger railway stations. When on duty they were distinguished by wearing the Bahnhofswach Ringkragen. As part of their duties they were responsible for the control of military personnel and civilians passing through railway stations, the patrol of passenger railway areas, and the checking of travel and leave passes. They had the power of arrest over those persons who by their manner gave rise to suspicion.

The Bahnhofswach gorget was to be worn with the Service, and Field Service Uniforms and the Greatcoat.

2.8(4). *The Kommandantur Ringkragen* was worn by

115. *The Imperial German Army Standard Bearers' Gorgets continued in use prior to the introduction of the new National Socialist pattern. Here the tradition standards of the old Imperial Guard Regiments are handed over to the young German Wehrmacht. Königsplatz, Berlin, 5th May 1935.*

116. *The Wehrmacht pattern Fahnenträger Ring-kragen seen here worn by a Standard Bearer from a Gebirgsjäger Regiment.*

117. *An example of the BeVo quality German Army Regimental Standard Bearers' armshield. The 'shield' shaped background is dark green, the Wehrmacht style eagle and swastika is black picked out with silver-grey stitching. The background colouring to the regimental standards is in the colour of the wearer's waffenfarbe. Reproduced here is an example for an artillery regiment.*

those army personnel appointed by military district commanders to act as street patrols within their areas of command. This gorget was intended to be worn on the Service and Field Service Uniforms as well as the Greatcoat and Motorcycle Coat.

2.8(5). *Feldjägerkorps Ringkragen.* Feldjägerkommandos were army units consisting of officers, NCOs and men all of whom had front-line experience; they had been formed late in the war for the purpose of arresting military deserters, apprehending looters and insubordinates as well as 'press-ganging' rear area soldiers in an attempt to fill gaps in the front during times of emergency. In addition to exercising special emergency measures, commanders of Feldjäger units had the power to conduct 'flying courts-martial'.

When carrying out these duties these troops wore the Feldjägerkorps Ringkragen. This could be used with any form of military uniform being worn.

2.8(6). *The Feldherrnhalle Ringkragen* was used in the army on parade occasions by those Army personnel acting as an 'Honour Guard' for units from the 60.Panzer-Grenadier-Division 'Feldherrnhalle' and the 271.Infanterie-Regiment 'Feldherrnhalle'.

The gorget used by these units was identical to that used by the élite S.A. unit of the same name. It was worn by these army troops as a mark of distinction which, along with the 'Feldherrnhalle' cuff-title (see page 79) and special S.A. shoulder strap insignia (see page 32), emphasized the direct links these army units

had with the National Socialist Sturm Abteilung formation.

2.9. The Army standard bearer's arm shield
Das Heeres Fahnen Träger Ärmel Schild

The original standard bearer's arm-shield was first introduced for wear in the German Army by an Allerhöchste Kabinetts-Ordre (A.K.O.) dated 15th June 1898. This emblem ceased to be used after 1919.

On 4th August 1936 a new version of the original standard bearer's arm-shield was introduced (plate 117). It was initially intended to be worn on the right upper arm only on the Field Service, the Service and the Uniform Tunics but not on the Greatcoat. This last stipulation was, however, later withdrawn and the Greatcoat was included in the list of military clothing that could display the arm-shield.

Like the Fahnenträger Ringkragen, the arm-shield distinguished the wearer as holding a special position within his military unit, that of a standard bearer. But, unlike the gorget which was easily removable once the necessity for it to be worn had passed, the arm-shields were of a more permanent nature (plate 118).

Those branches of the army who had been

presented with Fahnen and Standarten, and therefore had appointed standard bearers, were as follows: Infanterie, Jäger, Pioniere, Artillerie, Kavallerie, Kraftfahrkampftruppe, Fahr- und Kraftfahr-Einheiten, Pioniere (mot.), Nachrichtentruppe, Nebeltruppe, Schützentruppe, Aufklärungs-Abteilung, Führer-Begleitbataillon.

The predominant colour used in the arm-shields matched the wearer's Waffenfarbe and the colour of the standard being carried. These colours are listed along with the details of the arm-shield design to be found on the opposite page.

2.10. The Army standard bearer's carrying sash
Das Heeres Fahnen Träger Schärpe

The German Army standard bearers' carrying sashes consisted of a wide leather-backed, heavy gauge silver braid, incorporating silk embroidery in the colour of the wearers' Waffenfarbe. There was a leather cup to hold and support the base of the standard pole, and the sash was worn over the left shoulder across the body with the cup lying against the wearer's right thigh (plate 119).

2.11. 'Swallows' nests'
Schwalbennester

Swallows' nests (Schwalbennester) or, as they are referred to in the British Army, 'Musicians' Wings' were a traditional item of dress decoration worn by German military musicians (plate 120). They served to show, by the use of colour, the wearer's branch of service as well as showing him to be a military musician.

Swallows' nests were worn in the German Army by three groups of musicians. These were:
1. Drum and fife musicians (Spielmann und Spielleute) had their nests constructed with dull grey braiding on a backing of appropriate waffenfarbe cloth. There was no fringe to these nests.
2. Regimental bandsmen and trumpeters (Musiker und Trompeter) had their nests constructed with bright aluminium braiding on a backing of appropriate Waffenfarbe cloth. There was no fringe to these nests.
3. Battalion buglers (Bataillonshornist) had their nests constructed with bright aluminium braiding also on a backing of appropriate Waffenfarbe cloth. They wore a 7cm deep fringe to their swallows' nests.

Schwalbennester were worn in matching pairs one to each shoulder on the Field Service, the Service and Uniform Tunic but not on the Greatcoat, and by all arms including Panzer troops wearing the black Special Panzer Uniform. The swallows' nests were removable, being held in position on the jacket by five metal hooks which clipped into five eyelets stitched around both the shoulder seams (plates 121, 122, 123).
(See also the Uniform Section dealing with the German Army Bandsmen's Service Uniform with Swallows' Nests.)

118. A regimental Fahnenträger with the rank of Feldwebel giving instruction during rifle firing practice. Unlike the Fahnenträger Ringkragen the Standard Bearers' armshield was not readily removable.

119. *Standard Bearers' Carrying Sashes. General der Artillerie von Reichenau, commanding general of the Armee Korps VII and senior commander in Wehrkreis VII, presenting new Fahnen and Standarten at a ceremony held at Munich, 19th April 1937.*

120. The use of Army Swallows' nests. A parade of the fife and drum section from the honour company of Wachtruppe Berlin.

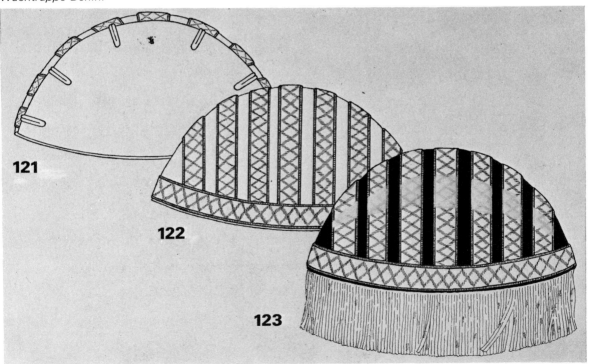

121, 122, 123. German Army Swallows' nests: 122, Drum and Fife, 123, Drum Major, 121, the reverse of a Swallows' nest showing the arrangement of hooks.

2.12. Troddel, Faustriemen and Portepee

In peacetime Germany, and during the war in those areas of the Greater German Reich where the military conditions were considered stable enough to warrant the wearing of this decorative feature, a system of coloured sidearm tassels were used by the Germans below the rank of Fähnrich. As well as being a decorative feature of the Parade and Walking-out uniforms they also allowed an initiated observer to place with precision the exact whereabouts of the soldier in his regiment. (The soldier's branch of service and his regimental and company number or designation could be established from the colour of his 'Waffenfarbe' and the numbering used on his shoulder straps and shoulder strap buttons.)

The Troddel was worn by Infanterie-, Artillerie-, Pioniere-, Nachrichten-, Panzerabwehr- (Kraftfahrkampf-) and Nachschubtruppe. Faustriemen were worn by troops of Kavallerie and Schützenregimenter.

The German Army Troddel was divided into the following parts (plate 125):

1. The Strap (das Band), coloured dark green for regimental and battalion staff as well as the 13th and 14th companies: grey for the rest
2. The Slide (das Schieber) in the company colours
3. The Stem (der Stengel) in the battalion colours
4. The Crown (der Kranz) like the slide, in the company colours

5. The Tassel (der Quast) in grey or dark green to match the strap

The German Army Faustriemen was divided into the following parts (plate 126):

1. The Leather Strap (der Lederriemen) in field-grey
2. The Slide (der Schieber) in the 'Abteilung' colour
3. The Crown (der Kranz) in the squadron colour
4. The Tassel (der Quast) in dark green for staff and light grey for squadrons

A full colour chart of all colours used both for Troddel and Faustriemen can be found on page 25.

The sequence of battalion and company colours used for these sidearm tassels was based on the colour seniority introduced with the Prussian Army reforms after 1808.

The NCOs and men of the 3rd battalion Headquarters and the 10th, 11th and 12th companies from the 67th Infantry Regiment wore, to commemorate the 1st Regiment of (Prussian) Grenadier Guards, their Troddeln on a strap of red Russian leather.

Fahnen Junker-Gefreiter, Unteroffizier, Unterfeldwebel and Unterwachtmeister wore their Troddeln and Faustriemen of a special design without relation to their Company colours (plate 124).

The German Army NCOs Troddel was divided thus (plate 127):

1. The strap was dark green material with three thin silver stripes on each side

124. The Troddel of a special design worn by Army Unteroffizieren.

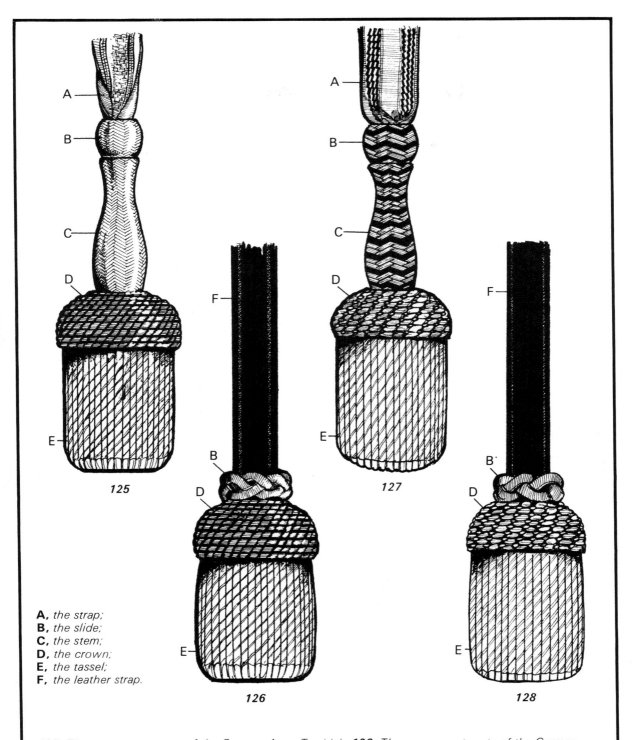

A, the strap;
B, the slide;
C, the stem;
D, the crown;
E, the tassel;
F, the leather strap.

125. The component parts of the German Army Troddel. **126.** The component parts of the German Army Faustriemen. **127.** The component parts of the German Army Troddel for NCOs. **128.** The component parts of the German Army Faustriemen for NCOs.

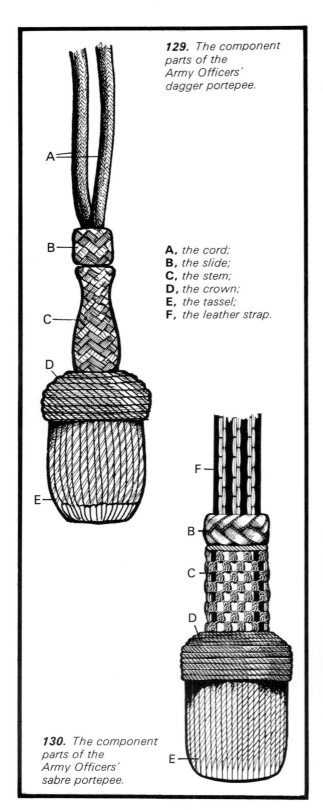

129. *The component parts of the Army Officers' dagger portepee.*

A

B

A, *the cord;*
B, *the slide;*
C, *the stem;*
D, *the crown;*
E, *the tassel;*
F, *the leather strap.*

C

D

E

F

B

C

D

E

130. *The component parts of the Army Officers' sabre portepee.*

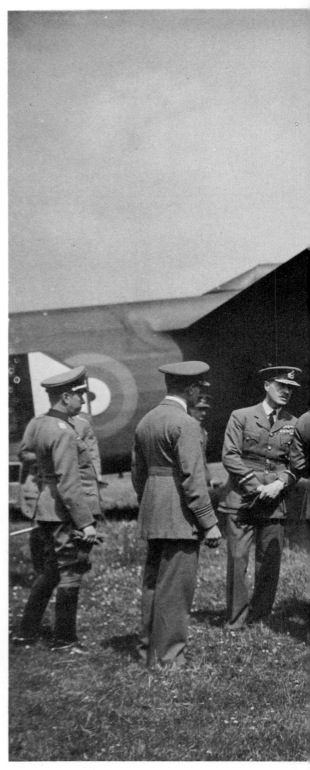

131. *The German Army Officers' dagger Portepee.*

Generaloberst Werner von Blomberg, on an official visit to England before the war, with senior R.A.F. officers.

132. *The German Army Officers' sabre Portepee. Generaloberst von Blomberg, Minister of War and Commander-in-Chief of the Wehrmacht (1935—38), is seen here with other senior German Army officers in*

conversation with visiting foreign politicians in front of the Ehrenmal, Berlin.

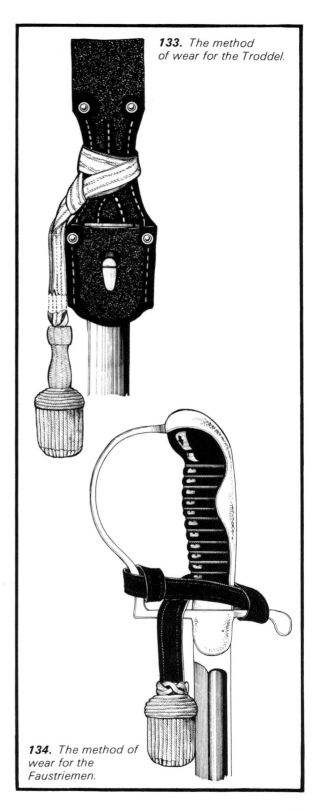

133. The method of wear for the Troddel.

134. The method of wear for the Faustriemen.

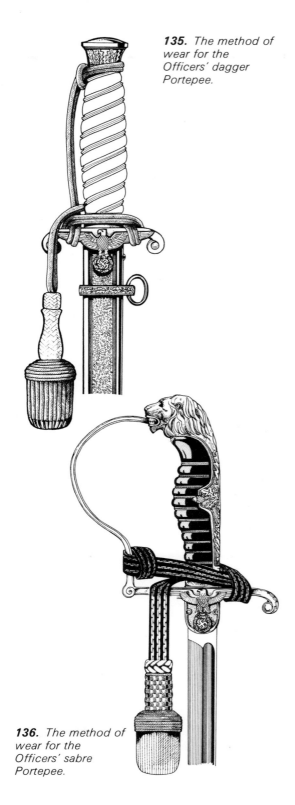

135. *The method of wear for the Officers' dagger Portepee.*

136. *The method of wear for the Officers' sabre Portepee.*

2. The slide, the stem and the crown were in dark green with silver thread patterning
3. The tassel was of dull matt silver

The German Army NCOs Faustriemen was divided thus (plate 128):
1. The strap was of light grey leather
2. The slide was a narrow loop of field-grey leather, sometimes plaited
3. The crown was dark green with silver decoration
4. The tassel was of dull matt silver

The German Army Portepee was worn in place of the Troddeln and Faustriemen by all ranks from Fähnrich upwards. When worn on the officer's dagger it was all silver. The 'strap' on this sidearm tassel consisted of a continuous loop of silver cord, which when laid flat was 42cm long, the slide, stem, crown and tassel all being in silver (plate 129). The Portepee worn with the army sabre and bayonet was also in silver with the wide strap of field-grey leather decorated with four silver strips (plates 130, 131, 132).

Illustrations showing the method by which all these four types of sidearm tassels were worn can be found overleaf and on this page (plates 133–136).

2.13. German Army cuff-titles

Cuff-titles worn in the German Army can be divided into three groups.
1. Those cuff-titles awarded as a battle honour and were the equivalent of a campaign medal.
2. Those cuff-titles worn by certain élite army units and formations.
3. Those cuff-titles worn by personnel of a training school, command staff or special formation amongst others.

Cuff-titles known to have been issued and worn by army personnel are listed below along with other information. This list does not include slight variations of colour and manufacture occurring in the issued title.

The following are of type 1 in the list given above, awarded as battle honours.

2.13(1). *1936 SPANIEN 1939.* Instituted on 21st June 1939 to commemorate the German Troops who served in the 'Panzer Lehr- Regiments' and the 'Nachrichten Lehrabteilung' in Spain (Traditionstruppenteile der 'Imker-Verbände' der 'Legion Condor'). The title was 3·2cm wide with gold gothic lettering and dates on a red band edged in gold. It was prescribed to be worn on the Service Blouse 15cm above the lower edge of the tunic sleeve and on the Uniform Tunic when it was worn on the right cuff 7·5cm above the 'Swedish cuff-facing'. On the Officers' Piped Field Service Tunic and on the Greatcoat for Parade and Walking-out it was worn 1cm above the upper edge to the right cuff turn-back.

2.13(2). *AFRIKAKORPS.* Instituted on 18th July 1941, it was authorized for wear by members of the Deutsches Afrika Korps fighting in North Africa. The title was 3·3cm wide with silver block lettering on a dark green background. This was edged top and bottom with a band of silver 0·3cm wide and these

137. *The 'Afrikakorps' cuff-title.*

138. *The 'Afrika' with palms cuff-title.*

silver bands were themselves edged in a tan coloured material. This title was worn on the right cuff of Service, Field Service and Uniform Tunics as well as the Greatcoat (plate 137).

2.13(3). *KRETA.* Instituted on 16th October 1942 for wear by those German troops who took part in the successful battle for Crete. The title was 3·3cm wide with the word *KRETA* in roman lettering worked in yellow thread on a white band. The edging and the two acanthus leaf emblems either side of the word were also in yellow cotton thread. This title was intended to be worn by all eligible personnel on the left cuff of all uniform jackets including the Greatcoat.

2.13(4). *AFRIKA* with Palms. Instituted on 15th January 1943 and intended to replace the earlier *AFRIKAKORPS* cuff-title. The title was in a soft khaki coloured cloth 3·3cm wide with the wording, the edging and the two representations of palm trees positioned either side of the lettering all in silver-grey cotton thread. This title was worn on left cuff of all army uniforms including the Greatcoat (plate 138).

2.13(5). *METZ 1944.* Instituted on 24th October 1944 for wear by those troops who took part in the fighting for the citadel of Metz from 27th July to 25th September 1944. This cuff-title was considered as a campaign badge (Kampfabzeichen) for all troops in Kampfgruppe von Siegroth and as a tradition badge (Traditionsabzeichen) for all officers, officials, NCOs and men from the VI Schule für Fahnenjunker der Infanterie in Metz, all of whom took part in the fighting. The title was in black cloth 3·3cm wide with the lettering, date and edging in silver wire. It was worn on the left cuff of all Tunics as well as the Greatcoat.

2.13(6). *KURLAND.* Instituted on 12th March 1945, this proved to be the last cuff-title ever instituted in the Wehrmacht. It was intended to be awarded to those German forces surrounded and cut off in the Courland region of Latvia. The *KURLAND* cuff-title was approximately 4cm wide and made from silver-grey to grey-white cloth edged in black. The wording and the two emblems—the shield on the left that of the Grand Masters of the Order of Teutonic Knights and that on the right bearing an elk's head (the arms of Mitau, the principal town in Courland)—were all worked in black thread. Those troops who actually received a cuff-title wore it on the left cuff.

The following were worn by élite formations.

2.13(7). *GROSSDEUTSCHLAND.* Instituted on 15th September 1939 for wear by all members of Infanterie Regiment 'Grossdeutschland'. It was a band of dark green material with silver edging and silver machine-woven gothic lettering and was worn on the right cuff. This title is illustrated in plate 279, and details regarding its wear can be found on page 153.

2.13(8). *INF. REGT. GROSSDEUTSCHLAND.* Instituted in May 1940 to replace the above title for wear by all personnel from Infanterie Regiment 'Grossdeutschland'. The title was in black cloth with silver gothic lettering and silver edging. This too was worn on the right cuff.

139. *The 'Grossdeutschland' cuff-title.*

140. *The 'Propagandakompanie' cuff-title.*

2.13(9). *GROSSDEUTSCHLAND.* Instituted on 7th October 1940 this new title was introduced to replace the previous two. It was issued to be worn by all ranks of Infanterie Regiment 'Grossdeutschland' and the Führer-Begleitbataillon. It was 3·2cm wide in black material with silver edging and silver hand stitched German script lettering (plate 139).

2.13(10). *GROSSDEUTSCHLAND.* Instituted about the same time as the above title this version was in fact a variation of lettering style. The colours and size were the same but the lettering used on this cuff-title was in silver handwritten (copper plate) script.

2.13(11). *BRANDENBURG.* Silver gothic lettering on a black band.

2.13(12). *FELDHERRNHALLE.* Originally awarded to all members of Infanterie-Regiment 271, known as Infanterie Regiment 'Feldherrnhalle' on 4th September 1942. The title, 2·7cm wide, was in S.A. brown cloth edged in silver-grey cotton thread and with the silver lettering machine woven in German script. It was worn on the left cuff of the Uniform Tunic 7·5cm above the 'Swedish' cuff-facings, on the Service Tunic 15cm from the lower edge of the sleeve and on the Greatcoat 1cm above the upper edge of the turn-back cuff.

2.13(13). *INFANTERIE REGIMENT LIST.* Awarded to all ranks of the 199.Grenadier-Regiment from the 57.Infanterie-Division during the winter of 1944 to commemorate the Imperial German regiment in which Hitler had served as a Gefreiter. It was a 3·2cm wide band of dark green cloth with grey-white edging and copper-plate style lettering. It was worn on the left cuff.

2.13(14). *FELDMARSCHALL VON MACKENSEN.* Instituted on 6th December 1944 it was issued to be worn by all ranks of 5.Kavallerie-Regiment. A number of variations existed of this title. The one described here was in black cloth with white edging and white block lettering.

The following titles were issued to special formations.

2.13(15). *PROPAGANDAKOMPANIE.* Instituted before the war, this cuff-title was worn by all army personnel engaged in army propaganda. It was a black band 4.3cm wide with machine embroidered silver gothic lettering (plates 140, 142). It was worn on the right cuff.

2.13(16). *FELDPOST.* Instituted on 29th September 1939 for wear by Army Field Post personnel. It was a black band 4·3cm wide and, like the above cuff-title, had machine embroidered silver gothic lettering.

2.13(17). *HEERESMUSIKSCHULE.* Instituted before the war for wear by members of the Army School of Music, it was a dark green band with white-grey edging and gothic lettering and was worn on the right cuff.

2.13(18). *UNTEROFFIZIERVORSCHULE.* Also instituted before the war for wear by the staff and personnel of army preparatory schools for NCOs. It was in dark green material with machine-woven silver edging and gothic lettering. It was worn on the right cuff (plate 143).

141. The 'Führerhauptquartier' cuff-title.

2.13(19). *FELDGENDARMERIE.* Worn by all ranks of German Army Field Police units, it was a brown band 3cm wide with grey cotton edging and machine-woven gothic letters and was worn on the left cuff.

2.13(20). *FÜHRERHAUPTQUARTIER.* Worn by all army personnel entrusted· with the personal safety of the Führer and the security of all personnel and members of the Führer's Headquarters. A black band 4cm wide with gold edging and gold machine woven gothic lettering, it was worn on the left cuff (plate 141).

2.13(21). *FÜHRERHAUPTQUARTIER.* Worn by all personnel as described above, this cuff-title was introduced on 15th January 1941 to replace the earlier black and gold version. The new title was a band of black material edged in silver and with silver hand stitched German script lettering. This title was worn on the left cuff. It was often worn together with the black and silver *GROSSDEUTSCHLAND* cuff-title displayed on the right sleeve.

2.13(22). *O.K.H.-AUSBILDUNGSFILM.* This was instituted on 19th May 1941 to be worn by personnel of Army Film Units. It was a 3cm wide black band with silver gothic lettering. It was worn on the right cuff of the Greatcoat and the Service Tunic.

2,13(23). *STABSHELFERINNEN DES HEERES.* Introduced during the autumn of 1942, it was worn by female assistants working in army offices. The band was moss-green with silver edging and a double row of silver gothic lettering (plate 144). When in these colours it was worn by the rank and file of these female

142. The 'Propagandakompanie' cuff-title.

143. The 'Unteroffiziervorschule' cuff-title.

144. The 'Stabshelferin des Heeres' cuff-title.

145. The German Army stretcher bearers' arm band.

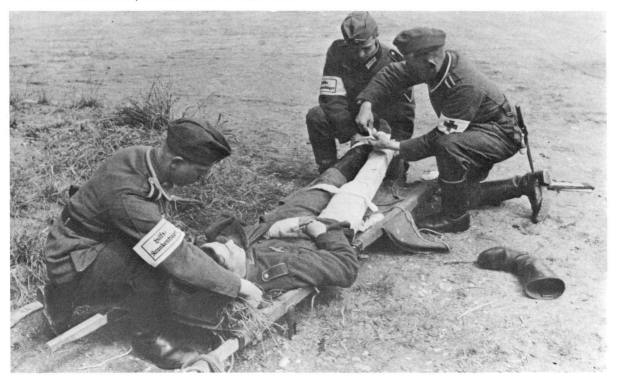

146. Army stretcher bearers receiving instruction for first aid from a medical orderly. Shown here are both the Hilfs-Krankenträger and the Red Cross emblem arm bands.

147, 148. *'In Service of the German Armed Forces': two versions of the same arm band. In accordance with international law persons engaged to serve as noncombatants within the German Armed Forces were obliged to wear an identification armband to be protected as 'soldiers'. Failure to wear such identifying arm bands meant that these 'Wehrmachtmitglieder' or Armed Forces Members were liable to be considered as 'franc-tireurs'.*

149. *A Ukranian auxiliary employed in the service of the German Army.*

helpers, but for the senior personnel known as 'Führerinnen' the title displayed gold lettering.

2.14. Arm-bands
Militärische Ärmelbinden

Armbands or brassards were worn for two reasons. When worn with the military uniform they indicated that the wearer held a special but temporary appointment or position or was fulfilling a particular task, and when worn with civilian clothing they served to indicate that the wearer was officially employed or engaged in a military or ancillary role.

In the German Army armbands were not the property of the individual wearer, but were issued out as necessary and returned to the unit stores when no longer required. In some cases armbands were methodically marked with the ink-stamp of the issuing unit.

A large number of Official armbands were known to have existed; all of them were issued to be worn for a variety of reasons. Colours, size, style of lettering and wording varied accordingly as did the arm and position on the arm that these bands were to be worn. Some armbands were properly manufactured to precise specifications, colours and style of lettering whilst others were more of a makeshift nature, of simple

150. *Frau Hoppe, acting as a military secretary and wearing the yellow and black 'Deutsche Wehrmacht' arm band, seen here after having been taken prisoner by British troops near Verden, April 1945.*

151. *German Armed Forces arm band.*

152. *Field Police arm band.*

153. *The black cloth mourning arm band. Four Generals of the German Army act as a guard of honour during the State Funeral of Generaloberst Dietl, the 'Hero of Narvik', on 3rd July 1944.*

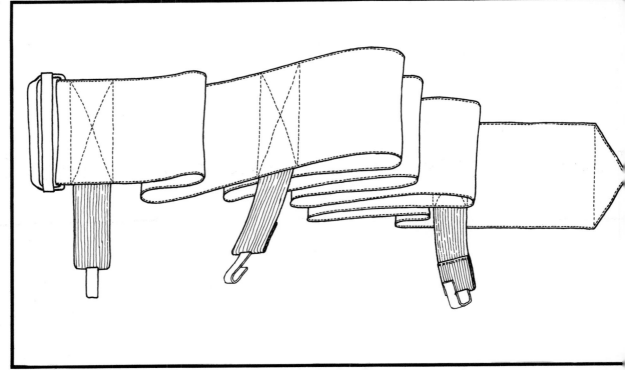

154. *The German Army red and yellow Battle Practice Helmet band.*

construction and lettering but achieving the same purpose.

Below are listed some of the more common types of military armbands:

Hilfs-Krankenträger (plate 145)   Stretcher bearer. Black gothic lettering inside a white, black edged, rectangle on a white band 41cm×10·3cm. Worn on the right upper arm
(Red Cross symbol)   Medical personnel including motor drivers of medical units; a bright red cross on plain white band, it was worn on the left upper arm (plate 146)
Bahnhofswache   Railway station patrol; black gothic lettering on yellow band
Bhf.O.   Bahnhofsoffizier (Bhf.O) below which appeared the number appointed to that particular officer; an army officer appointed to a main-line railway station with the task of the control, discipline and welfare of those troops passing through his area of control
Ausladekommissar   Officer in charge of a transport service centre; black latin block letters on white band, it was worn on the right upper arm
Im Dienst der Deutschen Wehrmacht (plates 147, 148)   In the service of the German Armed Forces. Issued and worn by those persons (usually non-Germans) employed in any military capacity not requiring the issue of a German military uniform; black latin lettering on white band and correctly worn on the left upper arm. Examples of this type of arm-band sometimes incorporated the use of a small band of colours based on the wearer's national flag and representing the wearer's non-German nationality (plate 149)
Deutsche Wehrmacht (plate 151)   German Armed Forces; black gothic lettering on a bright yellow band, it was worn on the left upper arm by those persons employed in the German Armed Forces including the army (plate 151)

Feld-Gendarmerie (plate 152)   Field Police; orange latin lettering on an emerald (police) green band, it was worn by military troops performing as temporary Field-Police
Hilfsgendarmerie   Police Helper; black lettering on a green band and worn by military troops assisting in police work

It should be noted that the 'Deutsche Volkssturm Wehrmacht' armband has not been included in this coverage as it is felt that the Volkssturm is a subject outside the scope of this book.

Black cloth mourning armbands approximately 12cm deep were worn by all ranks of all services on the left sleeve of the uniform jacket or Greatcoat just above the elbow or above the left cuff. It was used whilst the wearer was participating in a military or state funeral, including funeral parades, and when on parade during an official period of state mourning (plate 153).

Plain white cloth armbands approximately 12cm deep were worn by military umpires during army training and demonstration manoeuvres, see section 2.16.

2.15. Red-and-yellow Battle Practice Helmet Band
Rotes und Gelbes Gefechts-Übung Helm Band

When the German Army held demonstration and training manoeuvres, and especially those that took place before the outbreak of the war they were organized in such a way as to simulate actual battle

155, 156. The battle practice helmet band in position.

157. The Military Umpires' white cap band, seen here being worn by the Army Officer on the left of the picture acting as a military umpire during prewar military exercises held in Germany.

conditions. For this purpose the military units taking part were usually divided into two temporary opposing sides.

In order to identify these two sides a Battle-Practice Helmet Band was worn on the steel helmet and which was made in such a way as to be able to show a red band of colour or a yellow band of colour around the body of the helmet depending on which way the battle practice band was fastened to the helmet.

The band itself was made of two lengths of strong hard wearing cotton drill, separately coloured bright red and bright yellow, stitched together to form a reversible band 70cm long and 4cm wide. At one end of the band was a simple light alloy buckle and slide, the other end being shaped and stitched into a shallow point (plate 154).

The band was fixed on to the helmet by being buckled on around the body of the helmet and the three small metal hooks attached to the band by three short field-grey cloth straps hooked on to the rim of the helmet holding the entire battle practice band in position (plates 155, 156).

2.16. Military umpires' white cap band
Militärisches Scheidrichter weisses Kappen Band

During these military exercises and training manoeuvres certain army personnel were appointed to act as umpires and staff to the umpires. These personnel were

distinguished by the simple expedient of wearing a plain white cloth band worn around the cap-band of the Uniform Cap, the Officers' Field Service Cap (both old and new styles) and for NCOs on the body of the Feldmütze. They also wore a white armband on the left arm (plate 157).

2.17. Tradition badges worn on German Army head-dress
Errinnerungsabzeichen an Heeres Kopfbedeckung

In order to perpetuate the traditions of former German Army units certain formations of the 1933–45 period were given the honour of wearing emblems on their head-dress (not the steel helmet) which, in miniaturized form, were adopted from the tradition emblems of those older Imperial and pre-Imperial units with distinguished military history.

Three such tradition emblems existed in the German Army of the Wehrmacht (plates 158, 159, 160) all of them being worn positioned on the front of the cloth form of head-dress between the National Emblem and the oakleaves cluster or, in the case of the Feldmütze, between the National Emblem and the cockade.

2.17(1). *The Totenkopf*, with the bones positioned directly behind the skull, was originally worn by the Prussian 1st and 2nd Bodyguard Hussars. The insignia worn by the 1.Leib-Husaren-Regiment was continued by the 1st Squadron of the 5.Reiter-Regiment in 1921.

158. *Totenkopf tradition cap badge worn by the regimental staff, 1, 2, 4, 5 and 11 squadrons of the 5th Cavalry Regiment, and by all units of the 4th Cavalry Division except the 41st Cavalry Regiment (1944-5).*

159. *Dragonadler tradition cap badge worn by the regimental staff, 2 and 4 squadrons of Reiter-Regiment 6, the 3rd Motor-cycle battalion and all units of the 3rd Cavalry Division (1944-5).*

160. *Totenkopf tradition badge worn by the regimental staff, I and II battalion headquarters, 1, 4, 13 and 14 companies of Infanterie Regiment 17. Also worn by the 2 Abteilung and 4 squadron of Reiter-Regiment 13. Also worn by all members of the 41st Cavalry Regiment from the 4th Cavalry Division (1944-5).*

161. *Oberleutnant Draeger, adjutant to Auf-klarungsabteilung 328, killed on the Donetz on 23rd August 1943 while acting as squadron chief.*

162. *An unnamed Unteroffizier from Infanterie-Regiment 17.*

In 1933 it was worn by the Regimental Staff and the 1st, 5th and 11th Squadrons of 5.Kavallerie-Regiment (plate 161).

The insignia worn by the 2.Leib-Husaren-Regiment was, in 1921, worn by the 2nd Squadron of 5.Reiter-Regiment. In 1933 this Totenkopf was worn by the Regimental Staff, the 1st Abteilung, and 2nd and 4th Squadrons of 5.Kavallerie-Regiment.

2.17(2). *The Totenkopf,* with bones crossed directly below the skull (plate 162), was originally worn by the Brunswick Infantry Regiment 92 and, sometime after 1921 during the Reichswehr period, this tradition badge was passed on to the 1st and 4th Companies of

163. *Ritterkreuzträger and General der Panzer-truppen Cramer accompanied by his aide, Major von Meyer, North Africa 1943.*

165. *An unnamed Major and holder of the Knight's Cross from one of the Army units entitled to the honour of wearing the 'Schwedteradler' tradition badge. Of especial interest is the Army Honour Roll Clasp (Ehrenblatt Spange des Heeres).*

164. *Members of Reiter-Regiment 6 captured during the fighting for the Normandy beach-head, 6th June 1944.*

17.Infanterie-Regiment. On 10th February 1939 this honour was extended to include the Regimental Staff, the 1st and 2nd Battalions and 13th and 14th Companies of 17.Infanterie-Regiment.

The insignia worn by the Brunswick Hussar Regiment 17 was continued on in 1921 by the 4th Squadron of 13.Reiter-Regiment, and in 1939 by the 2nd Abteilung of 13.Kavallerie-Regiment.

2.17(3). *The Dragoon Eagle* correctly known as the *Schwedter Adler* (plates 163, 164, 165) was originally worn by the 1st Brandenburg Dragoon Regiment Nr. 2, sometimes referred to as the 'Schwedter Dragoons'.

This tradition badge was in 1921 worn by the Regimental Staff and the 2nd Squadron of 6.Reiter-Regiment and in 1926 the honour was extended to include the 4th Squadron of the same regiment.

166. A German Army chaplain. Clearly shown being worn on the Officers' Old Style Feldmütze is the Gothic Cross emblem. Normally of white metal, it is of particular interest that this emblem is made from cloth.

There was a change of units holding this tradition emblem sometime during 1933 but on 12th October 1937 Kradschützen Bataillon 3 was also given this distinction.

2.18. Official and semi-official Army cap emblems
Heeres offizielle und halbämtliche Mützen Abzeichen

In addition to the three tradition emblems worn on German Army head-dress described on page 87 certain other forms of insignia were instituted at various times and authorized to be worn on the head-dress of selected German Army formations. These were as follows:

1. The Gothic Cross worn by German Army chaplains and field bishops.
2. The Edelweiss cap badge worn by German Army mountain troops.

167. The Edelweiss cap badge as worn on the Bergmütze.

3. The oakleaf cap badge worn by troops of rifle divisions and rifle battalions.
4. The oakleaf-and-ski cap badge worn by Ski-Jäger troops.
5. The semi-official divisional emblem cap badges worn by certain élite formations.

2.18(1). *The Gotisches Kreuz.* In the Imperial German Army of 1915 and later, army chaplains wore a small white metal cross, with arms of equal length, positioned between the State and the National Cockades on the Schirmmütze. This practice was continued in the Wehrmacht and chaplains in the 'new' German Army wore a small white metal gothic cross. The Gotisches Kreuz was worn on both the Officers' Old-style Feldmütze and the Officers' Schirmmütze positioned below the National Emblem and above the oakleaf cluster surrounding the Reichskokade (plate 166).

2.18(2). *The Edelweiss metal cap badge* was first introduced for wear by members of mountain troop formations on 2nd May 1939. It was introduced at the same time as the Gebirgsjäger Edelweiss arm badge. It was issued in two styles to be worn on both the

168. *The Edelweiss cap badge as worn on the Schirmmütze.*

169. *The Jäger cap badge.*

Bergmütze and the Schirmmütze; the Bergmütze emblem consisted of a white metal Edelweiss flower with stem and leaves showing yellow metal stamens. This was intended to be worn on the left side of the Bergmütze. The stem of the Edelweiss was to be set at an angle of 45° to the lower edge of the cap and positioned with the tip of the stem 2·5cm above the lower edge of the cap and 2cm back from the end of the cap peak (plate 167). The Edelweiss emblem used on the Schirmmütze was without stem and the petals of this flower were in white metal with the stamens in gilt coloured metal. This was worn positioned on the front of the Uniform Cap between the National Emblem and the oakleaf cluster (plate 168).

2.18(3) *The Jäger oakleaf cap badge.* German Army Troops of Jäger divisions and Jäger battalions were, from 2nd August 1942, issued with an aluminium coloured metal badge consisting of a sprig of three oakleaves with a small acorn. This was worn on the left side of the Bergmütze and the Feldmütze (plate 169).

2.18(4). *The Ski-Jäger oakleaf-and-ski cap badge.*

170. *The Ski-Jäger cap badge.*

German Army troops from the Ski-Jäger Brigade 1 were authorized to wear a very similar cap badge to the Jäger badge. This was also made from aluminium coloured metal and consisted of the same style sprig of three oakleaves and small acorn but with the addition of a single snow-ski laid across the leaves; the Ski-Jäger cap badge was introduced on 21st August 1944 and issued to be worn on the left side of the Bergmütze and Feldmütze (plate 170).

2.18(5). *Divisional cap emblems.* Towards the latter half of World War II, certain élite German Army formations, as an outward sign of ésprit de corps and unit pride took to wearing small metal cap emblems representative of their divisional sign. Manufactured in metal and coloured with enamels they were allowed to be worn normally on the left side of the Einheitsfeldmütze (plate 171) and in the centre of the cap band on the left side of the schirmmütze.

171. *An example of the semi-official divisional emblem cap badge. Troops from the 116th Panzer Division receiving mail: on the left side of the Einheitsfeldmütze of the Obergefreiter handing out the post can be seen a small metal badge representative of the 'Windhund' Panzer Division emblem.*

3. Uniforms
Tunics, Military clothing, Head-dress and Footwear

3.1. German Army head-dress
Heeres Kopfbedeckung

The known varieties of German Army Head-dress were as follows:

3.1(1). *The Steel Helmet (der Stahlhelm).*[1] Although it was distinctive in appearance and was universally issued throughout the German Army, the steel helmet changed slightly in design and appearance during those years it was in production. The Model 1916 steel helmet was issued to the troops of the Imperial

German Army to replace the pickelhaube which unlike the new steel helmet, and although very decorative, did not afford the wearer sufficient head and neck protection. The steel helmet was originally designed to protect the wearer's head, neck and—to a certain extent—the shoulders from shrapnel and exploding missiles, falling rocks and earth.

Born out of necessity it became such a common-place item that the helmet, along with the jackboot epitomized for most people the German fighting soldier of two World Wars.

---

[1] For the colouring of German Army steel helmets see page 107.

172. *The early pattern Model 1916 Army Steel Helmet. Reserve troops from Wehrkreiskommando VIII returning to their barrack rooms after a training session. June 1935.*

173. *German Army helmet transfers: on the right side of the steel helmet is a tricolour shield displaying the national colours of black, white and red and, on the left, a silver-white 'Werhrmachtadler' on a black shield.*

174. *The Model 1935 Steel Helmet worn without insignia.*

The Model 1916 continued to be worn unaltered throughout the Reichswehr period and, with the addition of the helmet transfers of the Third Reich (plate 172), right up to 1935 when from 1st July it was replaced by a much smaller and lighter redesigned version. However this early Model 1916 helmet was worn by German Army troops up to 1939 and it continued in use right up till the end of the war, normally being only worn by civilians, Volkssturm personnel and foreign units.

The basic size and shape of the Model 1935 steel helmet varied very little. The most noticeable alterations being the gradual phasing-out of the two helmet transfers (these are both shown in plate 173). During 1940 the tricolour shield displayed on the right side of the helmet was dropped, followed later by the Wehrmacht style Eagle and Swastika.

By 1943 steel helmets were being manufactured without insignia and painted in plain field-grey (plate 174).

The Model 1943 helmet saw a slight alteration to the basic shape when, for reasons of economy, the helmet manufacturing process was simplified and the helmet 'shell' was stamped out of one piece of metal without having the helmet rim crimped inwards around the edge. This tended to give the Model 43 helmet a much sharper appearance and at the same time made it appear slightly larger around the base (plate 175, 176).

All these Wehrmacht steel helmets were painted

94

175. *The Model 1943 Steel Helmet shown here being worn by the soldier with the camouflage jacket thrown over his left shoulder. German prisoners taken in the Battle for Normandy, 12th June 1944.*

176. *The Model 1943 Steel Helmet worn here by the soldier holding the Red Cross flag. An incident during the fighting for the fortress city of Metz, November 1944.*

177. *Early pre-war Army manoeuvres. A clear example of the Model 1918 'Cavalry Helmet'.*

both inside and out in matt finish field-grey paint, with the actual shade of field-grey varying from light to dark grey. Painting the helmets internally was to prevent the formation of rust. Helmets came in five basic sizes, enough variety to fit all head sizes. They weighed from 29oz to 42oz (0·82–1·20kg). They had two small ventilation holes, one each side of the helmet. The helmet suspension consisted of an adjustable leather padded spring aluminium band held in place at the sides and rear of the helmet by three 'cotter' keys. The leather lining was cut out from a single piece of thin flexible leather which was threaded with a draw string in such a way as to allow all the leather flaps to be drawn together. This acted as a form of cushion for the wearer on the crown of the head.

The chinstraps to the steel helmets were removable and adjustable and were normally made from black leather (plate 178).

Three other helmets require mentioning, these were:

1. The unusual pre-war style, sometimes referred to as the 'cavalry helmet' which had a 'kink' in the sides of the neck protection (plate 177).
2. The prototype Model 1935 helmet which can be seen illustrated on page 123.
3. The special lightweight plastic helmets used by Senior Army Officers and Generals—especially aged or injured persons—for parade purposes. They were identical in shape and colour to the M35 version. They weighed only a few ounces and, having all the outward appearances of being the

standard issue helmet, were undetectable as plastic helmets except on very close inspection and handling.

3.1(2). *The Uniform Cap (die Schirmmütze).* The Uniform Cap was worn by all ranks as well as by administrative personnel. It was prescribed to be worn with Service Dress and Undress Uniforms, by officers and NCOs with Parade Dress, by officers when not actually on duty and with Walking-out Dress and with Dress Uniforms by officers.

It had (for all ranks) a field-grey top, a dark blue-green material capband and a black shiny peak. Other cap distinctions depended on the wearer's rank and position.

All Mannschaften and Unteroffizieren[2] wore shiny black leather chinstraps and black chinstrap buttons to their caps, with metal National Emblem and oakleaf cluster in white metal, (the Reichskokade remaining the same colouring for all ranks of army personnel). Piping used on this Schirmmütze was 0·2cm thick, appearing around the crown of the cap and around the top and bottom edges to the dark blue-green cap band and was in the Waffenfarbe of the wearer (plate 179).

Army officers below the rank of general wore the same style and basic colouring to their Uniform Caps as shown above but they used silver cap cords with small silver buttons to hold the cords in position on the cap.

The peak of the cap, like all Uniform Caps was shiny black made with a slight ridge running along the edge to the peak. The insignia on the Officers' Schirmmütze was in white metal, and the cap piping was that of the wearer's Waffenfarbe. These Officers' Uniform Caps were usually of a much better quality than those worn by NCOs and men (plate 180).

Army generals and army administration officials of equivalent rank wore the same basic style of Schirmmütze as worn by officers, but in place of the silver cap cords they wore gold cords and small gilt cap cord buttons.

The cap was piped—regardless of the wearer's branch of service—in gold, both around the crown and the edges to the cap band (plate 181).

Prior to 1st January 1943 Army generals and above wore a silver white metal or silver embroidered National Emblem to the Schirmmütze as well as a silver oakleaf wreath surrounding the Reichskokade. From 1st January 1943 they were instructed to wear gold coloured cap insignia.[3]

The Schirmmütze worn by chaplains and field bishops differed from the above in the following details: Heerespfarrer and Heeresoberpfarrer wore, in keeping with their officers' status, silver cap cords, silver cap cord buttons, silver coloured National

178. *The Model 1935 Steel Helmet clearly showing the black leather chin strap.*

179. *The Army NCOs' Schirmmütze; the 'soft' appearance of the crown to the cap is due to the cap spring having been removed.*

---

[2] Oberfähnriche, Unterärzte, Unterveterinäre, Oberfeuerwerker and Offizier Anwärter plus Zahlmeisteranwärter in the Oberfeldwebel rank range were permitted from 22nd February 1936 to wear officers' quality silver cap cords to their NCOs Schirmmütze (plate 182)

[3] For details regarding the National Emblem, the Reich Cockade and the oakleaf surround worn on Army Uniform Caps see page 10

180. A fine example of the Army Officers' Schirmmütze.

181. General der Panzertruppen Lemelsen, holder of the Knight's Cross. The Schirmmütze worn by Army Generals was piped in fine gilt cording and had gold coloured cap cords.

182. A German Army Sanitätsoberfeldwebel taken prisoner near Frankfurt by an American reconnaissance unit. Although only a non-commissioned officer, he was permitted by an order dating from November 1936 to wear Officers' quality silver cap cord.

Emblem and oakleaves plus a small metal silver coloured 'Gothic Cross'. The cap was piped in violet around the crown and top and bottom edges of the dark blue-green cap band. For a Feld Bischof the cap cords were gold, as were the cap cord buttons. The crown of the field-grey cap was piped in gold and the dark blue-green cap band was piped on the top edge in violet and on the bottom edge in gold piping. The National Emblem, the oakleaves and the 'Gothic Cross' were in silver white metal.[4]

3.1(3). *The Field Service Cap (die Feldmütze).* The Feldmütze was worn in various styles and qualities by all ranks of the army and was officially described as being for use on those occasions other than prescribed for the steel helmet and the Uniform Cap. The various types of Feldmütze worn by all ranks below that of Officer were as follows: the Model 1938 Feldmütze was manufactured in field-grey cloth. A small inverted chevron (soutache) of 'Russia Braid' in the wearer's Waffenfarbe was worn positioned at an angle of 90° surrounding a cloth version of the Reichskokade. The National Emblem, also in cloth, was worn displayed on the front of the upper part of the Field Cap (plate 183).

This cap was designed to allow the sides to be pulled down and worn around the wearer's ears. The sides of the cap towards the front were 'scalloped' to allow for clear vision when the cap was worn in this fashion: however, this was seldom done. The Model 1938 Feldmütze could also be worn under the steel helmet.

The Model 1942 Feldmütze was very similar in design to the earlier 1938 style cap, but this model was in fact a much earlier Field Cap which was updated with the use of the National Emblem and cockade and was reintroduced on 21st July 1942 as the M42 Feldmütze.

---

[4]For details regarding the 'Gothic Cross' see page 90.

183. *The Model 1938 other ranks' Feldmütze. An Obergefreiter from an infantry instruction unit.*
184. *The Model 1942 other ranks' Feldmütze, shown here being worn by an Obergefreiter awarded the Drivers' Service Badge (Kraftfahr-Bëwahrungs-abzeichen).*

185. The Army Officers' Old Style Field Service Cap, being worn here by an unnamed Ritterkreuzträger.

186. The Army Officers' New Style Field Service Cap, shown here being worn by the Oberleutnant and Kompanieführer seated between RKT Obergefreiter Rausch (left) and RKT Unteroffizier Ruhnke (right).

187. The Bergmütze worn here by a Gebirgsjäger Officer.

188. The Bergmütze worn with a white wool knitted cover.

On the front of the cap the Waffenfarbe 'soutache' was no longer displayed; instead there were two small field grey metal buttons which when undone allowed the sides of the cap with their scalloped sections in the front to be worn down around the user's ears, the sides being buttoned up under the chin. The National Emblem and Reichskokade were now being machine-embroidered in one piece as one single badge and worn positioned in the centre of the front of the cap just below the crown (plate 184). Officers' Field Service Caps, which were worn by all officers, including generals and above, were in two basic styles. Those referred to as the 'Officers' Old Style Field Service Cap' (die Offizierfeldmütze älterer Art) and those known as the 'Officers' New Style Field Service Cap' (die Offizierfeldmütze neuer Probe).

The 'Old Style' were in general appearance similar to the Officers' Schirmmütze, but in detail they differed considerably. On these Old Style Service Caps no cap cords were worn. There was no hat spring to stiffen the crown of the cap and the peak was of softish black leather without a moulded rim. The National Emblem was normally in cloth and, so too, was the specially manufactured oakleaf cluster and cockade, both of which, were machine-embroidered in silver aluminium and coloured silks on to a backing of dark blue-green cloth which in turn was stitched directly on to the front of the dark blue-green cap band. Piping around the crown of the cap as well as to the top and bottom edges of the cap band was in the wearer's Waffenfarbe (plate 185).[1]

These Old Style Field Service Caps when worn by Generals displayed gold piping. German Army clergy who were permitted to wear this form of head-dress used exactly the same system of coloured piping as described in the paragraph on the chaplains' and field bishop's Schirmmützen on page 97. It will be seen that the 'Gothic Cross' used on the Officers' Old Style Service Cap is in cloth and not as normally used in white metal.

This Officers' Old Style Field Service Cap was intended to be worn until 1st April 1942, when it was to be finally discontinued—but in practice it proved so popular that it continued to be widely worn right up till the end of the war.

The Officers' New Style Field Service Cap which was introduced for wear from 6th December 1938 was in principle very much like the M38 Field Service Cap worn by all other ranks below officer. The officers' cap was however made from much better quality material and had the addition of silver aluminium piping worn around the crown of the cap and on the upper edges of the turn up at the front; generals wore gilt coloured piping. The cockade was also surrounded with a fine edging of silver wire. A chevron of appropriate waffen-farbe was worn over the cockade (plate 186).

3.1(4). *The Mountain Cap (die Bergmütze).* The Bergmütze was worn by all ranks of mountain units,

---

[1] Officers' Old Style Field Service Caps of a particular colouring were known to have been worn by officers of Panzer-Späh-Kompanien during 1943—4. The top of the cap was in field-grey cloth but the cap band was in black and not the dark blue-green material. The cap was also piped in red.

ski units and Jäger personnel. It was worn in preference to almost all other forms of head-dress permitted to be worn by these troops almost as a form of pride. It had a short field-grey cloth peak (shorter than the Einheitsfeldmütze described below) and was based on the design of the Austrian Army service cap.

With the exception of the National Emblem, the cockade and the two cap buttons worn on the front of the cap and the metal Edelweiss badge worn on the left side of the Bergmütze[2] no other features were displayed on this cap (plate 187).

By an order dated 3rd October 1942, officers and Wehrmachtbeamten with officers' rank were to wear silver aluminium piping around the crown of the Bergmütze and generals and Wehrmachtbeamten with generals' rank were to display gold coloured piping in the same way.

For snow camouflage purposes the Bergmütze was often worn with a pure white woollen cover. This was knitted in such a way as to allow it to be pulled on over the Mountain cap (plate 188).

3.1(5). *The 1943 General Issue Field Cap (die Einheitsfeldmütze).* This was a new form of military head-dress introduced on 11th June 1943 and which subsequently became (apart from the steel helmet) the most widely worn form of service head-dress used throughout the German armed forces.

Its design was based on the cap used by German troops in North Africa. It was field-grey for all army troops and all ranks, although Panzer troops had their version in black and there were examples of this cap made from camouflage material. The National Emblem and the Reichskokade were displayed on the centre front of the cap combined in a 'T' shape form as one badge (plate 189). The movable sides to this cap were extended to the front, curving down to where they were held in position by two small field-grey metal buttons. The cap's semi-stiff peak was covered in field-grey cloth and was slightly longer than the peak of the Bergmütze (plate 190).

Army officers, and administration officials of equivalent rank, wearing this Einheitsfeldmütze displayed silver piping around the crown of the cap (plates 191, 192) and generals and their Beamten equivalent had gold piping on the crown.

3.1(6). *The Panzer Beret (die Schutzmütze).* The black Panzer Beret was a distinctive feature of the black Panzer Uniform worn by all members of the youngest arm of the Wehrmacht. The beret and the special uniform was first worn before the war at the time of the creation of the first German Army Panzer formations (plate 290).

The Schutzmütze was in two parts. A soft, fairly large beret 'cover' was worn pulled and shaped towards the back of the head-dress which was detachable from the crash liner. This liner was faced on the outside in black wool cloth of a quality matching the beret and on the inside it was constructed from thick

[2]For details regarding the positioning of this metal Edelweiss on the Bergmütze see page 91.

189. *The 1943 Einheitsfeldmütze, as worn by other ranks of the German Army.*

192. *The 1943 Einheitsfeldmütze as worn by Officers*

102

190. *The 1943 Einheitsfeldmütze, as worn by NCOs and ORs of the German Army.*

191. *The 1943 Einheitsfeldmütze as worn by Army Officers, showing the silver piping around the crown.*

and General class Officers of the German Army.

193. *The Panzer Schutzmütze.*

194. *The issue fur cap with a hard liner worn here by Generalfeldmarschall von Manstein, talking to troops who had fought in the encirclement at Tscherkassy, 14th March 1944.*

195. *The fur pile cap worn here by a Stabsfeldwebel on patrol on the Eastern Front.*

196. *Fur covered head-dress in use during sub-zero temperature. A breast emblem has been stitched onto this cap in place of the normal form of head-dress National Emblem.*

felt padding and covered with a lining of six panels of black oil cloth. The liner also had a leather sweat band and six rubber ringed ventilation holes.

On the front of the black beret were displayed a machine-woven version of the National Emblem and the oakleaf cluster all in silver thread with cockade in coloured silks worked on to a backing of black material and stitched in position on the beret (plate 193).

The wearing of these Panzer Berets was discontinued during the winter of 1939–40 and they were replaced by a black cloth version of the Model 1938 Feldmütze. For additional information on the forms of military head-dress worn by Panzer troops refer to page 160 under the heading 'The Special Black Panzer Uniform'.

3.1(7). *Fur covered caps (Pelz Mützen).* During the winter of 1942–3 German troops serving in the East began to be issued with a field-grey fur trimmed form of head-dress. Remaining stocks of crash liners from the old discontinued Panzer Beret were utilized in the making of these fur caps. The outside of the hat with its hard liner was covered in field-grey cloth and they had fur covered neck and side flaps which could be worn either tied up across the crown of the cap or worn tied down under the wearer's neck and chin. There was a small area of animal fur worn at the front of the cap across the wearer's forehead which sometimes displayed a metal or cloth form of the National Emblem (plate 194).

Other forms of 'Pile-Caps', both with and without insignia were worn by German Troops in the East but these may not have been of official issue (plates 195–198).

Two other forms of cold weather 'head-dress' remain to be mentioned. These were the Helmet Toques and the tight fitting camouflage reversible hood designed to be worn under the steel helmet as part of the reversible winter uniform.

1. The Helmet Toque was a shapeless sleeve of field-grey woollen material open at both ends which was worn by being pulled on over the wearer's head. When worn in this manner one end of the sleeve was around the base of the wearer's neck and the other end around the face (plate 199).

2. The tight fitting hoods—not to be confused with the reversible hoods attached to the padded winter jackets—were made with a thick blanket lining. They had a large 'collar' which, when the hood was worn, spread out over the wearer's neck and shoulders; when used with the winter jacket this provided excellent insulation against the cold. The hoods were shaped to fit the contours of the head and the neck could be closed over and tied with one long and one short tape, the long tape being wound right round the neck and tied in the front (plate 200).

This form of close fitting 'head-dress' was designed for warmth and was manufactured in both patterns of army camouflage as well as mouse-grey all of which were reversible to white. They formed part of the

197. Another example of a fur covered cap. *198.* An unofficial style of fur covered cap, worn here in combination with the issue Toque.

199. *The Army issue Toque as it was intended to be worn with the Steel Helmet.*

201. *German Army Tropical Sun Helmets. These tropical helmets used by Army personnel displayed two embossed metal helmet plates. On the right side, as can be seen in this photo, the embossed plate or shield bore the National tricolour of black, white (plain silver metal) and red. The shield on the left side displayed a dull silver metal Wehrmacht-adler raised from a black painted shield.*

200. *The close fitting reversible headwear worn in cold weather as part of the heavy winter uniform.*

202. *The Deutsches Afrikakorps Feldmütze, the forerunner of the 1943 Einheitsfeldmütze.*

203. *An example of the Steel Helmet treated with a coating of white-wash for use in snow covered terrain.*

padded Winter Uniform, details of which can be found on page 177.

3.1(8). *Tropical Head-dress (Tropische Kopfbedeckung).* German Army tropical head-dress originated with the German troops sent to North Africa in 1941. All ranks were issued with, and wore, the army Sun Helmet (plate 201). The Sun Helmet was shortlived, as it proved cumbersome and its value as a form of protective head-dress dubious. German troops took to wearing a simplified version and forerunner of the Einheitsfeldmütze (plate 202). It was light in weight, being made from cotton drill and with all extra thicknesses of unnecessary material discarded. The longish peak afforded shade to the user's eyes. Badges in keeping with the colour of this tropical cap were machinewoven in dull copper-brown and grey thread. Officers displayed dull silver piping to the cap as specified for the Einheitsfeldmütze.

3.2. Helmet colourings

German steel helmets issued to all army personnel were usually field-grey in colour although the actual shade of field-grey varied according to the firm manufacturing them and the paint being used. Both matt and semi-matt finishes were achieved on the helmet.

Helmets used in North Africa and those countries with hot dry climates were required to blend with the yellow sand and soil. Field-grey helmets were overpainted in a sandy-buff colour sometimes with sand being thrown over the still wet paint which when dry gave a perfect non-reflective surface.

204. *The regulation German Army issue camouflage helmet cover.*

205. (above) Helmets worn with elasticated rings cut from motor tyre inner tubes. German infantry prepare to move forward during the attack on Poland, September 1939.

206. (below) Foliage held in place on the helmet by use of these rubber rings. A heavy machine-gun in operation somewhere on the Eastern Front.

For service in snow covered country it was necessary to have a matt-white helmet. This was simply achieved by painting the helmet with a thick coating of white-wash. Whitewash was used instead of white paint so that, when the spring came and the snow disappeared, the whitewash could be scrubbed off in water and the helmet restored to its original field-grey colour (plate 203).

3.3. Helmet coverings

Apart from the regulation army issue camouflage helmet cover (plate 204) which was first manufactured and issued to the troops on the introduction of army camouflage clothing there were numerous ways carried out both on a unit basis and by individual soldiers of camouflaging the steel helmet.

Perhaps the commonest and easiest way was by the use of a strong rubber ring cut from a motor tyre inner tube which was forced down around the body of the helmet, under which could be held foliage or grass (plates 205, 206, 207, 208).

Other methods were used to varying degrees but all of them had the desired effect of breaking up the sharp outline of the helmet's shape, to a certain extent making the helmet surface non-reflective and adding cover to the hidden soldier.

Chicken wire mesh was used in such a way as to be shaped to the helmet's roundness and held in position by crude wire hooks attaching the wire mesh to the rim of the helmet (plate 209). This method allowed the wearer, if required, to garnish the entire helmet with twigs, grass or foliage.

Sacking was also used which was positioned on the helmet, folded into place and held down usually with the rubber inner-tube ring already mentioned (plate 210 shows a variation of this sacking cover).

White cloth rags were also used more as a makeshift snow camouflage helmet cover. These unshaped pieces of white cloth were held in place on the helmet again either by the inner tube ring or string (plate 211).

Camouflage material was usually of the German Army pattern (although the author has seen original German photographs which show Army personnel wearing Waffen-SS manufactured helmet covers as well as Waffen-SS pattern camouflage material) and was used to form a helmet cover very simply by cutting out a fairly large circular shape from the material, stitching a draw string around the edge of the material, fitting the cover over the helmet and drawing the string together, gathering the bottom of the cover up together under the rim of the helmet (plate 213). Wear along the rim of the helmet caused the material cover to fray badly.

Individual soldiers sometimes utilised the Army issue canvas carrying straps and by shortening these they were able to fit them on to the helmet to form a simple system of straps to hold camouflage. The four ends of the canvas straps with their leather reinforced metal spring clips were used to hold the straps in position on the helmet rim (plate 214).

207. *Foliage held in place on the helmet by use of rubber rings. A pause during the march on Petrograd.*

208. *Foliage held in place on the helmet by the use of rubber rings. A Croatian volunteer serving in the German Army trains in infantry tactics.*

209. Steel Helmets covered with chicken wire mesh. A break in the vicious fighting for Warsaw, autumn 1944.
210. A variation on the sacking helmet covers.

211. *MG unit from Infantry Regiment 'Grossdeutschland'. An example of early makeshift snow camouflage.*
212. *The woven string helmet net, here worn in combination with the regulation camouflage helmet cover.*

213. *Helmet covering made from a single piece of camouflage material.*

214. *A form of helmet covering constructed from canvas carrying straps.*

215. *A wounded officer is assisted to the rear. St. Malo, France, August 1944. The Obergefreiter, on the right has utilised an Allied issue helmet net.*

216. *Leather straps used on the helmet to allow the helmet to be camouflaged with foliage.*

217. Prewar early attempts at using leather straps on the steel helmet.

218. The regulation issue helmet cover worn with the white side outermost.

Strong woven string nets were used made of a fairly large mesh and worn on the helmet being drawn up tight under the helmet rim (plate 212). It was not uncommon to find German soldiers making use of British Army helmet nets, these were distinctive by their fine khaki-green mesh (plate 215).

During the earlier stages of the war as well as prewar, leather straps were a popular form of helmet camouflage attachment, one leather strap passing right round the body of the helmet sometimes being attached to the rim by two (one on either side of the helmet) or more short leather straps with metal clips (plates 216, 217).

The regulation issue Army patterned camouflage helmet cover was constructed from five pieces of material, each panel stitched together so as to shape themselves to the contours of the helmet. There were seven single cloth loops made from short lengths of camouflage material which were stitched in position on the helmet cover and were intended to allow the wearer to stuff grass and small twigs into the loops to further garnish the helmet. The entire cover was held in position on the helmet by having the draw string tightened up under the helmet rim and tied in position.

The material used for this issue cover was a fairly hard-wearing cotton cloth printed on one side in Army pattern camouflage colours, the other side being left unprinted in plain white. During those months with snow fall this helmet cover was often worn with the white side outermost. It was recognizable as the issue helmet cover when worn in this manner for, although it did not show any loops—as these were not required in snow landscapes—it could be distinguished from the shapes of its stitched cloth panels (plate 218).

3.4. Footwear
Fussbekleidung

Footwear worn in the German Army consisted of the following:

1. The black leather marching boots (Marschstiefel) (plates 219, 221, 222)
2. The leather riding boots with adjustable straps to the top (Reitstiefel mit verstellbaren Oberiemen) (plate 132)
3. The officers' leather riding boots, normally worn with spurs (Reitstiefel mit Anschnallsporen) (plates 132, 220, 223)
4. The short lace-up ankle boots (Schnürschuhe) (plate 224)
5. Climbing boots used by mountain troops (Bergschuhe) (plate 226)
6. The canvas and leather lace-up tropical boots (Leinen und leder tropische Schnürschuhe) (plate 303)
7. Running shoes for sports events (Laufschuhe) (plate 236)

In addition to footwear, green canvas and leather-reinforced gaiters (Stoff Gamaschen) were issued for wear with the lace-up ankle boots. They were introduced in 1943 and issued in increasing quantities to replace the shortage of leather marching boots (plates 225, 227, 229).

White waterproof 'spats' were used by Gebirgsjäger troops and worn together with their mountain climbing boots (plate 242). Army issue puttees (Wickelgamaschen) in field-grey cloth were also worn by these and other units (plates 228, 230, 242).

Waterproof covers for the feet and legs of motorcyclists were sometimes worn in very wet weather or muddy road conditions (plate 231). Tall leather gaiters were worn with short lace-up boots (plate 305).

The special heavy duty winter footwear introduced to combat the sub-zero weather conditions encountered on the Eastern Front were as follows: in compressed and moulded felt, worn as an overboot (plate 232): in a combination of thick felt and leather (plate 233); or made from thick layers of plaited straw large enough to be worn over the issue leather marching boots (plate 234).

219. *The black leather marching boots in peacetime. Sentries from the Guard Regiment Berlin salute 'Il Duce' on his departure from the German monument to the Unknown Soldier (Ehrenmal); Berlin, 29th September 1937.*

220. *Officers' riding boots worn with spurs. The Commandant for Berlin, Generalleutnant von Hase, greeting the Hungarian War Minister (Vitez Bartha) at the Berlin Ehrenmal in Unter den Linden. 24th January 1941.*

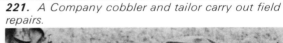

221. A Company cobbler and tailor carry out field repairs.

222. The black leather marching boot in wartime. An Obergefreiter on the Eastern Front takes time off to write home. June 1942.

223. Officers' riding boots. An Oberleutnant from a Jäger regiment taken prisoner in France, 1944.

224. The short lace-up ankle boots. Generalleutnant von Arnim arriving in Britain sometime after his capture in North Africa.

225. German Army issue canvas and leather reinforced gaiters.

226. Detail of the soles of the climbing boots worn by German Army mountain troops.

227. German troops taken prisoner after the fall of St Sauveur (France), all of whom are wearing the short lace-up ankle boots with canvas gaiters.

228. German troops taken prisoner in North Africa, most of whom are wearing mountaineering boots with issue puttees.

229. An honour guard of German Army troops, July 1943. All but the officers are wearing Army issue gaiters in place of the leather marching boots.

230. *A German officer wearing climbing boots and Army issue puttees.* :

231. *Generalfeldmarschall Model speaking with a motor-cycle rider somewhere on the southern sector of the Eastern Front, May 1944. Note the use of waterproof leggings and overboots.*

232. Specially manufactured felt overboots, a design of Russian origin, issued to German troops during the sub-zero winter months in the East.

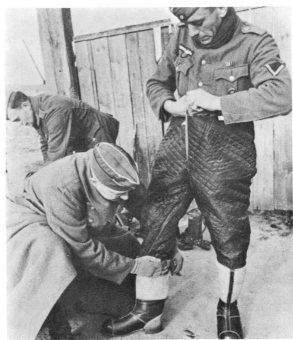

233. Special felt and leather boots introduced for wear in cold climates. The Gefreiter is preparing for patrol duty and is also wearing quilted overtrousers especially designed for extra warmth.

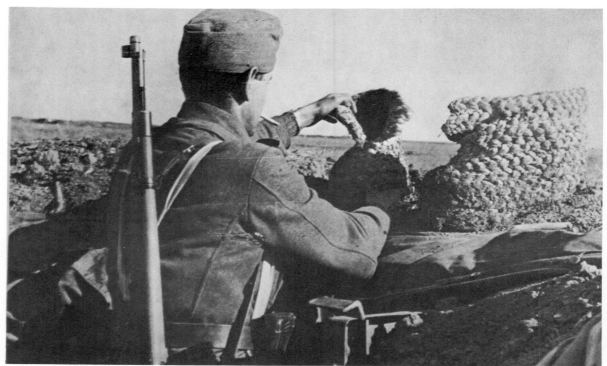

234. *Plaited straw overboots, made especially large to fit over the normal marching boots and used on sentry duty in the severe cold encountered on the Eastern Front.*

235. *The German Army Denim Fatigue Uniform. Recruits from Infanterie-Regiment 67 in Ruhleben under instruction.*

3.5. The Army Denim Fatigue Uniform
Heeres Drillichanzug

In the years preceding World War II, and for those war years until stocks were exhausted, the off-white Denim Fatigue Uniform was a standard issue garment to all recruits on entering the German Army.

Of unbleached denim material with a fine 'herringbone' pattern it was a hardwearing uniform consisting of a shapeless single-breasted jacket (Drillichrock) and equally shapeless trousers (Drillichhose). The jacket, when worn correctly, was closed at the neck by the top button of five field-grey detachable buttons arranged down the front of the jacket. It had the normal turn-down collar and two patch pockets without pocket flaps, one each side of the skirt to the jacket.

The trousers were made in the same material as the jacket and were of a simple cut with two side pockets. Because of its quality and wearing ability the uniform was easily washable and was used extensively for fatigue duty, work details, instruction both on the parade ground and the field, training manoeuvres, weapon cleaning and motor vehicle maintenance (plate 235).

Insignia of rank worn on this uniform can be found on page 44.

3.6. Army issue sports kit
Heeres Sportanzug

This was another separate item of clothing issue. Every recruit on entering the German Army was issued with a sports vest (Sporthemd), shorts (Sporthose) and sports shoes (Laufschuhe—running shoes) (plate 236). In addition to this there was a pair of swimming trunks (Badehose) which were only intended for wear at water sports.

The vests were white cotton and the shorts were of black cotton, pocketless with an elasticated waistband: the sports shoes were lace up brown leather. No mention can be found of any special issue socks for this outfit.

Regulation vests were sleeveless without collars and were officially to display the appropriate vest emblem for the wearer's branch of service. The army sports vest insignia has been dealt with in Part 2 on Insignia to be found on page 58.

3.7. Service Tunic Model 1936
Heeres Dienstanzug Modell 1936

This was a single breasted tunic which incorporated smartness with practicality and, with only slight difference in quality and minor modifications, was worn by all ranks in the German Army.

The Service Tunic as worn by Mannschaften was field-grey in colour and manufactured from wool/rayon mixed material. It had four box-pleated patch pockets. Five field-grey finished metal buttons were positioned down the front of the coat with another button to each of the four three pointed pocket flaps, a style of pocket adopted from those worn on the Austro-Hungarian Army tunics of World War I. The

236. German Army Sports clothing. Wounded German troops exercising during convalescence. The man second from the left is an Army soldier.

237. *The German Army Model 1936 Service Tunic, worn in the field under combat conditions.*

collar was faced with dark blue-green material and this was also used as the backing cloth to the National Emblem positioned across the right breast of the jacket and running parallel to the top of the right breast pocket. The material was also used as backing cloth to the collar patches, to trade and specialist insignia as well as arm rank insignia.

Three reinforced belt hook eyelet holes positioned one above the other were situated on either side of the waist in the front and at the back of the tunic. Four removable metal belt hooks could be positioned at one of three slightly varying heights to support the wearer's leather belt and thus the equipment hung from the belt.

Shoulder straps, constructed from dark blue-green material, were normally removable from this tunic, an advantage when the tunic was being cleaned. The Service Tunic was slightly waisted, giving a slight flair to the jacket 'skirt'. There was a small 'inner' pocket 17cm to 18cm deep, fastened with a single horn button which was located on the inside lower edge to the right side flap of the tunic front. This pocket was designed to hold the German Army issue field dressing pack. There was a small 15cm deep vent in the centre at the rear of the jacket skirt.

The ends of the sleeves were without cuff turn backs and were split in order that the sleeve ends could be wrapped tighter round the wearer's wrist and buttoned in position.

A removable neck band (Kragenbinde) was worn inside the collar of the tunic and attached to the collar with the use of three small flexible metal collar studs built into the tunic collar. The tunic was correctly buttoned up when used as the Service Dress and as the Service Dress it was worn when attending classes, on duty in an office or performing other duties not calling for the Field Service Uniform.

When worn as the Field Service Uniform (that is, worn with field equipment) the top button and collar hooks were allowed to be undone if required (plate 237). However, during the war troops returning to Germany during the summer months from warm climate countries—which were listed as Bulgaria, Rumania, Jugoslavia, Greece and southern France— were warned that the top button of the Field Blouse must be buttoned up and the neck band had to be worn. Army patrols and street patrols were to enforce this order.

The steel helmet or the field cap would have been worn with the Service Dress, depending on requirements and normal Army issue footwear was also worn.

For the trousers worn with this jacket see information on the Service Tunic as worn by Unteroffiziere.

3.8. Service Uniform Model 1936, as worn by non-commissioned officers

In exactly the same design, colour, quality and cut to the Service Uniform worn by Mannschaften, the only differences were the visible signs of rank. These were the 0·9cm wide rank braiding worn down the front of,

238. *The prototype Reichsheer Service Tunic, introduced for field use sometime during 1934. It was from this tunic that the Model 1936 Service Tunic was evolved. Of special note is the very interesting prototype steel helmet—the forerunner of the Model 1935 helmet. The collar to the tunic is field-grey, the dark blue-green material not being introduced until 1936. Pleated patch pockets are introduced for the first time.*

and around the lower edge to, the tunic collar; shoulder straps would also have indicated the wearer's rank as would the double rings of 0·9cm braiding worn on both cuffs by 'der Spiess' (plate 239).

The trousers worn with this tunic both for Mannschaften and Unteroffiziere were normally field-grey in colour. When field-grey trousers were worn with this jacket they were straight-legged and cut in such a way as to be fairly high waisted. The trousers had four fly buttons plus a top waist button, with three sets each of two buttons stitched to the outside of the waist band, one set on either side of the front and one set at the back for attachment to the braces. The waist band at the back of the trousers had a 'V' cut into it with a small cloth half-belt in two sections joined with a small metal buckle and used to draw the waist of the trousers tighter. Sometimes extra buttons, horn 'plastic' or metal were stitched on to the waist band next to the braces buttons as added security.

There were two slanting side pockets situated on each side of the trousers slightly to the front. These sometimes had pocket flaps or no flaps at all, depending on manufacture, but both types were worn with one button to each pocket opening or pocket flap. A small 'fob pocket' was positioned on the right hand side of the trouser front. A metal ring stitched on to the outside of the waist band or a small cloth loop stitched just above this pocket was intended to hold the pocket watch chain. One more pocket was to be found at the rear of the trousers on the right hip. This was normally

239. *The Model 1936 German Army Service Tunic as worn by 'der Spiess'.*

240. *(opposite page) German Army Officers' Service Uniforms worn by Army Beamten Officials in France, 1940. It can clearly be seen from this photo that a certain amount of latitude was tolerated when it came to Officers' Service uniforms. This photo illustrates the range of slight variations in the basic Officers' Service Uniform. The two officials on the right have utilised, with the use of their own insignia of rank, the form of tunic normally worn by Army other ranks. The official on the left of the picture is wearing the regulation form of Officers' Service Tunic with its deep turn back cuffs. The shape of the pocket flaps is a further point of interest and it would seem that the official at the back of the group has more than the required number of tunic buttons.*

without pocket flap and was secured with a single button.

Normal German Army black leather marching boots were worn with this Service Uniform jacket and trousers by all NCOs and men, although Cavalry personnel would (and some senior non-commissioned officers could) wear riding breeches with riding boots.

Short ankle boots could also be used and later when anklets were introduced for universal wear they were worn as a matter of course.

3.9. Service Uniform for officers Dienstanzug für Offiziere

Very similar in design and cut to that worn by Mannschaften and Unteroffiziere, the Service Tunic worn by army officers was usually of better quality material and had the noticeable difference of plain deep turn-back cuffs.[1] There were four patch pockets with box pleats, five field-grey metal buttons down the jacket front with one button to each of the three pointed pocket flaps. As with the other tunics dark blue-green material was used on the collar and as backing cloth to the officers' quality National Emblem worn on the right breast, as well as to the Officers' collar patches (plate 240).

The Officer's Service Tunic could be worn with either trousers and lace up ankle shoes or, as was usually the case, with officers' breeches and high riding boots. Officers' brown leather Service Belts were used with this uniform, cross straps (Schulterriemen) being worn only in peacetime and during the early part of the war. During the 1939 Polish Campaign, field officers were known to have dyed their tan coloured leather belts, holsters and cross straps black in an effort to make themselves less conspicuous to the enemy. They also covered their shoulder straps with cloth covers.

Officers had a choice of head-dress to be worn with the Service Uniform. The Uniform Cap, the Officers' old and new style Field Service Caps as well as the

---

[1] These deep turn back cuffs were often used as a convenient form of extra 'pockets'. Papers that were required for use, and which were thin enough, could be tucked into these cuffs rather than being buttoned into the tunic pocket or held in the hand.

Steel Helmet could be worn with this dress, depending on the period the uniform was being worn and the officer's preference or necessity.

During the last months of the war in Europe, army officers were permitted to wear issue shirts with collar and tie under the Field Service Tunic, the top button and neck hooks of which were allowed to be worn open to show the shirt and tie.

3.10. Service Uniform for generals and above
Dienstanzug für Generäle und General-feldmarschälle

Like those tunics worn by officers, the Service Tunic worn by generals and above was of a fine quality material and usually of a much higher degree of finish than the issue tunics (plate 241).

Generäle and Generalfeldmarshälle rank insignia was worn, red and gold collar patches set against a dark blue-green collar with generals' style shoulder straps worn on the jacket. The National Emblem worn as for all Army tunics on the right breast was worked in fine gold wire on to the dark blue-green backing cloth. Gilt buttons were used five down the front of the jacket and one to each pocket flap of the four patch pockets. This tunic also had sleeves with deep turn-back cuffs.

Trousers or riding breeches could be worn with this Service Jacket although it would seem that most general-class officers preferred breeches. Displayed on these trousers or breeches was the very distinctive Army Generals' 'broad red stripe'. This 'red stripe' was in fact made up of two strips of red material each 3·3cm wide stitched along the outer leg of the trousers or breeches and positioned 0·4cm away from, and on either side of, a single line of red piping 0·2cm thick set into the seam of the trousers or breeches.

Brown leather service belts were worn, officers' quality boots were worn and the head-dress was that as for generals.

3.11. Field Service Uniform for mountain troops
Dienstanzug für Gebirgstruppen

The jacket to this uniform was the Service Jacket, the same as that worn by all ranks and previously described.

The main difference in the Service Uniform worn by army mountain troops (Gebirgstruppen) was in the variety of 'trousers' used. They could wear with the normal issue Field Service Jacket, knickerbockers worn with long thick woollen socks and climbing boots, ski-trousers worn with ski-boots and short socks

241. The Service Uniform worn by Army Generals. Generalmajor Max Joseph Pemsel, holder of the Knight's Cross, Chief of Staff and deputy Commander of Marshal Graziani's 6th Ligurian Army, is seen here after the surrender of this army to the allies in 1945.

242. The Field Service Uniform for Army Mountain troops. General der Infanterie Dietl, the first officer in the German Wehrmacht to be awarded the Oakleaves to the Knight's Cross of the Iron Cross seen here in the company of his staff officers.

243. *General Dietl with other Gebirgsjäger officers. This photo illustrates the variety of clothing that could be worn by German Army mountaineering personnel.*

rolled over the top of the boots or mountaineering boots worn with trousers, slightly tapered at the ends and worn bound round with puttees (plates 242, 243).

The Field Service Jacket would display the Edelweiss arm badge on the right upper sleeve and the head-dress, normally the Bergmütze, would be that used by army mountain troop formations.

3.12. Service Tunic Model 1943
Die Feldbluse Modell 1943

The economies forced upon the German uniform manufacturing industry by the prolongation of the war beyond 1942 and by the ever increasing shortage of uniform materials effected changes in the basic Service Uniform that were introduced to conserve materials and at the same time to cut back on the skilled labour needed in the manufacturing of future uniforms.

The Model 1943 Service Tunic, and to an even greater extent the M44 Field Blouse (pages 128–131) went a long way towards helping on these two counts.

In the Model 1943 German Army Service Tunic we see for the first time since it was introduced in 1936 the absence of the familiar dark blue-green collar material. Shoulder straps constructed entirely from field-grey cloth began to be issued, at first specifically with this tunic, but later as a matter of course for all

army issue shoulder straps.

The four patch pockets to this tunic no longer had box pleats and the pocket flaps were reduced slightly in depth and were cut straight without having the three points to them. In all other details this tunic was the same as the earlier Model 1936 Service Tunic (plate 244).

Prior to 1935 German Army uniforms were manufactured from an all wool fabric but, in 1935, this was modified with the introduction of 5% rayon stable fibre. Later this proportion was increased to 20% and during the war it rose as high as 65%. It was found that in the spinning of these mixtures the smooth rayon fibres moved into the core of the yarn leaving the crimpy woollen fibres on the outside, so that after fulling the cover of the cloth was largely formed by the wool. Because of this it became possible when dying the bulk material field-grey to use the rayon-sulphur dyes rather than the much more expensive vat dyes which had previously been the only type permissible.

The wool content of uniform cloth was drawn from imported scoured wool, combed wool, shoddy and wool waste. By 1943 about 90% of uniform cloth was produced from shoddy or wool waste; often the waste wool was of a field grey colour and as such did not require any additional dyeing.

244. *German Army prisoners captured by French forces in Italy. This photo clearly shows the Model 1943 Service Tunic. Of interest are the slight variations in design. On the far left patch pockets with pleats have been used on the M43 tunic whilst in the foreground the bareheaded Unteroffizier is wearing a dark blue-green collar together with early pre-war pointed 'Feldbluse' pattern shoulder straps.*

The wool content of the Model 1943 Service Tunic was drastically reduced while at the same time the rayon content was increased. Added to this lowering of quality, the wool used in the manufacture of the tunic tended to be low-quality reworked wool which together gave the Model 1943 Service Tunic a shoddy appearance even when new (plate 245). It also had poor thermal insulation and when wet lacked strength.

The German Army Belted Trousers (Rundbund-hosen). In 1943 the German Army was issued with field uniform trousers with a built-in cloth belt after the style of the 'Afrika Korps' trousers. The decision to discontinue production and issue of the suspender trousers was governed by two considerations: the impracticability of braces when only the shirt and trousers were worn and the inconvenient and, under battle conditions, dangerous necessity of removing the coat and battle equipment to let down the trousers. These trousers were cut high, and the legs were tapered to fit into gaiters or tops of ankle boots.

3.13. The Model 1944 Field Blouse
Die Feldbluse Modell 1944

The pressure of economic war conditions against Germany resulted in the introduction on 25th September 1944 of an entirely new style of Field Service Tunic, the Model 1944 (or M44) Field Blouse. This was a complete break with German Army uniform tradition in so far as it was a new form of uniform jacket, the Germans adopting a style which for all its radical design was very similar to the British Army Battledress Blouse, and which did not retain any of the features of styling normally associated with the traditional German Service Uniform (plate 246).

The colour of this new uniform was more slate grey-green than field-grey and the most noticeable feature of the Field Blouse was the replacement of the jacket skirt with a waist band 12cm deep. Because of the lack of a skirt to the jacket only two patch pockets were worn, both on the chest. Each were without pleats and each had a simple straight-edged pocket

245. *A clear example of the inferior quality of the M43 Service Tunic.*

flap. The collar of the jacket, slate grey-green in colour was normally worn open but it could be closed if required. There were six field-grey or dark grey metal buttons worn down the front, the lower two being positioned on the waist band. The cuffs to the sleeves were like the normal other ranks quality Service Tunics cut in such a way as to be gathered in and buttoned to fit more closely around the wearer's wrists. The back of the tunic was made of one unseamed piece of material. Metal belt hooks were fitted to this blouse to hold up the belt and to help support the wearer's equipment, but the normal triple belt hook positions had been reduced to only one position. There were two inside breast pockets, each closed with a single fibre button, but there was no field dressing pocket inside the blouse.

Normal shoulder straps of the wearer's rank and with his Waffenfarbe piping were worn, sometimes made of the same material as the jacket but often use was made of older shoulder straps. The collar was of

246. *The M44 Field Uniform. The 'Feldbluse' was distinctive for its two unpleated breast pockets, wide waist band and lack of 'skirt' to the jacket. The 'fob' pocket can be seen on the right side of the trousers.*

247. *The BeVo quality National Emblem designed especially for use on the M44 Field Blouse.*

248. *16-year-old Grenadier Joseph Voss taken prisoner defending the German town of Lemgo. Clearly shown are the 'economy' pattern insignia used on the Model 1944 field blouse, the triangular National Emblem and the mouse-grey collar patches.*

249. *Generalleutnant Graf von Schwerin, holder of the Knight's Cross with Oakleaves and Swords, Commanding Officer of the 76th Panzer Corps. He is seen here wearing a slightly modified form of the M44 Field Blouse.*

the same material and colour as the blouse and the late-pattern mouse-grey collar patches were worn (these did not show the wearer's Waffenfarbe).

Although the accepted design of the National Emblem was often worn on the right breast of this Field Blouse there was a new economy style of National Emblem manufactured and intended to be used with this model uniform. When sewn in position it gave the appearance of being a triangular piece of dull grey material with the Eagle-and-Swastika design machine-woven in dull grey yarn (plates 247, 248).

The M44 Field Blouse was issued to all ranks both in the German Army and the Waffen-SS (but with the exception of Panzer crews) to be worn when existing stocks of the old Model 1936 Service Uniform were exhausted.

Non-commissioned officers did not normally wear any rank braiding sewn around the edge of the collar, the only indication of their rank being the shoulder straps. Generals, however, were permitted to wear normal rank insignia including collar patches.

3.14. The M44 Field Blouse worn by generals
Die Feldbluse M44 für Generäle

As can be seen from the illustration opposite (plate 249) the M44 Field Blouse was worn by officers of the rank of general. The photograph shows that the tunic being worn, although it conforms to the issued pattern of the M44 blouse, differs in a number of interesting points.

The two breast patch pockets have box pleats and curved edges to the pocket flaps, there are no buttons visible down the front of the blouse because the blouse has been made with a fly front, and full general's rank insignia is being worn including a gilt embroidered National Emblem worn over the right breast pocket. The two buttons showing on the breast pockets would appear to be of gilt coloured metal.

Also on this blouse, and just visible, is the 'Afrika with palms' cuff-title being worn on the left cuff.

3.15. The reed-green Denim Field Service Uniform
Schilfgrüner Drillich Felddienstanzug

Identical in cut and design to the normal Service Uniform jacket and trousers this item of clothing was introduced for summer wear by the fighting troops. It could be worn by officers as well as NCOs and men. Both the trousers and the jacket were made of matching reed-green 'herringbone' pattern denim. Hard wearing, lightweight and readily washable, this uniform proved both popular and successful in warm and hot climates (plate 250).

The jacket was single breasted. It had four patch pockets generally without pleats but with points to the pocket flaps and ten field-grey metal buttons, six arranged down the front of the jacket and one to each pocket. All buttons were removable being held in place by split rings or 'S' shaped wire rings. When worn closed at the neck and as well as being buttoned up,

250. *The reed-green denim version of the German Army Field Service uniform. An Unteroffizier from a Panzer-Grenadier-Regiment taken prisoner by 8th Army troops in the Lake Trasimeno area, near the village of Castiglione, Italy, July 1944.*

the tunic collar could be fastened together with the small metal neck hooks. The issue neck-band could be worn with this tunic. Located on the inside of the neck opening were two small horn buttons positioned there to allow the neckband—which was simply placed around the wearer's neck—to be buttoned across the front of the neck, each end of the band being fastened to one of the two buttons.

The sleeve ends were cut to allow them to be buttoned up tight around the wrists. There was a 17cm deep slit in the centre of the jacket skirt at the rear. Belt hook holes were also located at the rear on each side of the tunic. As with the normal Service Tunic there was a field dressing pocket inside the tunic flap.

The jacket carried normal insignia and military decorations could also be displayed on this tunic. Dull grey NCOs' rank braiding was also worn stitched around the base of the collar.

The trousers to this jacket were made from the same quality material as the tunic and were cut in the same style as normal field-grey service trousers. They had two side pockets, a fly-front, an adjustable waist half-belt at the rear and no turn-ups to the straight cut trouser legs. It should be stressed that these trousers were not always worn with the issue coat.

3.16. Army Bandsman's Service Uniform with 'Swallow's nests'
Heeres Musiker Dienstanzug mit 'Schwalbennesten'

Apart from their musical instruments, bandsmen were distinguished as musicians by the practice of wearing Swallows' Nests (Schwalbennester).

These were worn in matching pairs one to each shoulder of the military tunic. They were each attached to the tunic shoulder by five 1·5cm long metal hooks positioned at evenly spaced intervals on the curved underside edge of the 'nest'. These hooks were clipped on to five corresponding eyelets stitched at regular intervals around the shoulder seam of the jacket.

Swallows' Nests were worn on the Service and Uniform Tunics, but not on the Greatcoat and were normally only worn when the musicians were employed as bandsmen. Normal day-to-day military service did not require them to wear these 'nests' as part of their military dress (plate 251).

Information regarding the various types of Swallows' Nests used in the German Army can be found on page 67.

3.17. Service Uniform for Military Field Police
Dienstanzug für Feldgendarmerie

The Feldgendarmerie was a military body having police powers and forming part of the German Army in the Field. Units of Military Police were employed with army divisions and higher formations.

They were responsible in occupied areas for traffic control, for control duties at ports and aerodromes, for administrative control of aliens, and cattle diseases,

251. *German Army Bandsman, the Service Uniform with Swallows' Nests.*

hunting, fishing, business, agricultural and forestry police duties and for patrol duties. During an advance Feldgendarmerie units followed closely behind the fighting troops acting as and establishing temporary town majors and army stragglers' posts, rounding up of enemy stragglers and terrorists, collecting refugees and prisoners of war, guarding booty and ensuring that weapons in the hands of civilians were surrendered. They also were responsible for the organization of civilian labour and erection of military and civil signs.

wreath. On the cuff of the left sleeve they wore a brown cuff-title inscribed with the word *FELD-GENDARMERIE* in silver-grey gothic lettering. When on duty the Field Police wore a metal gorget (Ring-kragen) on a chain around their necks (plate 252). Because of their unpopularity amongst the rank and file of German troops they were often referred to as 'chained dogs', a reference to their wearing of the duty Ringkragen.

The Feldgendarmerie were organized into battalions of three companies, each of three platoons. A typical company consisted of 4 officers, 90 NCOs and 22 men with 22 lorries, 7 trucks and 28 motor-cycles.

Establishments provided various types of Feldgendarmerie detachments which were self-contained units under the command of army divisions. They worked in close co-operation with the Secret Field Police (Geheime Feldpolizei) and with district commanders and town majors.

252. The Field Service Uniform and insignia as worn by Feldgendarmerie personnel.

In the home areas of the German Reich they were responsible for discipline amongst troops, the rounding up of deserters, military traffic control, marshalling refugees and the evacuation of prisoners. All ranks of the Field Police received full infantry training and all personnel wore army uniforms with the addition of certain insignia.

They used orange Waffenfarbe and wore on the left upper arm of the Field Service Tunic the police style Eagle-and-Swastika emblem surrounded by an oakleaf

253. A member of an Army Field Post unit sorting mail for troops on the Russian front.

3.18. Service Uniform for Army Field Post personnel
Dienstanzug für Heeres Feldpost Personal

Classed as Beamten officials, these personnel fulfilled a very important and necessary task with the collecting, conveying and delivering of military mail to and from German and Axis troops throughout all the spheres of German military influence.

They wore normal issue German Army uniforms, Service Dress and Greatcoats, and were only distinguished as Field-post personnel by their distinctive Beamten collar patches, yellow and dark-green shoulder straps and in some cases the *FELDPOST* cuff-title (plate 253). For details regarding these items see the colour plates of shoulder straps and collar patches on pages 26–28 and the section on cuff-titles on page 76.

254. *A German Army Sonderführer being questioned by British Naval and Air Force Officers. France, June 1944.*

3.19. Army Sonderführer Field Service Uniform and insignia
Sonderführer des Deutschen Heeres, Felddienstanzug und Abzeichen

Army Sonderführer were those persons who, during the war, were posted to do officers' duties in many areas of work without reference to their military ability but simply because of their professional qualifications.

They were only promoted to such positions if it was officially necessary to take over a position for which they were qualified and for which no active officer of equivalent qualification was available.

They retained for the period of the posting officers' rank, but without commission, and had officers' authority only within the area of their job.

The grades of rank for Sonderführer were:
Sonderführer (Z), designated with the rank of Leutnant, were interpreters (Z), and Sonderführer for specialist purposes (Z).
Sonderführer (K), designated with the rank of Hauptmann, were interpreters (K), and doctors in the rank of Hauptmann (K).
Sonderführer (B), designated with the rank of Major, were specialist doctors in the rank of Major (B).

They were issued with uniforms similar to those of army officers. Those Sonderführer in the army were distinguished by their grey-blue Waffenfarbe, simple embroidered collar patches and shoulder straps interwoven with very small chevrons of black/white/red silk. All other insignia, including the National Emblem, and decorations as well as head-dress and footwear was the same as that for active serving officers (plate 254).

256. Army Officers' Old Style White Summer Tunic.

3.20. Officers' Old Style 'Reichsheer' Service Tunic
Feld Rock des Reichheers älterer Vorschrift

The photograph illustrated here (plate 255) gives a very good example of the old Reichsheer and new Wehrmacht—Heer—styles of Service Tunics worn by general-class officers.

The general on the left is wearing the Reichsheer pattern Service Tunic with its distinctive slashed side pockets plus the addition of the National Emblem, whilst the general on the right of the photograph is wearing the regulation Service Tunic introduced for army officers in 1936.

Although the old style tunic was superseded by the more recent Service Tunic it was still retained for wear by a considerable number of officers and generals some of whom continued to wear it right up to the end of the war.

3.21. Officers' Old Style White Summer Tunic
Weisser Rock für Offiziere, älterer Vorschrift

The old-style White Summer Tunic could be worn by all ranks of army officers up to the rank of General-feldmarschall including Wehrmachtbeamten of equivalent officers' rank.

The jacket was a separate item. White trousers were not used as they did not form part of this outfit; instead the White Summer Jacket was worn with the officers' grey or field-grey trousers (Uniform or Service trousers).

The old-style jacket had a stand-up collar worn

255. *The two patterns of the Army Officers' Service Tunic. Two unnamed Army Generals.*

257. *The Army Officers' New Style White Summer Tunic worn here by two Army Beamten Officials.*

without collar patches and worn closed at the neck with collar hooks. The entire jacket was completely white and had two box-pleated patch pockets on the chest and two slanting slash pockets in the skirt of the tunic in the same style as those worn on the old Reichsheer officer's tunic. The tunic sleeves had straight ends to the cuffs with no cuff turn-backs. Six metal buttons were arranged down the front of the coat with one more to each pocket flap. These buttons were all removable, as were any insignia worn on the coat, for ease of cleaning. Buttons and the pin-on National Emblem worn over the right breast pocket were in white metal for officers and gilt coloured metal for generals and above. It is interesting to note that in the photograph reproduced here (plate 256) the National Emblem is not being worn.

3.22. Officers' New Style White Summer Tunic Weisser Rock für Offiziere, neuerer Vorschrift

A new-style of Army Officer's White Summer Tunic was introduced by an order dated 9th July 1937 to be worn in the place of the Old Style Reichsheer White Summer Tunic. However, it would seem that both styles were worn after 1937 by individual officers as a matter of choice.

The New Style Summer Jacket could only be worn, weather permitting, from 1st April to 30th September each year and it was prescribed to be worn for the following reasons:
1. As a Walking-out Uniform
2. As an ordinary Dress Uniform when worn in the Officers' Mess or officers' clubs, or for social family gatherings or garden parties
3. At gymnastic, running and sports meetings within Germany and abroad, both for participating in the sports events and as a spectator

Unlike the Old Style Summer Jacket this tunic had a high neck turndown collar, a single row of eight buttons down the front, four box pleated patch pockets, two on the chest and two more with slanting pocket flaps on the tunic 'skirt'; there were deep officers' style turn-back cuffs to the sleeves. But, like the Old Style Jacket, rank was only indicated by the shoulder straps, no collar patches being worn. The pin-on National Emblem worn on the right breast and all buttons were removable. These were in white metal for officers and gilt coloured metal for generals and above. Two buttons were set at waist level at the rear of the jacket's vented tail. There was also one button to each pocket flap (plate 257).

There were no white trousers to be worn with this

258. *Deputy Führer and Reichminister Rudolf Hess, on the occasion of the 15th anniversary of the German National Socialist Student Bund, greeting officers of the German Armed Forces, all holders of the Knight's Cross and all of whom had been members of the NSD-Studentenbund. Munich, 27th January 1941. The Army Officer shaking hands with Rudolf Hess is wearing a fine quality example of the Army Officers' Piped Field Service Tunic.*

all white coat. The New Style Summer Tunic was intended to be worn by all ranks of officers including Generalfeldmarschall and Wehrmachtbeamten with officers' rank.

3.23. Officers' Piped Field Service Tunic
Die Feldbluse mit Vorstössen

This was a mixture of two styles of officers' tunics; the Service Tunic and the Uniform Tunic and, as the name implies, this was a service tunic with piping (plate 258).

The quality and design of the Piped Service Jacket was the same as that found in the normal quality officer's Service Tunic. It had the noticeable addition of 0·2cm wide Waffenfarbe piping worn down the front overlap of the coat, down the front edge to, and around the lower edge of, the tunic collar and around the upper edge of the deep turn-back cuffs. The collar patches worn on this tunic were the type as used on the Uniform Tunic. The buttons to this jacket were silver-white metal, five in a row down the front of the single breasted coat and one to each three pointed pocket flap on all four pockets.

The trousers worn with this tunic were those worn

with the Uniform Tunic, grey in colour with 0·2cm wide waffenfarbe piping displayed down the outer seam of each trouser leg. Officers' riding breeches could be worn with this tunic. Head-dress and foot-wear were normal.

Use of this style of uniform was restricted to those senior NCOs entitled to wear officers' silver cap cords to their peaked caps, Fähnriche, Wehrmachtbeamten, officers and general officers including Generalfeld-marschälle.

3.24. Field Service Uniform as worn by
army clergy
Dienstkleidung für Heeresgeistliche

Clergy in the German Army were issued with the standard Service Uniform and it was intended to be worn on the following occasions: when accompanying troops in the field, for attendance at troop training and manoeuvres, when administering to the troops, for study in the barracks, when visiting the sick in hospital, for reporting purposes, for riding and on all other official occasions reserved for the wearing of the Service Uniform. Shoulder straps were not worn on any uniform

259. *Three unnamed German Army chaplains at Regen, Germany, June 1945. Clearly shown on the central officer is the breast cross (crucifix) and also the special armband issued for wear by German Army clergy and worn on the left upper arm.*

260. *The Field Service Uniform as worn by German Army chaplains. There are no shoulder straps in wear and, as well as the breast cross and chain, the gothic cross can be seen on the Shirmmütze. Of special interest is the pistol and holster being worn, no doubt, for self-protection but nevertheless contrary to the regulations which forbade the carrying of weapons and side arms by German Army clergy.*

used by the army clergy. The only visible signs indicating rank were the use of buttons and collar patches. Gilt buttons were worn on the Service Tunic by field bishops (Feldbischöfe) and silver-white metal buttons on the uniform worn by army chaplains (Heerespfarrer) and senior army chaplains (Heeresoberpfarrer). The collar patches also showed the difference in rank. These were the same design as the normal pattern of officers' Field Service collar patches, the main difference being that the background colour to the embroidery was a rich violet instead of the dark blue-green. Heerespfarrer and Heeresoberpfarrer wore collar patches of silver thread embroidery inlaid with purple thread whereas Feldbischöfe wore gold embroidered patches inset with purple thread.

The National Emblem worn on the right breast was in gilt for Feldbischöfe and silver for Heerespfarrer and Heeresoberpfarrer.

All German Army clergy wore as part of their Service Dress a crucifix in gold hung on a chain around their neck. There were two versions of this crucifix, one for Protestant ministers and one for Catholic priests (plate 259). All ranks of clergy wore normal issue service trousers without piping as well as black leather lace-up short boots. Riding breeches with officers' high boots were also worn.

Officers' quality grey doe-skin gloves were used with the Service Dress. Regulations were laid down that army clergy were not to carry weapons or wear sidearms, but the photograph reproduced here would indicate that this order was not adhered to as it is evident that there is a pistol and holster being worn on the officer's leather service belt (plate 260).

When conducting normal religious services German Army Ministers wore the garments or vestments peculiar to their religious denomination.

3.25. Field-grey Frock Coat as worn by army clergy
Langer feldgrauer Rock (Überrock) für Heeresgeistliche

Two other distinctive items of dress were peculiar to German Army chaplains and field bishops. These were the long field-grey Frock Coat and the Greatcoat.

The Frock Coat was completely field-grey in colour, single breasted and tailored to reach to the height of the wearer's knees. The coat was waisted giving a slight flair to the coat tails (plates 261, 262). Violet piping, the distinctive colour for German Army clergy 0·2cm thick was displayed right around the upper edge to the simple upright field-grey collar, down the entire length of the front edge to the Frock Coat and around the upper edges to the deep turn-back cuffs.

A single row of eight silver-white metal buttons were worn down the front of the coat, the last button in the row being positioned in line with the waist seam. Two more silver-white buttons appeared on the back of the coat at waist level. Field bishops wore gilt coloured metal buttons.

An officers' quality silver National Emblem was worn

261, 262. *The field-grey Frock Coat for wear by German Army Chaplains and Field Bishops, as seen from the front and the rear.*

on the right breast, gilt for field bishops. The upper edge of the emblem was in line with the second button hole down from the collar. Medals, if worn, were positioned on the left breast, the upper edge of the ribbons also being in line with the second button hole.

No shoulder straps were worn, nor collar patches or any form of belt. Arms were not carried. The correct form of head-dress for this uniform coat was the Schirmmütze with its gothic cross emblem.

Long grey trousers, with violet piping 0·2cm thick displayed on the outer seams of the trouser legs, were worn with this coat as well as white gloves and black lace-up high shoes.

The field-grey Frock Coat was intended to be worn on those occasions not calling for the chaplains'/field bishops' style of Service Dress.

3.26. Greatcoat for German Army chaplains and field bishops
Mantel für Heeresgeistliche und Feld Bischöfe

German military clergy were issued with one other item of uniform which was intended to be worn on those occasions calling for a top coat when the Frock Coat was not required.[1] Regulations allowed them to

wear the officers' quality Greatcoat but with two distinct features. They wore no shoulder straps on the Greatcoat, in keeping with all their other items of military dress. The top two buttons of the Greatcoat were normally worn undone and the lapels of the coat were folded back to reveal violet facings in exactly the same fashion as the bright red Greatcoat facings worn by Generäle and Generalfeldmarschälle and the dark green facings worn by Wehrmachtbeamten with the rank of general.

Two rows each of six buttons were worn down the front of the Greatcoat, silver-white for Heerespfarrer and Heeresoberpfarrer and gilt metal for Feldbischöfe.

Officers' brown leather Service Belts could be worn with this coat, and regulations stated that no side arms were to be carried.

3.27. The German Army Greatcoat, basic styles and variations

There were at least thirteen known styles of German Army Greatcoat and variations on these styles, some of which only just qualify for the description of 'greatcoat', introduced at various times and intended to be

[1] German Army clergy were also permitted to wear the regulation Army Officer's Cloak if they so wished.

263. *The standard pattern Army Greatcoat. This was normal issue throughout the Reichsheer period and was worn in the Army of the Wehrmacht, being issued until stocks became exhausted, when it was superseded by the later pattern Greatcoats of inferior quality. This photo shows General Freiherr von Hammerstein, Chef der Heeresleitung, inspecting the Berlin Wachtruppe on the parade ground at Berlin-Moabit.*

worn by personnel of the German Army. These were as follows:

1. The standard pattern field-grey Army Greatcoat with dark blue-green collar worn by all ranks up to but not including the rank of army general and above, by all arms of service.[1]
2. The standard pattern field-grey Army Greatcoat worn by generals and above. A colour and quality variation on (1)
3. The standard pattern field-grey Greatcoat worn by German Army Wehrmachtbeamten of general's rank and above. A colour and quality variation on (1)
4. The standard pattern field-grey Greatcoat worn by German Army clergy. A colour and quality variation on (1)
5. The specially designed field-grey Greatcoat worn by personnel of the Infantry Regiment 'Grossdeutschland'
6. The standard pattern field-grey Army Greatcoat with field-grey collar
7. The Deutsches 'Afrika Korps' khaki Greatcoat; colour variation on (1)
8. The inferior quality all field-grey Greatcoat with large collar
9. The inferior quality all field-grey Greatcoat with

large collar and two extra side pockets
10. The army pattern field-grey Greatcoat with reinforced leather patches to the shoulders
11. The grey-green quality leather Greatcoat worn by army officers and generals
12. The Greatcoat lined with fur, sometimes with thick fur collar
13. The Greatcoat made from animal skins and fur

Details regarding these thirteen styles of coats are as follows:

3.27(1). *The standard field-grey Greatcoat, dark blue-green collar.* Designed and introduced before the war, the basic German Army pattern Greatcoat was worn by all ranks with only differences in quality, rank insignia, colour of buttons and lapel facings indicating the wearer's military position.

The standard pattern Greatcoat was a long double breasted garment, which when correctly tailored reached at least to the wearer's calf. It displayed a 9cm deep dark blue-green collar and two rows of six field-grey metal buttons worn down the front of the chest. It was slightly waisted giving a flare to the bottom of the coat. There were two side slash pockets set at a slight angle both with rounded pocket flaps. All ranks had 15cm deep turn back cuffs (officers' cuffs were slightly deeper: 23cm)[2] (plate 263).

There was a 6cm deep half-belt with two field-grey buttons in the centre of the back at waist level. This could be adjusted to one of two positions. For officers there was a long inverted pleat at the back of the Greatcoat reaching from the lower edge of the collar right down to the tail of the coat. For all personnel below the rank of officer this inverted pleat only started from the waist reaching down to the tails. In the 'skirts' of all Greatcoats at the back there was a deep vent designed to give extra freedom of movement to the wearer. It was fastened in place with four horn buttons. Sometimes this pattern of Greatcoat was made with an extra thick blanket lining for added warmth.

Shoulder straps were worn on this Greatcoat by all ranks.

The Greatcoat was correctly worn buttoned up to the neck, the collar fastened with the neck hook and folded down in place. Holders of the Knight's Cross were permitted to leave undone the top two buttons and to fold the lapels back in order to display their neck decoration worn on the neck of their uniform tunic.

264. *Field-grey standard pattern Army Greatcoats were normal wear during cold weather by Panzer crews until about 1942, when they were discarded in favour of the newly introduced winter clothing.*

[1] It should be noted that crews of armoured fighting vehicles, contrary to what one would expect, were not issued with a black Greatcoat in keeping with their Black Panzer Uniforms. Instead they received the normal issue field-grey Greatcoat with its dark blue-green collar (plate 264). This impractical situation of having to wear this long cumbersome garment during the winter months whilst inside the confined space of their armoured vehicles lasted until the heavy winter clothing was introduced. Thereafter the Greatcoats were discarded in favour of this new form of warm and practical garment.

[2] Cuffs of this design were originally intended to be turned down to provide extra protection to the wrists and hands in cold weather. On almost all German Army Greatcoats this was impossible to do without first cutting through the sleeve material and stitching on the inside of the cuffs used to hold the turn-backs in position.

265. *The standard pattern Greatcoat as worn by Army Generals and above, clearly showing the bright red lapel facings. Seen here is Generalfeldmarschall Gerd von Rundstedt, the former supreme commander of the German armies on the Western Front and one of Germany's ablest generals, together with his son (Leutnant Hans von Rundstedt) at the time of their capture by troops of the Seventh U.S. Army. Bad Tolz, Bavaria, 2nd May 1945.*

In cold weather the Greatcoat collar could be worn turned up around the wearer's neck and lower jaw. This was done by the collar being turned up and buttoned across the throat by a small cloth flap positioned on the left underside of the coat collar and attached to a small horn button on the opposite underside of the collar.

Army personnel from senior non-commissioned officers and above could privately purchase their own Greatcoats for Walking-out dress. These were usually of fine quality material and only differed in very minor points to the standard pattern German Army issue Greatcoat.

3.27(2). *Generals' field-grey Greatcoat.* Identical in design and cut to the Greatcoat worn by all other ranks below that of general. The quality was usually of a high standard, normally of a fine quality doe-skin. All buttons were in gilt coloured metal and appropriate rank shoulder straps were worn. The two top buttons were normally worn undone, the lapels of the coat being folded back to reveal bright red facings. The red material used on these lapel facings was continued inside both the coat flaps reaching down to and level with the last two of the twelve gilt buttons worn in two rows of six down the front of the Greatcoat (plate 265).

3.27(3). *Field-grey Wehrmachtbeamten Greatcoat.* The description of the Greatcoat is as for (2) above. The lapel facings on this Greatcoat showed dark green.

3.27(4). *Field-grey Greatcoat for Army Clergy.* The description of this Greatcoat is as for (2) above. It was worn without shoulder straps and the lapel facings showed violet. For further details of this coat see 'The Greatcoat for German Army Chaplains and Field Bishops', page 140.

3.27(5). *The special 'Grossdeutschland' Greatcoat.* The description of this Greatcoat is as for (1) above. It was designed with an extra large dark blue-green collar piped in white Waffenfarbe as were the upper edges to the turn-back cuffs. For additional information regarding this coat see 'Infantry Regiment 'Grossdeutschland' Special Greatcoat, page 153.

3.27(6). *Field-grey Greatcoat with field-grey collar.* Introduced sometime after the standard pattern army Greatcoat, it differed only in having a field-grey collar of the same colour as the coat which replaced the earlier dark blue-green collar. The depth to the collar remained the same, but in appearance the new field-grey collar was slightly stiffer (plate 266). Shoulder straps manufactured for this all field-grey Greatcoat worn by Mannschaften and Unteroffiziere were constructed from field-grey cloth. For other details of description see (1) above.

3.27(7). *Deutsches Afrika Korps khaki Greatcoat.* This was yet another colour variation on the basic pattern Greatcoat. While it retained all those features covered within (1) it was manufactured from a khaki-coloured material (plate 267).

3.27(8). *Field-grey Greatcoat with large collar.* This was a new style of Greatcoat manufactured and issued

266. *The standard pattern Army field-grey Greatcoat with field-grey collar shown here being worn by German troops arriving at a British port. These troops were some of the first to be taken prisoner during the initial Allied landings in Northern France, June 1944.*

267. *The 'Afrikakorps' khaki Greatcoat. General der Panzertruppen Gustav von Varest (saluting), General-major Krause, Generalmajor Neuffer, Generalmajor Bassange and Generalmajor Borowietz, with aides: all had surrendered to the Allies in Tunisia, here seen being received by Major-General E. C. Gepp, C.B., D.S.O., on their arrival in Britain. May 1943.*

in the German Army during 1943 when, for reasons of economy and practicality a modified version of the standard issue Greatcoat was introduced.

Made from inferior quality material, its appearance tended to be more shoddy than the prewar Greatcoat. Noticeably the dark blue-green collar was discontinued and in its place was a much larger field-grey collar made of the same material as the coat. The collar being much larger than the earlier dark blue-green version it afforded more neck and head protection when turned up (plate 268).

All other features were retained: the two rows of six metal buttons, the deep turn-back cuffs and the half-belt at the rear. Long inverted back pleats and the button-up vent in the rear coat tails were also retained. These Greatcoats were sometimes made with an extra thick lining of blanket material for added warmth.

268. *The inferior quality all field-grey Army Greatcoat with large collar.*

269. *The inferior quality all field-grey Army Greatcoat with large collar and two extra side pockets.*

3.27(9). *Field-grey Greatcoat with large collar and extra pockets.* This was identical in quality and cut to the Greatcoat described in (8) above but with the following exceptions: there were two pocket openings, without flaps, let into the coat on either side of the chest (plate 269). Some examples of this Greatcoat had a field-grey cloth hood, made from blanket material, attached to the inside of the coat collar at the back of the neck (plate 270). The two normal pockets had square cut pocket flaps. A full length inverted pleat ran down the entire length of the back. Some coats also had extra thick linings.

3.27(10). *Field-grey Greatcoat with reinforced shoulders.* This was a variation in manufacture on either of the two Greatcoats described under (8) or (9) above. It had the noticeable addition of leather shoulder patches (plate 272).

3.27(11). *The grey-green leather Greatcoat.* If required, German Army officers and generals were entitled to purchase for their own use fine grain quality leather overcoats for Service and Field Service use. No insignia other than detachable shoulder straps were permitted to be worn on this form of Greatcoat (plate 273).

3.27(12). *Fur-lined Greatcoat.* As the title aptly describes it, this was a fur-lined Greatcoat sometimes with the fur extending to the collar. Worn in very cold climates (plate 271).

3.27(13). *Animal-skin Greatcoat.* These skin coats varied greatly in colour, size and shape but they all had one thing in common, they were designed to be worn for extremes of cold climates. They were worn mostly by officers, but soldiers used this type when on guard duties in very cold weather (plates 274, 275).

270. *German prisoners are searched by American Military Police, Germany, March 1945. Shown on the left of the photo is the 'blanket' material hood attached to the inside neck of the Army Greatcoat.*

271. *The Army Greatcoat lined with fur. Generalmajor Scherer (right), holder of the Knight's Cross to the Iron Cross and awarded the Oakleaves by the Führer for his command of the Cholm garrison. This consisted of 5,500 miscellaneous troops who held out in an area of one square mile for 105 days of bitter fighting from 21st January 1942 to 5th May 1942, before being finally relieved.*

272. *(centre) The Army pattern field-grey Greatcoat with reinforced leather patches to the shoulders.*

273. *(right) The grey-green leather Greatcoat worn here by Generalmajor Graf von Sponeck at the time of his arrival in England. Holder of the Knight's Cross and ex-CO of the German 90th Light Division.*

3.28. The Army Officers' Cloak
Der Ümhang für Offiziere des Heeres

In peacetime the German Army pattern cloak was worn on informal occasions by all ranks of officers including Wehrmachtbeamten with officers' rank. The regulation cloak was field-grey in colour and had a dark blue-green collar.

The example illustrated here (plate 276) shows the Officers' Field-Grey Cloak but with a field-grey collar. It can also be seen that apart from the cloak reaching down to the wearer's calf it has five horn buttons, collar neck hooks and two side 'pocket' openings.

3.29. Motorcyclists' Waterproof Coat
Schutzmantel für Kraft Radfahrer

Members of motorcycle units and individual motorcyclists, regardless of rank, were issued with a very practical double breasted rubberized motorcycle coat. Loose fitting, the tail of the coat could be gathered in around the wearer's legs and buttoned in position to allow for easier and safer movement whilst on the motorbike.

This waterproof coat tended more towards field-grey-green in colour; it had a woollen field-grey material faced collar as well as two large pockets in

274. An example of a type of animal skin fur coat issued for use to German troops driving vehicles or on guard duties on the Eastern Front during winter.

275. Oberst Graf Strachwitz, holder of the Knight's Cross with Oakleaves and Swords, shown here wearing another variety of animal skin fur coat and speaking with a Panzer commander on the Narwa front, 1 April 1944.

276. *The German Army Officers' Cloak. Shown here being worn by Generalleutnant Scheurlein, the former commander in Macedonia. Both he and Luftwaffe Generalleutnant Oberhausser are seen here passing through Euston station, the departure point for a number of senior German prisoners in transit through London. 17th May 1945.*

277. *The German Army issue waterproof motor-cycle coat, showing both the front and rear.*

the front of and each side of the coat each with large button down pocket flaps (plate 277).

When in use, the Motorcycle Waterproof Coat was worn with army canvas and leather issue gloves or cloth mittens, with overshoes and leggings or just with normal army boots. When required, equipment was worn over the rubberized motorcycle coat.

3.30. The Uniform Tunic as worn by other ranks
Der Waffenrock des Deutschen Heeres für Mannschaften

The Uniform Tunic, introduced on 29th June 1935, was worn by all ranks of the German Army with only the rank insignia to indicate difference in ranks. The Uniform Tunic as worn by those army personnel classed as Mannschaften was as follows (plate 278): the jacket was field-grey in colour with collar and 'Swedish' cuff-facings in dark blue-green material. Waffenfarbe piping 0·2cm thick was used down the edge of the front overlap to the tunic, down the front edge of the collar and around the collar base, on the upper edges of the cuff-facings and down the two tunic flaps at the rear of the uniform.

Uniform quality collar and cuff-facing patches, all of which were worked on a backing cloth of the

278. *The German Army regulation issue Uniform tunic (Waffenrock) worn here by members of an Artillery Observation unit, all of whom are taking*

part in a parade in honour of the Führer's birthday. The fact that these troops are wearing normal Service Uniform trousers with the Waffenrock tunic, and not the correct Uniform trousers, would suggest that these soldiers were seated in troop carriers in which they would only have been seen from the waist up.

279. *The new style Waffenrock especially designed for personnel of the élite Infantry Regiment 'Gross-deutschland'. The rare photograph reproduced here was taken on the first day of its introduction, 16th March 1939.*

appropriate waffenfarbe, were worn on this tunic. There was a single row of eight silver-white metal buttons worn down the front of the tunic, the last in the row being in line with the waist seam of the jacket. Six more silver-white metal buttons decorated the two tunic flaps at the back, three to each flap. Four 'dummy' buttons were used, one to each cuff-facing patch and two more buttons were used one to each of the dark blue-green shoulder straps.

Other than the two 'hidden' pockets in the tail of the tunic there were no pockets on the tunic.

The appropriate National Emblem was worn on the right breast of the jacket stitched against an outlined background of dark blue-green material.

Normal rank insignia and military decorations were worn on this uniform where appropriate. The trousers worn with this Uniform Tunic were of a plain grey colour with Waffenfarbe piping, matching that of the tunic, 0·2cm thick running down the length of both outer seams of each trouser leg.

The Uniform Tunic and trousers were used for parades, walking-out and for all ceremonial occasions.

3.31. Special uniform for the Infantry Regiment 'Grossdeutschland' Sonder Waffenrock für das Infanterie-Regiment 'Grossdeutschland'

A specially designed uniform jacket was proposed for the Infantry Regiment 'Grossdeutschland' to be worn as from 15th September 1939 (plate 279). It was modelled on the normal army Uniform Tunic of field-grey material. It had white Waffenfarbe piping worn down the front overlap of the tunic, down the front of and around the collar base, on the upper edges of the cuffs and around the cuff-patterns as well as on the edging to the jacket tails at the rear. All buttons were in matt finish white metal.

This jacket had two especially notable features. Both the collar-patches and the cuff-patterns were of a design completely different to any other German Army uniform introduced during the Third Reich period. These features were deliberately chosen for this 'new' formation in order to convey a sense of continuing tradition with the Imperial German Army of 1914. Élite regiments of all old Imperial States wore 'dopplelitzen' collar patch lace of an elongated design and the 'French cuffs' were a feature of Imperial German Army uniform worn only by the Garde Schützen Bataillon and the 2.Garde-M.G.Abteilung. By adopting this particular style of collar patch and cuff-pattern it was a deliberate attempt to identify this élite unit with the traditions of the old Imperial Army.

The collar patches were of a special elongated design 13cm long in silver embroidery and worked directly on to the dark blue-green collar and, unlike normal Infantry Parade collar patches, were without any white Waffenfarbe underlay cloth.

On both cuffs of this special tunic were worn 'French cuff' patterns. These French cuffs were constructed of dark blue-green backing cloth, they were

piped around the edge with white Waffenfarbe piping 0·2cm thick and on each cuff pattern there were three separate silver embroidered cuff-patches each with a matt finished white metal button and, like the special elongated collar patches, were without any white Waffenfarbe underlay. Shoulder straps worn on this tunic carried the entwined 'GD' shoulder strap monogram in white. The straps themselves were of dark blue-green material piped white.

On the lower right arm, 1cm above the top edge of the French cuff was worn the newly issued 'Grossdeutschland' cuff title, 3·2cm wide with gothic style lettering in fine silver aluminium thread machine-embroidered on to a dark green band.

The National Emblem backed with dark blue-green material was worn on the right breast.

The special uniform worn by NCOs from this unit differed from the one described above in three points. 0·9cm wide rank braiding was worn around the upper edges to the Swedish cuffs—behind the French cuff facing patterns. This rank braiding was also displayed around the upper edge to, and down the front of, the collar, necessitating the use of only a single bar of patch 'litzen' instead of the double lace braiding worn by other ranks and officers. The 'GD' monogram shoulder straps displayed the NCOs' rank.

Owing to the outbreak of the war this jacket was not issued and during the war manufacture of new jackets was not carried out.

3.32. Special greatcoat for the Infantry Regiment 'Grossdeutschland' Sonder Mantel für das Infanterie-Regiment 'Grossdeutschland'

Very similar in style and colour to the normal pattern of Greatcoat worn throughout the German Army in peacetime by all ranks (other than generals), this Greatcoat had two interesting features (plate 280).

The collar was much larger than normal with deep collar points and, although it was faced with the universal dark blue-green material, it was edged with 0·2cm wide white waffenfarbe piping. This white piping was also carried around the upper edges to the deep turn-back cuffs.

On the right sleeve 1cm above the turn-back cuff was worn the silver on green cuff-title 'Grossdeutschland'. All other details were as for the standard pattern German Army Greatcoat.

This Greatcoat was introduced for wear by all personnel of the 'Grossdeutschland' Infantry Regiment at the same time as the special 'Grossdeutschland' Uniform Tunic. There is no evidence that it was actually issued for wear in any numbers.

3.33. Utilisation of the basic German Army Uniform for various forms of dress

Certain basic types of uniforms were used for a wide variety of purposes covering most military and social occasions. This was achieved by the addition of particular uniform accoutrements to the basic uniform,

the use of military decorations or the wearing of certain types of head-dress, footwear or equipment.

The correct methods used to convert the army officers' and soldiers' military uniform into a style required for a particular function were carefully prescribed in German Army Dress Regulations. Plates 281–9 show a few of the many forms of German Army dress utilised from the basic uniform.

3.33.(1). *The Parade Dress worn by German Army Generals (Paradeanzug für Generäle).* For this style of dress the Waffenrock—Uniform Tunic—for generals was worn with full military decorations. The parade belt for army generals (in silver and dark green braiding with gold buckle) and the gold parade aiguillettes were worn. Generals' red 'striped' breeches and officers' black leather riding boots were also used and, to complete the Parade Dress swords were carried and steel helmets normally worn (plate 281).

3.33(2). *The German Army Parade Dress for Officers, NCOs and Men (Paradeanzug für Offiziere, Feldwebel und Mannschaften).* Plate 282 shows the style of Army Parade Dress as worn by army officers—the officer behind Reichsprotektor Freiherr von Neurath shown saluting—and by NCOs and men of the Ehrenbataillon, (the Guard of Honour). Generaloberst von Brauchitsch on the far left is wearing the General Officers' Service Tunic for parade purposes.

3.33(3). *The German Army Officers' Parade Dress worn with long trousers (Paradeanzug für Offizier mit langer Hose).* In the photograph shown here (plate 283) it can be seen that, in addition to the officers' riding breeches, the long piped trousers were permitted to be worn with the officers' Waffenrock when the Uniform Tunic was used as Parade Dress.

The officers' parade belt and aiguillettes, full military decorations, Schirmmütze, white gloves (normally grey) black leather shoes and sword were all used with this style of dress.

3.33(4). *The Full Dress Uniform as worn by German Army Officers (Grosser Gessellschaftanzug für Offizier).* The Full Dress Uniform worn by army officers consisted of the Uniform Tunic (der Waffenrock) worn without the silver and green parade belt but with the officers' silver parade aiguillettes. Military decorations and ribbons were also worn. The long piped trousers were worn over the black shoes (plate 284).

3.33(5). *The German Army Officers' Undress Uniform (Kleiner Dienstanzug für Offiziere).* The 'Undress Uniform' could be worn by all army officers including generals and above. It consisted of the Service Tunic worn without belt or decorations but with medal ribbons being permitted, and with Service Uniform trousers worn over black shoes.

The Officers' Uniform Peaked Cap, the Schirmmütze, was also worn as was the army officers' dagger. This was carried hung from the dagger straps on the left side of the tunic (plate 285).

3.33(6). *The Undress Uniform worn by a War Administration Official (Kleiner Dienstanzug für Kriegsverwaltungsbeamte).* The photo shown here

280. The new style Greatcoat especially designed for the élite Infantry Regiment 'Grossdeutschland'.

281. *General Dr. Edmund Glaise von Horstenau. A fine example of the General Officers' Uniform Tunic worn as the Parade Dress. The use of decorations, medals and sashes completed this form of dress as described in the text. It is interesting to note that there are 14 medals showing on the medal bar, 5 different neck orders worn at different positions down the front of the tunic, 4 breast orders and 1 sash order.*

283. The German Army Officers' Grossen Gesellschaftsanzug.
282. Reichsprotektor Freiherr von Neurath accompanied by Generaloberst von Brauchitsch inspecting the honour company drawn from the 31st Infantry Regiment, 24th Infantry Division. Prague, 5th April 1939.
284. The German Army Officers' Kleiner Gesellschaftsanzug.

285. *The German Army Officers' Undress Uniform.*

(plate 286) illustrates a type of uniform used as an 'Undress Uniform' by a War Administration Official. **3.33.(7).** *A form of Dress Uniform worn by a German Army Administration Official.* The photo shown here (plate 287) illustrates a form of Dress Uniform worn by a Wehrmachtbeamter. The Service Dress has been utilized with the addition of the officers' green and silver braided belt and silver aiguillettes.

3.33(8). *The Walking-out Dress for an Army Gefreiter (Ausgehanzug für Mannschaften).* This was the Service Uniform utilised for the purpose of walking-out. Individual soldiers, NCOs and officers were allowed to purchase for themselves uniforms of better quality material and finish than those Service Uniforms issued by the army. These were often bought for walking-out purposes. The photo illustrated here shows such an example (plate 288).

In the photo, the cavalry Gefreiter is wearing an officers' quality National Emblem and parade quality collar patches. The sleeves of this tunic have deep turn-back cuffs, a feature of Officers' Service Tunics not normally found on tunics worn by other ranks. The Schirmmütze worn by Mannschaften and the cavalry sabre were also used with this Walking-out Uniform.

286. *The Undress Uniform worn by a War Administration Official.*

287. *A form of dress uniform worn by a German Army Administration Official.*

288. *The Walking-out Dress for an Army Gefreiter.*

289. *The German Army Reporting Uniform, seen here being correctly worn by an Unteroffizier acting as 'der Spiess'. Note the Blood Order ribbon worn on the right breast pocket flap and the reporting pouch tucked into the tunic.*

3.33(9). *The German Army Reporting Uniform, as worn by 'der Spiess' (Meldeanzug für 'der Spiess').* The German Army Service Uniform was correctly utilised for the purpose of a Reporting Uniform by the wearing of the NCOs' Schirmmütze and the use of the reporting pouch. Plate 289 shows this pouch tucked inside the jacket, the second tunic button being left undone for this purpose. Service Uniform trousers and lace-up boots were worn. See also plate 292 for the Reporting Uniform used by Panzer troops.

3.34. The Special Black Panzer Uniform Sonderbekleidung der Deutschen Panzertruppen

With the creation of the new Panzer arm of the German Army, a special style of uniform was designed, manufactured and issued to be worn by all ranks serving in armoured fighting vehicles (plate 290).

This special uniform consisted of a short black double-breasted jacket worn with long black trousers. The uniform was used both as a Service Uniform, including Field Service, and as a Dress Uniform.

The short double breasted jacket was normally worn open at the neck with the two top buttons undone in order to fold back the wide lapels. When

290. *The Black Panzer Uniform, shown being worn by a Panzer Oberleutnant at the time of its intro- duction. It is interesting to note that on this early example of the Panzer Uniform the National Emblem normally worn both on the Panzer beret and on the jacket are not displayed. The wreath of silver oakleaves has been embroidered directly onto the beret and the Reichs- kokade is of the same type (a metal rosette) found on the Officers' Schirmmütze. The collar to the jacket is much narrower than that on the later models and the Totenkopf collar patches are slightly larger than those of wartime manufacture. The grey doe-skin gloves were retained for wear by officers with this type of uniform when used for parade and walking-out purposes. The use of the leather cross strap was discontinued during the early part of the war.*

worn in this fashion it showed the mouse-grey shirt and black tie that were intended to be worn with this uniform. When serving in the field the jacket could, if required, be buttoned across at the neck which, in cold weather, gave extra warmth.

The jacket was made in such a way that few buttons were worn on the outside of the coat. With the exception of the two small black horn buttons worn positioned one above the other on the far right side of the chest which were intended to secure the left lapel when the jacket was worn closed up at the neck, and with the two field-grey metal buttons used to secure the shoulder straps no other buttons were visible on the outside of this jacket.

291. *The use of the Officers' field-grey Schirmmütze worn together with the Special Black Panzer uniform was fairly common. The photo shows an unnamed Ritterkreuzträger, a former member of the Hitler Youth.*

292. *'Panzer Spiess'.*

The large buttons used on the inside of the double breasted fly-fronted jacket were made of black horn.

Rose pink piping was worn by all ranks around the outer edge to the wide jacket collar although this practice was discontinued during 1942. The pink piping was also used as edging to the Death's head collar patches as well as piping and underlay to the shoulder straps.[1]

This Special Black Panzer Uniform was of the same design and colouring for all ranks of the Panzer arm including Generals of Panzer Troops, the only discernable difference being in the following points.

1. Rank Insignia: unlike other forms of German Army uniforms which used collar patches and shoulder straps to show the wearer's rank, only the shoulder straps served this purpose on the Special Panzer Uniform. The collar patches were a form of distinctive 'traditional' decoration. These have been described in the section dealing with the subject of German Army collar patches. A known exception to this rule was

[1] Gold yellow Waffenfarbe piping was used by all members of the 24.Panzer-Division in exactly the same way as described for the rose-pink piping. They were allowed to wear this gold-yellow piping as a distinction to commemorate the fact that they had originally been the 1.Kavallerie-Division and were the only cavalry division in the Wehrmacht to be converted to a Panzer division. This yellow piping used on the edge to the collar was also discontinued at the same time as the rose-pink piping.

that of Generalleutnant Hoppe, the commanding officer of the 278.Volksgrenadier-Division, who wore generals' normal red and gold collar patches on the collar of his Black Panzer Uniform.

Shoulder straps which, for Mannschaften and Unteroffiziere, were constructed from black cloth and not from dark blue-green material were sometimes stitched on to the shoulder of the jacket all around the strap. This was done to prevent the strap from getting caught up on any projections inside the armoured vehicle.

2. The National Emblem: the quality and colour of the National Emblem worn over the right breast varied according to rank. It was manufactured in white or grey cotton yarn or in fine aluminium thread for wear by all ranks below that of officer and, normally (but not always) in heavy silver wire embroidery for officers and in gilt embroidery for Generals of Panzer troops.

All National Emblems, as well as arm rank insignia, were worked on to a backing of black cloth, not on to dark blue-green material. It should be noted that, except for the collar of the field-grey Greatcoat and the cap band to the Officer's Old Style Field Service Cap as well as the field-grey Schirmmütze which was often worn by all ranks with the Panzer Uniform (plate 291), no dark blue-green material appeared at all with this form of special clothing.

3. Other Insignia: double bands of rank braiding were

worn on the sleeves of the Panzer jacket by 'der Spiess' (plate 292). Cuff-titles, standard bearers' gorgets, arm-shields and carrying sashes were worn on this uniform depending on the wearer's position and requirements. However what was not worn on this jacket was the 0·9cm wide rank braiding normally used around the lower edge of tunic collars by non-commissioned officers.

Officers wearing the black Panzer Uniform for official parades would normally wear the officers' quality Parade Belt, the officers' silver aiguillettes—gilt for Generals—and grey doe-skin gloves.

The trousers to this uniform were exactly the same style for all ranks. They were worn full length and gathered in around the tops to the short black leather lace-up ankle boots. There was no piping used on the outer seams to these trouser legs. Generals of Panzer troops who choose to wear the Special Black Panzer Uniform did not wear the generals' 'broad red stripe' on the trousers. Two slanting side pockets, both with button down pocket flaps were used on these trousers as well as a small 'fob pocket' and a hip pocket.[2]

The black Panzer Beret, which has been covered in the section on German Army Head-dress, was first issued to be worn with the Special Panzer Uniform (plate 293). This was replaced during the winter of 1939–40. In its place Panzer troops were issued with a black Feldmütze of a shape and design identical to the army officers' field-grey Feldmütze and the Feldmütze worn by other ranks (plate 294 and 295). How-

293. The Black Panzer Schutzmütze or Panzer Beret. A clear indication of the round shape of the inner crash liner can be seen being worn by the Unteroffizier on the left of the photo. The elasticated strap to the goggles has pulled the soft beret cover in tight around the crash liner.

[2]It is interesting to note that by an order dated 10th May 1940 this special black clothing was extended to be worn by members of Panzer-Pioniere-Kompanien. Instead of the rose-pink piping—still being used at this time—they were to wear a twisted black and white piping on the uniform in the following positions: as a 90° inverted Waffenfarbe chevron on the black Feldmütze, around the edge to the jacket collar and as piping around the collar patches and on the shoulder straps.

294. The Black Panzer feldmütze for other ranks.
295. (right) The Black Panzer feldmütze for officers.

ever it was not uncommon to see Panzer crew members wearing the Army issue field-grey Feldmütze together with their black uniforms although this practice was later forbidden. As late as the summer of 1944, the wearing of what was described as the field-grey service cap worn with the black Panzer Uniform, both in and out of service, was again forbidden.

In 1943 a new form of head-dress, the Einheitsfeldmütze, was manufactured to be worn universally throughout the German Army with only slight differences in finish and cap insignia between the various ranks. Panzer troops were issued a black version of this cap which was intended to be worn when stocks of the earlier black Feldmütze were exhausted.

The field-grey German Army steel helmet was issued to all Panzer crews as part of their regulation clothing issue (plate 296). This helmet was worn by crew members inside the armoured vehicle when crossing over rough terrain.

The original intention of producing a black uniform with a double breasted jacket was no doubt motivated by the fact that oil and grease stains would be harder to see on black material and that, by being double-breasted, the jacket would provide additional frontal

296. *The normal pattern field-grey Army steel helmet was issued for wear to all panzer crews.*
297. *Crew members from a 'Grossdeutschland' Tiger tank. All are wearing the reed-green Panzer denims with the large patch pocket.*

298. *The Special field-grey uniform for wear by Tank Destroyer and Self Propelled Assault Gun units. Hauptmann Lützow, holder of the Knight's Cross seen on the left of the photo is wearing the complete field-grey uniform with the Officers' quality field-grey Einheitsfeldmütze. The Oberwachtmeister on the right is wearing the special reversible winter trousers, field-grey side outermost, as part of his uniform.*

protection to the wearer from wind as well as extra warmth.

However, one suspects that the designers of this uniform jacket were not just governed by the need to produce a black double-breasted uniform which combined practicality with warmth, but that they were influenced by the historical aspect of the old Imperial German Death's head Hussar uniform.

Even the choice of metal Death's heads used as a distinctive form of collar patch decoration, rather than the practical use of the patches to show differences of rank and waffenfarbe, can be attributed as an acknowledgement to the Imperial Death's head Hussars. Indeed it is not uncommon to find in early prewar German publications which featured pictures of these black uniformed troops from the new Panzer arm to see them referred to as 'The new Black Hussars' (Die neuen Schwarzen Husaren).

The Germans were so successful in establishing this black uniform as the accepted form of dress for the crews of their armoured fighting vehicles that the British tank crews from the Royal Tank Corps Regiments, who were issued with a somewhat similar tank suit in black denim, discontinued wearing this in order to avoid confusion with their German opposite numbers.

3.35. The reed-green two-piece Panzer Denims Schilfgrüner Drillichschutzanzug für Panzertruppen

A two piece reed-green denim suit, hard wearing, light and easily washable, identical in cut to the Special Black Panzer Uniform was issued to the crews of army panzer formations.

It was intended to be used during the summer months, especially in warm climate countries, as a separate item of clothing. It was also used as an outer garment worn over the normal panzer uniform.

The jacket of this suit sometimes had the addition of a large patch pocket, with pocket flap, set at an angle on the front left side of the chest.

Normal insignia including the National Emblem, shoulder straps and panzer totenkopf collar patches as well as military decorations were worn on the jacket (plate 297).

3.36. Special field-grey uniform worn by crews of tank destroyer and self-propelled assault gun units Feldgrauer sonderbekleidung für die Besatzung der Jagd. Pzkw. und S.F.L. Artillerie Einheiten

The Special Black Panzer Uniform proved to be a very

299. *Ritterkreuzträger Oberleutnant Ludwig instructing his battery officers during the fighting in Normandy, 10th July 1944. Five different varieties of collar patches can be seen in this one photo all worn on the Special Field-Grey uniform.*

300. *A Panzerjäger Oberleutnant, taken prisoner by Canadian forces west of Deventes, Holland. The Totenkopf collar patches of black material edged with rose pink piping are being worn.*

301. *Normal pattern Army field service collar patches piped with 'Russia braid' in the appropriate Waffenfarbe gradually replaced the Totenkopf collar patches.*

practical garment for members serving in armoured fighting vehicles. However there was only one major drawback to the uniform in that it was black. Traditional considerations, oil and grease stains apart, the Special Black Panzer Uniform was completely unsuitable for camouflage purposes. Its wearer became conspicuous immediately on leaving his armoured vehicle. Enemy reconnaissance teams and advance detachments often prematurely recognized the presence of Panzer units.

When designing a uniform for crews of tank destroyers and self-propelled assault guns serving in Panzer and Panzergrenadier divisions with their need for close observation work both inside and away from their armoured vehicles, the Germans decided on using the same style and practical cut of the black Panzer Uniform but to produce a new version in field-grey to give better camouflage qualities (plate 298).

This special uniform was made entirely of field-grey cloth with all details of cut and design the same as those for the black Panzer Uniform. It did however differ in respect to certain insignia.

The collar patches used on this short field-grey

double-breasted jacket by those crews of different types of military units entitled to wear the uniform were as follows (plate 299): metal Death's head emblems were mounted on patches of dark blue-green cloth and edged with bright red Waffenfarbe piping; metal Death's head emblems mounted on patches of black material edged with rose-pink Waffenfarbe piping (plate 300). Normal style field-service quality collar patches which, for those personnel below the rank of officer, were sometimes mounted on dark blue-green patches edged in bright red Waffenfarbe piping or stitched directly on to the field-grey collar inside a rectangular surround of bright red 'Russia braid' (plate 301).[1]

---

[1] The practice of wearing the metal 'Death's head' emblem on the collar patches of those units permitted to wear the Special Field-Grey Uniform was gradually forbidden. As a temporary measure the Death's head was removed (plate 9) but eventually in place of the Totenkopf collar patches these personnel were issued with normal army field-service quality collar patches. For those ranks below officer these displayed a rectangular edging of 'Russia braid' in the colour (Waffenfarbe) appointed to their particular unit or formation. Normal army officers' quality field service collar patches were worn by all officers which also showed their particular Waffenfarbe as part of the embroidered design to the collar patch.

302. Officers' field service quality collar patches were worn on the special field-grey uniforms by Army officers in place of the original Totenkopf collar patches. The photo shows some of the first Germans to have been taken prisoner in France at the time of the Allied landings arriving at a British port. 8th June 1944.

For all those officers, including generals and above, entitled to wear this style of uniform normal field-service and generals' collar patches were worn on the collar (plate 302).

No piping to the edge of the collar was used; nor was the 0·9cm wide rank braiding normally used by those ranks of non-commissioned officers who, in other units of the German Army, would be entitled to wear it. Shoulder straps were those as used on the normal Service Uniform.

Black leather marching boots were worn with this uniform; the ends of the long field-grey trousers were worn over the boots and gathered in tight around the lower calves. Anklets and short black leather ankle boots were also used and all forms of German Army field-grey head-dress were worn with this uniform.

3.37. Army Tropical Field Service Uniform
Tropenanzug für das deutsche Heer

A variety of military uniform styles existed for wear by German Army personnel both in North Africa, southern Russia and those Mediterranean countries occupied by the Axis and where German troops were garrisoned.

The clothing, including the tropical Einheitsfeld-mütze, was made of lightweight canvas drill dyed either to a light sage-green or to a sand tan colour. However, after prolonged wear the colours of the tropical clothing and head-dress tended to vary considerably. The bleaching effects of the combination of sun, heat, desert air and washing quickly altered the original colours to many lighter shades of green and brown, and in many cases almost reducing the original colour to that of the natural uncoloured fabric.

The photographs illustrated here show the standard pattern issued Tropical Field Service Tunic as worn by a Private in the German Afrika Korps.

The correct insignia worn on this tunic was that peculiar to the D.A.K. being manufactured in copper-brown yarn instead of the silver-grey coloured thread.

Worn with this Field Jacket were shorts made from the same material as the jacket as well as the special canvas and leather high lace-up tropical boots (plate 303).

The photographs also show the Tropical Field Service Uniform for wear by an army officer, being worn here with long lightweight trousers. These were usually worn gathered in around the ankles of the lace-up boots (plate 304).

The Tropical Field Service Uniform, as worn by army generals, had a jacket and breeches like all other

303. *The German Army Tropical Field Service Jacket and shorts seen here worn together with canvas and leather high lace-up tropical boots.*

304. *The German Army Tropical Field Service Uniform. German prisoners taken by the First Army during an attack near Medjez-el-Bab in April 1943.*

issue tropical clothing, made from lightweight cotton drill. These Tropical quality jackets worn by army officers and generals retained all those features normally found on the European type of Officers' Field Service Tunics except with respect to the cuffs. Tropical jackets had plain sleeve ends without the characteristic deep turn-back cuffs.

In the photo shown here, it can be seen that tall leather gaiters are being worn over the tropical lace-up canvas and leather boots (plate 305).

A variety of tropical uniforms were worn by army officers as well as Generaloberst Rommel. The General to whom Rommel is talking is wearing the tropical version of the motorcycle coat normally worn in North Africa and other hot climate countries. This coat was identical in design to the European version but was made entirely from tan coloured heavy cotton drill and not from green rubberized material (plate 306).

3.38. The German Army Shirt
Heeres Hemd

Prewar, and during the early 1939 Polish Campaign, army issue shirts were white.[1] They had long shirt tails reaching down to mid-thigh length with long sleeves but without collars. It was soon found, however, that white shirts were very impractical from the point of view of camouflage. During the warm seasons of the year it was necessary for the German soldier to work without his uniform jacket, not only in the firing positions but in construction work and on labour duty. White shirts were very conspicuous even at a long range so the military authorities introduced, at varying times, shirts made of materials coloured field-grey and mouse-grey.

The mouse-grey coloured shirt was without breast pockets, had an attached collar, long sleeves, and was manufactured from a knitted wool like material (plate 307).

The field-grey shirt had two breast pockets both with button down pocket flaps, long sleeves, attached collar and was made of cotton 'aertex' type material which had certain stretch qualities (plate 308).

Neither of these two shirts undid right down the front. Each type had to be pulled on over the head, the neck and the front of the shirt being done up by a vertical line of four small shirt buttons. The cuffs of these shirts also had buttons.[2]

The shirt issued for wear to troops in North Africa and Italy was very similar in style to the field-grey army shirt, but this garment was made of a hard-wearing cotton drill dyed to a darkish sand colour. It was designed to take the place of the Tropical Service Tunic and, as such, it showed more attention to detail than the two preceding shirts.

This tropical shirt had two pleated breast patch pockets each with a button down pocket flap with two

305. The Tropical Field Service Uniform as worn by German Army Generals. This photo shows General-major von Ravenstein, holder of the Knight's Cross and commanding officer of the 21st Panzer-Division in North Africa. He was taken prisoner by New Zealand troops on 29th November 1941.

[1] These white shirts were issued to all arms of the German Army with the exception of the personnel of armoured units who, as part of their black uniform, were issued with grey shirts.
[2] See page 126 on the use of shirt and tie worn with Army Officers' Field Service tunic during the last months of the war in Europe.

170

306. Various styles of German Army tropical clothing.

307. The Army issue mouse-grey coloured shirts. Regimental commander Major Bäke, holder of the Knight's Cross with Oakleaves, seen here in the company of other Panzer officers talking with the regimental supply officer. 28th August 1943.

308. A young member of the Panzer-Division 'Grossdeutschland' shown here wearing the German Army issue field-grey shirt with button down pockets.

cuff buttons per cuff, four buttons down the front neck opening and an attached collar. Shoulder strap loops at the shoulder seams facilitated attachment of shoulder straps when the shirt was worn as a form of military dress. Shirt sleeves could be buttoned down or rolled up, when orders stated or at the individual's

309. *The German Army mountain troops sage-green windproof jacket.*

choice. Across the back of the shoulders was a reinforced collar yoke. The tail of the shirt at the back was longer than the tail at the front.

When wearing shirt sleeve order the shirt collar was normally worn open at the neck but holders of the Knight's Cross would wear the neck closed in order to display their neck decoration.

The special rank insignia 'bars' dealt with on page 43 were intended to be worn on these tropical shirts.

3.39. Mountain Troops' sage-green Windjacket
Windjacke für Gebirgstruppen

Made from heavy duty close woven calico material and coloured a sage-green, this was a comparatively early and little-used item of clothing issued to mountain troops (plate 309).

It was intended to be a waterproof and windproof jacket. It was double breasted, had adjustable cuffs, four pockets—two pleated patch pockets on the jacket skirt and two side pocket openings—with flaps positioned at an angle on either side of the chest. Rank was indicated only by the use of removable shoulder straps. The coat had a half-belt at the back with two buttons. The back of the coat had a full length inverted pleat.

The two rows each of five large buttons worn down the front of the coat and the four on the pocket flaps, as well as the two on the cuffs and the two worn on the back of the coat were all manufactured from a moulded form of grey-green plastic.

The Windjacket was a loose fitting garment, reaching to the wearer's thighs and could, if needed, be worn over the basic field-equipment.

3.40. German Army Anoraks
Windblusen

A number of varieties of anoraks or windjackets existed in the German Army. Some were of official issue and design while others tended to be the lightweight anoraks of civilian origin. The example illustrated here was one of the former.

This item of apparel was used fairly widely in the latter years of the war in Europe, Italy and on the Eastern Front. The most noticeable feature of the pull-on jackets were the three pockets arranged horizontally across the chest. Each one had a button-down pocket flap, the two pockets on either side had pleats and were not as large as the centre unpleated pocket. The garment had a draw string waist and it can be seen from the photograph reproduced here (plate 310) that there was a reinforced button positioned in the centre of the jacket skirt which was meant to allow a 'tail piece' to button up under the wearer's crotch in exactly the same way as the British Army Parachute Smock.

The sleeves were elasticated at the wrist for warmth and there was an attached draw string hood. It had a reinforced shoulder and neck yoke. This anorak was not camouflaged but was manufactured in plain field-grey windproof cloth. It could be worn over the outside

310. *The German Army issue windproof Anorak, here worn by a Panzer-Grenadier in Italy.*

311. *The four pocket German Army Camouflaged Field Service Jacket.*

312. *German troops taken prisoner near the Italian town of Lugo. An example of German Army issue trousers made from Italian camouflage material.*

313. The German Army issue lightweight camouflage smock, shown here being worn by the soldier kneeling and adjusting blankets on a crude sledge. The same type of smock worn with the white side outermost is worn by the soldier on the left of the photo. The unnamed Major, a Knight's Cross holder, in the centre of the photo is the commander of a Jäger battalion. He is holding a 'Wolchowstock', a wooden stick intricately carved with designs appropriate to the owner's formation. The sticks were a form of souvenir much favoured by German troops serving on the Eastern Front. He is also wearing the special felt and leather boots provided for wear in cold climates.

of or tucked into the wearer's trousers, usually over trousers, and was worn over the Field Service Uniform Tunic. It was not normally worn as a separate coat on its own.

3.41. The four-pocket Army Camouflaged Field Service Jacket
Heeres-Tarnungs Feld Dienst Jacke mit vier Taschen

In effect this was a camouflaged version of the Army Officers' Field Service Tunic. It retained all the visible features of the wool-rayon jacket but had the advantage of being light in weight and with better qualities for concealment.

It is doubtful if this style of jacket was used to any great extent but it did exist as can be seen from the accompanying photograph (plate 311).

The need for a camouflaged uniform which incorporated all or some of the various basic camouflage colours of tans, browns, greens, reds, pinks, greys and black in irregular patterns had been evident to the Germans from the outset of the war.

Early attempts to manufacture the normal Field Service woollen uniforms in various coloured patterns failed because of technical difficulties, since wool cannot be stamped without damage and it was very difficult to weave coloured woollen thread in irregular patterns.

Cotton fabrics were found to be most adaptable for this purpose, since they could be easily printed in various colours without causing damage to the cotton fibres. Cotton was the material used extensively for German camouflage clothing which proved successful for concealment purposes in every European country including Russia.

Although camouflage uniforms were never issued throughout the German Army as an item of clothing they did become increasingly widespread as the war progressed (plate 312).

3.42. The lightweight Army Camouflage Smock
Die leichte Tarnjacke des deutschen Heeres

Yet another variation of camouflage clothing in a distinctive style very similar in design to the camouflaged jacket used by the Waffen-SS was the lightweight reversible German Army camouflage smock. It was printed on one side of the water repellent material in German Army 'splinter' pattern green camouflage, the other side being plain white. The obvious feature of this pull-on garment was the lace-up neck. Without any collar, the neck opening was a simple hole with a shaped 'V' front reinforced to accommodate two rows of five eyelet holes through which a white cord was threaded to draw the neck opening together.

On either side of the chest were two openings intended to allow the wearer to reach into the breast pockets of his Service Tunic which was normally worn under the smock. These openings were very simple and each one had a flap of camouflage/white material which was meant to be tucked inside the opening thus closing the slit.

Under both the armpits of the garment was a large air hole to allow for good ventilation. These armpit holes were edged for added strength in white binding very noticeable on the camouflaged side.

In the waist of the garment was a 'tunnel' going right round the body and through which was threaded a grey tape the ends of which were knotted together. This draw string was used to gather the waist of the smock in around the wearer. The smock had a short skirt to it with a single gusset let into each side.

The sleeves of the smock were sewn on to the body of the garment approximately halfway along the upper arm. The cuffs to these sleeves were about 10cm deep with two buttons and a wrist tag which allowed the wearer to fold the cuff over and button the tag in a position which closed up the cuff opening (plate 313).

3.43. The Camouflage Body-Apron
Die Heeres Tarnungs Körper-Schürze

One of the simplest of all manufactured German Army reversible camouflaged garments, this was made from a large piece of thin cotton material printed on one side in German Army tan-coloured 'water' camouflage with the other side being plain white (plate 314). Without any collar, but edged for extra strength, it had a 'V' neck opening in the front of the garment attached to which were two pieces of grey coloured tape used to tie the neck opening together. The garment was completely open on both sides from the 'shoulder' seam down. On each side of both the front and the back of the garment there were two sets of camouflage material tapes intended for tying the garment close around the wearer's body. The upper set of tapes would have tied under the arms around the chest and the bottom set around the waist or lower. This smock or body apron was large enough to be worn over all personal equipment, or could be gathered in and worn with the wearer's field equipment over it.

3.44. Army Red Cross Medical Attendants' Vests
Heeres Rotes-Kreuz Hemd für Sanitäter

Not strictly an item of clothing but more of an identifiable emblem large enough and constructed in such a way as to be worn over the normal Service Uniform or Greatcoat was the Red Cross Identification Vest.

Made simply from a single piece of white cotton material was designed in such a way that when worn it displayed both on the back and on the front a large red cross. It was pulled on over the wearer's head and tied at the waist with tapes (plate 315).

Normally worn by German medical personnel, it proved to be much more prominent than the regulation issue Red Cross armband. It was worn extensively during all stages of the Normandy fighting and it continued in use throughout the remainder of the war.

315. The German Army Red Cross Medical Attendants' identification 'Vest'.

3.45. Camouflage 'string-vests' Das Tarn Schnur Hemd

At the time of the Allied landings in Normandy in June 1944 certain German Army infantry units experimented with an improvised string vest constructed in such a way as to allow the wearer to camouflage most of his body by completely garnishing the string netting with foliage. The vest was drawn over the wearer's head and held in position by means of his normal field equipment.

3.46. Reversible Winter Uniforms Umkehrbare Winteranzug des deutschen Heeres

Introduced during the winter of 1942–3 as the result of the bitter experiences of the previous winter when thousands of German troops fighting on the Eastern Front suffered from the extremes of cold (plates 317, 318).

These uniforms proved to be extremely comfortable and, as a combat uniform, they gave freedom of movement and use of equipment whilst at the same time affording protection against severe cold as well as overheating during periods of exertion.

Both patterns consisted of a heavy reversible double-breasted over jacket and matching over trousers. The uniform—and trousers—were designed large enough to be worn over the normal Field Service Uniform including basic field equipment, although

314. The German Army camouflage 'Body apron'.

316. The experimental camouflage 'string vests' first used by certain German Infantry units during the Normandy fighting. The Grenadier on the left is wearing an ungarnished version whilst the rest of his comrades are partially or fully camouflaged.

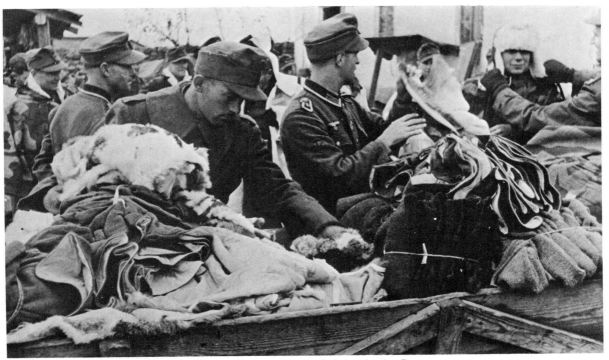

317. The issue of new winter clothing to German forces fighting in the East.

318. *The issue of new winter clothing to German forces fighting in the East.*

319. *With the enemy forces wearing white snow camouflage clothing, front line German troops were issued with coloured arm bands for use on their winter clothing. These enabled them to distinguish between friend and foe.*

320. *The trousers of the reversible winter uniform.*

321. *The trousers of the reversible winter uniform.*

German troops favoured wearing their equipment over the Winter Jacket.

Because it was a completely reversible item of clothing, including the trousers, features such as pockets, draw strings and buttons located on the camouflage or mouse-grey side were duplicated on the white side.

The jacket was double-breasted for extra frontal warmth, with double buttoned overlaps to the flaps of the jacket at the front which when securely fastened provided a windproof closure. There was a 'hidden' waist belt which could be gathered in around the wearer's waist from the outside of whichever side of the jacket was being worn outermost. The bottom edge to the jacket also had a draw string and the ends of the cuffs were also adjustable. The jacket had long sleeves as well as an attached draw-string adjustable hood, also reversible. Six buttons were visible worn down the front of the coat and there was one button to each pocket flap on both sides of the coat 'skirt'.

These metal buttons were field-grey when used on the camouflaged/mouse-grey side of the coat and white painted on the white side. Two small fibre buttons were located approximately 20cm from the shoulder seam on both sleeves and positioned on the two seams of both jacket sleeves. These were intended to be used to button on the bands of coloured cloth used by forward German Forces to help identify friendly troops. Like passwords, these bands of cloth were changed every day and a new colour was used for this purpose.

This arrangement could be used on both sides of the jacket as the small fibre buttons were sewn on to the white side as well as the coloured side of the jacket (plate 319).

The trousers worn with this jacket were of the same quality, colouring and manufacture. They were shorter in the leg than normal cloth trousers and could be worn either tucked inside the German Army marching boots or worn over the top of the boots with the ends of the trousers gathered in by the draw strings and tied around the calf of the boots (plate 320).

The trousers were extra thick, as was the jacket, and was completely reversible—which included the pockets. The buttons used on the trousers were large smooth black plastic ones each with four eye holes and used stitched on to both the camouflaged and the white side. There were built in braces made of white webbing. They were sewn into the waist of the trousers at the rear and crossed behind the wearer's shoulder blades passing over the shoulders and being buttoned in the front on either side of the front opening. The braces were adjustable to one of three positions on the front of the trousers (plate 321).

The trousers had two reversible pockets with large reversible button down pocket flaps. There were four buttons used down the fly front. Two tapes were sewn into the rear of the waist to allow the waist band to be drawn in tight. There were tapes at the bottom of each trouser leg.

Both the mouse-grey and the camouflage reversible winter uniforms were identical in design and manufacture (plate 322). Both patterns of German Army camouflage were used for the camouflaged version,

322. *Both the green splinter pattern Army camouflage and the mouse-grey camouflage versions (centre) of the winter uniforms are shown in this photo. The officer on the left is Oberstleutnant Dr. Bäke, holder of Knight's Cross, Oakleaves and Swords (latter not shown), and now a commander of heavy Panzer regiments.*

323. *The tan water pattern (left) and the green splinter pattern (right) versions of German Army camouflage material used on the heavy reversible winter uniforms can clearly be seen in this picture. The officer in the centre is Oberst Schulz, commander of a Panzer regiment, holder of the Knight's Cross, Oakleaves and Swords.*

324. *Early attempts at snow camouflage.*

325. *Snowshirts.*

326. *The two piece snow suit.*

i.e. the green splinter pattern and the tan water pattern (plate 323).

No form of insignia decoration or badge other than the special rank insignia designed for this type of clothing was worn on this uniform.

3.47. German Army snow camouflage: single and double garments

The newly introduced heavy reversible winter clothing proved so popular with the German troops fighting in the east that they tended to wear the uniform day and night for weeks on end. As the uniform was a warm garment designed to keep out the severe cold and at the same time to provide camouflage in the snow, the white side to the jacket and trousers soon became filthy thus defeating the object of the white camouflage. It was impossible for the troops to wash these garments as the thick blanket lining did not allow the uniform to dry out.

It was therefore found necessary to supply the front line combat troops with a thin white cotton cover, cape or suit that could be worn over all uniforms and equipment and which at the same time could be easily

washed and cleaned.

A number of different styles of white, lightweight covers existed, some of which are illustrated and listed below:

3.47(1). *Early snow camouflage.* Earlier attempts at white cloth covers had no bearing on the problem mentioned above but rather were crude attempts at snow camouflage (plate 324).

3.47(2). *Snow 'shirts' (Schneehemden).* A fairly tight fitting shirt-like garment without collar but with long sleeves and with the shirt tails reaching down to the wearer's knees. This item was pulled on over the wearer's head (plate 325).

3.47(3). *Two-piece snow suit (Schneeanzüge).* A shapeless two piece snow-suit consisting of a white jacket and white trousers. The jacket was buttoned right down the front with white painted buttons and had an attached white hood as well as extra long sleeves, the cuffs of which were rolled back up the wearer's wrists. The trousers, also white, were equally shapeless and were worn over the winter clothing and tucked into the boots (plate 326).

3.47(4). *Snow coveralls (Schnee-Tarnung Überzug).*

327. The single piece snow overalls.

328. The face mask as a form of snow camouflage.

Another form of white snow camouflage clothing was the long coverall coat which buttoned right down the front of the garment, had a deep collar, an attached hood and long sleeves. Large and shapeless it was worn without belt over any uniform and all equipment. However this item of clothing did not prove to be as practical as the snow suit as it tended to restrict the wearer's freedom of movement (plate 330).

3.47(5). *Single-piece snow overalls (Einzelstück Schnee-Tarnung Überzug).* Probably one of the most efficient forms of snow camouflage clothing the Germans produced. It was a single white cotton garment which buttoned up from the crotch to the neck. It had an attached hood and long sleeves. The ends of the trouser legs were gathered in and tied around the wearer's ankles and there were two large pocket openings on either side of the trousers. Whilst this garment afforded complete snow camouflage and excellent freedom of movement to the wearer it did have one drawback in that in order that the trousers could be removed, the entire garment had to be undone and taken off, a difficulty not experienced with a two piece garment (plate 327).

All these snow covers were properly manufactured garments, with reinforced seams, buttons, button holes, draw strings and strengthened flaps.

3.48. White and camouflaged face masks

The face mask was basically a cloth hood, the mask simply being made by having two eye holes and a nose piece cut away. They were worn in the German Army by combat troops, including snipers, but the practice was not widespread. The hoods were normally worn under the steel helmet and they served a dual purpose: as a face mask for snipers and observers, when both camouflage material as well as white cloth was used depending on the season of the year (plate 329), and with the white side outermost as a means of facial protection against extremes of cold weather. This last use also served as an additional form of snow camouflage (plate 328). The human face tends to stand out as a dark spot when seen against a background of pure white snow.

These face masks should not be confused with the German Army issue fine mesh green mosquito nets worn over the head and shoulders (plates 331, 332).

One other form of face mask is worth noting. German troops undertaking anti-aircraft defence duty on armoured, troop and war-freight trains were issued in cold weather with special leather face masks. These were intended to protect the face of the wearer against the bitter wind and cold to which they were exposed through necessity on their special flak cars.

329. *German Army camouflaged face masks. There are* **three** *German soldiers wearing these camouflage face masks or hoods, two on the officer's left and one on his right.*

330. *Snow coveralls.*

331, 332. German Army mosquito nets.

3.49. 'Zeltbahn' waterproof shelter triangle

Although this was essentially an item of German Army equipment it was designed and issued to be worn and used as a waterproof cape. The Zeltbahn—or waterproof shelter triangle—was manufactured from tightly woven water repellent cotton drill and issued universally throughout the German Army. It was triangular in shape being 203cm × 203cm × 240cm in size and was printed on both sides with army green splinter pattern camouflage, dark on one side and light on the other.

On both sides of the shelter were stitched 62 metal buttons, 31 to each side. There were 30 button holes (plate 338). In the centre of the Zeltbahn was a double flapped opening. This was positioned in such a way to allow the shelter when worn as a rain cape to be pulled on over the user's head (plate 333). The buttons, the positioning of which corresponded exactly on both sides of the Zeltbahn, and button holes were used to fasten this cover around the wearer's body in a number of ways. Each method was designed to give the wearer the maximum amount of protection while at the same time providing freedom of movement (plates 334–7).

When not in use the Zeltbahn was folded or rolled and worn strapped on to the wearer's field equipment (plate 339).

333. *German Artillerymen priming shells. All are wearing the issue Zeltbahn.*

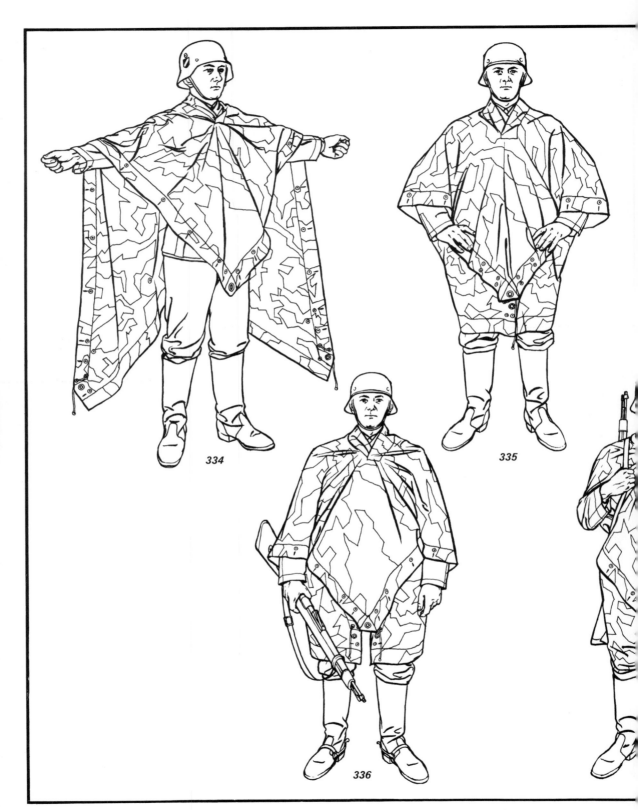

334

335

336

334. *The method of putting on the Zeltbahn.*
335. *The method of wear for marching.*
336. *The method of wear for horse riding.*
337. *The method of wear for riding a bicycle.*
338. *The Zeltbahn, plan view.*

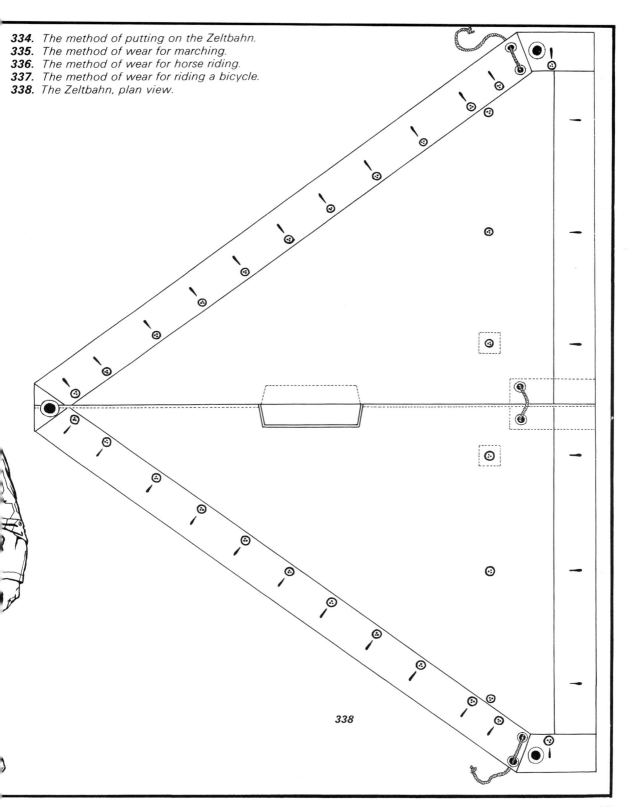

338

339. One method of carrying the Zeltbahn folded and strapped to the canvas carrying frame. In this manner it formed part of the assault equipment.

4. Personal Equipment

The following section comprises a selection of photographs which demonstrate the basic personal equipment in use by members of the German Army during the years 1933 to 1945. Whilst not entering the realm of specialised equipment, these illustrations should give the reader a clear impression of the principal accoutrements which completed the appearance of the soldiers of the German Army during this period.

340. *Swearing an oath of loyalty to the new Reichspräsident Adolf Hitler. Of particular interest are the rifle ammunition pouches and the normal pattern 'Y' straps. (The black arm bands are being worn as a sign of mourning for the late president Hindenburg.)*

341. British and German troops seen here at the control point during a 60 hour local truce at Dunkirk negotiated for the purpose of evacuating 20,000 French civilians from German-occupied territory, 4th October 1944. This clearly shows the 'D' ring 'Y' straps, as well as the map case, mess tins and bread bag.

342. Troops preparing to march out of barracks load their 'Tornisters' (fur-covered packs) onto a horse drawn wagon. Note especially the packs with rolled blankets and the wagon driver's method of wearing his gas mask canister.

343. Troops entraining with fur covered packs and rolled blankets as part of the German force used in the Austrian Anschluss.

344. *Manoeuvres for the VI Army Corps on Lüneburg Heath held from 2nd–7th September 1935. A heavy water-cooled machine-gun in use here in the anti-aircraft role. Note the map case and pistol holster.*

345. *German infantry resting after an attack during the early stages of the Polish campaign.*

346. *German infantry under instruction for close-quarter bayonet fighting practice. Shown here is the standard pattern military gas mask being worn.*

347. *German Grenadiers on parade. Note the gas mask canisters with rolled Zeltbahnen.*

348. *Gas mask canisters, when worn in vehicles or on motorcycles, were for comfort's sake normally worn slung around the neck instead of across the small of the back.*

349. *German Infantry prepare to advance during the Polish campaign of 1939.*

350. The German soldier was issued with a short-handled folding entrenching tool. This was worn hanging from the belt, the blade of the shovel being held in a special open leather case (see also plate 349).

351. *The fighting on the Don: soldiers detailed to collect food from the field kitchens. Of note are the mess tins and Schmeisser pouches.*

352. *An infantry Stosstruppführer in the Volkov area. Of special note are the canvas and leather Schmeisser pouches. It is also interesting to note that for security reasons this NCO is wearing his shoulder straps upside down.*

353. *German grenadiers wearing leather Schmeisser pouches move forward past a 'Tiger' tank.*

354. *German infantry pause for a rest during the course of their march into Russia.*

355, 356. *Two general views showing German infantry and their equipment in use during the early stages of the Polish campaign, 1939.*

357. *Equipment in profile — troops engaged in the battle for Stalingrad.*
358. *A machine-gun crew in action on the Eastern Front.*

Four photographs demonstrating the wearing arrangements for field equipment: *359.* German Infantry in the Kuban, crossing the Don delta. *360.* German Infantry advancing in the Lake Ilmen area of Russia.

361. German anti-tank crews in Jugoslavia. German troops manhandle an anti-tank gun onto a pontoon bridge.
362. German troops, a mortar crew and light machine-gun unit, on a training exercise.

365. *(above) Oberst Constantine Meyer, military commander of Metz, seen carrying an example of the German Army issue torch. These were issued throughout the Army to all ranks and were designed to be hung from a button on the uniform by fastening the small leather strap fixed to the back of the torch onto a convenient tunic or greatcoat button. The three small knobs that can be seen at the base of the front to the torch were used to slide a coloured screen in front of the bulb and reflector dish, thus converting the white light to either blue, red or green.*

363. *(above left) German infantry searching abandoned houses on the Eastern Front.*

364. *(below left) Fighting on the central sector of the Narwa front, April 1944. A wounded German is brought in on a simple sledge for treatment at a first aid post. Of special interest is the equipment hung from the belt of the soldier in the winter clothing and the special medical pouches worn by the orderly in the centre of the photograph.*

366. *(right) An Oberleutnant, commander of a Grenadier battalion, taken prisoner in the Trasimeno area of Italy, July 1944. Note the standard issue black leather map case shown here hung from the officer's field service belt.*

369. (above) German Transport crews operating somewhere in the Kuban area refresh themselves with slices of water melon. Of particular interest are the Army issue goggles, the issue and use of which was widespread. The glass lenses had, in this instance, a deep brown tint. The mask to the goggles was manufactured in a soft field-grey coloured leather and the strap was elasticated and adjustable.

367. (above left) Generalleutnant von Manteuffel, commander of the Panzer Grenadier division 'Grossdeutschland', holder of the Knight's Cross with Oakleaves, in conference with German and Rumanian officers in the spring of 1944. Note the various types of binoculars being worn.

368. (below left) Army issue goggles hang at this soldier's neck, as German troops enter Lemberg.

370. (right) A German Army Dispatch Rider. Goggles of the type shown here were normal issue to Luftwaffe flight crews and were also popular with German Army troops. Manufactured by Leitz, they had interchangeable curved 'lenses' in plain clear glass or brown tinted glass (the latter for use in bright sunlight or snow).

371. *Well equipped German infantry advance towards Polish positions in September 1939. Of particular interest is the carrying case for a single machine-gun barrel.*

372. *Generaloberst Model speaking with German infantry at the time of the heavy fighting in the Orel region of Russia, July 1943. Note the metal case for carrying two machine-gun barrels.*

373. *German replacement troops prepare to fly to North Africa. They have two water bottles per man, and the gas cape bags are being worn at the back instead of in the normal position across the front of the chest.*

374. *German Panzer-Grenadiers from the 15. Panzer-Division taken prisoner during the battle of Gabes Gap, North Africa, April 1943. Seen in this photo are the canvas field service belts and canvas 'Y' straps.*

375. Prisoner-of-war camp at Dieppe. Shown here is the method used when combining a number of Zeltbahnen to form four-man 'pup' tents.

5. Select Chronology
Significant dates relevant to the German military period 1933–1945

28th June 1919: Germany signed the Treaty of Versailles. The National Army of Germany was reduced to 4,000 Officers and 96,000 Men. The overall strength was to be maintained at this level and the composition was carefully prescribed. Men were recruited for 12 year periods of enlistment and new officers were engaged to serve for 25 years. The Allies considered that these long service requirements would prevent the accumulation of a large trained reserve. Under the Weimar Republic this 'limited' army of 100,000 troops was known as the Reichsheer, the Reichswehr being the term used to denote the entire armed forces of the German Reich.

12th March 1933: a decree issued by President von Hindenburg and communicated to the German people by Chancellor Hitler stated: 'On this day when the old black, white and red colours are flying at half mast in honour of our dead in the Great War, I order that until the question of the Reich colours is finally regulated the black, white and red and the Hakenkreuz flag of the NSDAP are to be flown together. . . . These flags united are to embody the might of this State and the internal unity of all National circles of the German People. Military buildings and ships are to fly only the War Flag.

20th March 1933: President von Hindenburg issued an order signed also by Hitler, Chancellor of the Reich and General von Blomberg, Minister for Defence in which it was laid down that the German War Flag was black-white-red with the iron cross in the middle and with black-red-gold in the left-hand top corner.

The Minister of Defence's flag was the same with a black and white edge. The Service Flag of the naval authorities was again similar but with the German Eagle instead of the Iron Cross.

From then on the German soldier wore only the black-white-red cockade. In a proclamation to the defence forces, the President declared that these measures were a visible sign of the bond between the German Defence Forces and the National Forces of the German people, and that these outward signs always kept before the eyes of the people the fact that a better future could not be secured without the will to defend the Fatherland.

7th April 1933: the German Cabinet decided to reintroduce titles, medals, orders and other signs of distinction abolished under the Weimar Republican Constitution in 1919.

16th March 1935: two years after he had come to power Adolf Hitler reintroduced military conscription. The 'Law for the Reconstruction of the National Defence Forces' decreed that all men of military age had to serve in the German Armed Forces for a year. The existing Reichsheer of 100,000 men consisting of seven infantry divisions and three cavalry divisions grouped under two corps headquarters was to be expanded to a National Force of 36 army divisions grouped in twelve army corps. The name 'Reichswehr' was to go and hence forth all the Armed Forces of Germany were to be known as the 'Wehrmacht' — Defence Force.

1st November 1935: A new Reichskriegsflag (War flag) was to be flown for the first time on 7th November 1935. On a red ground was superimposed a white cross at the juncture of which was a small circle containing a black swastika. A narrow black line ran along the centre of each arm of the cross to the circumference of the circle. In the upper left hand corner of the flag was a small black iron cross.

16th March 1936. The first anniversary of Hitler's repudiation of the military clauses of the Treaty of Versailles and the simultaneous proclamation of conscription was celebrated in Germany on 16th March. A special order of the day was issued by Hitler as follows: 'On the first anniversary of the rebirth of German military freedom I present the military forces with regimental colours. The glorious history of the old Army was ended by the events of 1918. The martial spirit of the soldier put to the proof through centuries can at times of national disaster be stifled but never destroyed. May the new colours be a symbol of this.'

Hitler also created a 'Service Medal' to be awarded for loyal service in the new fighting forces.

4th February 1938. From 4th February 1938 until 30th April 1945 Adolf Hitler was the Supreme Commander of the German Armed Forces and on 19th December 1941 he took on the additional office of Commander-in-Chief of the German Army. In accordance with German Law the title 'Führer' was never used as sole title unless referring to Hitler himself.

The Armed Forces of Germany were now collectively termed as 'die Wehrmacht' and they consisted of the Army (das Heer), the Navy (die Kriegsmarine) and the

Air Force (die Luftwaffe).

24th July 1944. An announcement was issued from the Führerhauptquartier to the effect that the German Greeting (Deutsches Gruss) would replace the customary military salute in the Wehrmacht as follows: 'Reichsmarschall Göring, as the most senior officer of the German Armed Forces, has in his name and in the name of Feldmarschall Keitel and Gross Admiral Dönitz reported to the Führer that all parts of the German Armed Forces on the occasion of the Führer's escape [referring to the attempt on Hitlers life, 20th July 1944.] have asked for the German Salute to be introduced in the Armed Forces as a sign of unbreakable loyalty and closest attachment between the Army and Party.

The Führer has complied with the request and given his approval. With effect at once the salute by lifting the right hand to the military headgear is replaced by the German Salute. The new regulations applies to all Officers and Men of the German Armed Forces both when on and off duty and the act of outstretching the right arm must be accompanied by the greeting "Heil Hitler". . . .'

18th October 1944. The German radio stated that 50,000 German Officers including 138 Generals had been killed in action since the beginning of the war.

8th May 1945. The final act of unconditional surrender was signed in Berlin at 00·16 hours in the early morning of 8th May 1945, the ceremony taking place in a building formerly housing the Pioneer College of the Wehrmacht in the suburb of Karlshorst.

The German delegates—Generalfeldmarschall Keitel, Chief of the German Army High Command, Generaladmiral von Friedeburg, Commander-in-Chief of the German Navy, and Generaloberst Stumpf of the Luftwaffe—were ushered at midnight into a room draped with the British, American, Russian and French flags.

In the presence of Marshal Zhukov, Keitel was asked by Air Chief Marshal Tedder whether he understood the terms of unconditional surrender, and on replying in the affirmative, he, von Friedeburg and Stumpf signed for Germany, the Allied signatures being Marshal Zhukov for the Soviet High Command and Air Chief Marshal Tedder for the Allied Expeditionary Force. Lieutenant-General Spaatz and General de Lattre de Tassigny also signed as witnesses.

13th May 1946. The Allied Control Council for Germany issued a directive on 13th May ordering the destruction of all military and National Socialist memorials and military museums 'tending to preserve and keep alive the German Military Tradition, to revive miltarism or to commemorate the National Socialist Party or of such a nature as to glorify war.'

The directive laid down that all such memorials dating from 1914 onwards would be destroyed, exception being made only for: (a) Monuments of artistic merit if containing no offensive features glorifying militarism or National Socialism, and (b) Gravestones or their equivalent.

20th August 1946. The Allied Control Council on 20th August passed a law formally dissolving the Wehrmacht, the German Armed Forces, which with their institutions and organizations were disbanded and proclaimed illegal and their reconstitution under any guise forbidden.

All quasi-military and war veterans' organizations were likewise disbanded and declared illegal, their property being subject to confiscation by the British, American, Russian and French Zonal Commanders.

6. Glossary

This glossary does not pretend to be exhaustive. It has been included for the purpose of giving the English equivalents of some of those German terms used for describing German Army badges, insignia and uniforms —some of which have been included in this book.

6.1. Glossary of Uniforms and Equipment

Below are listed all the basic items of Army equipment as well as items of uniform dress that went to make up certain basic styles of German Army Uniforms worn by all ranks below Officer.

This list corresponds to the dress regulations as laid down from 1936 to at least 1939. After the outbreak of the war it is probable that these lists underwent changes and as such no longer held true.

6.1(1). *Feldanzug. The Field Service Uniform*

Stahlhelm   Steel helmet
Feldmütze   Field cap
Feldbluse (Rock)   Field blouse (Jacket)
Kragenbinde   Collar band or neck band
Lange Tuchhose   Long trousers
 Schnurstiefel   Laced top boots   worn together
Reithose   Riding breeches
 Schnurstiefel   Laced top boots   worn together
Handschuhe   Gloves
Mantel (Angezogen oder gerollt am Tornister oder Sattel in Fahrzeugen)   Greatcoat (either worn or folded and rolled around the Pack or placed in a truck)
Tornister für Unberittene   Pack for unmounted use
Packtaschen für Berittene   Pack for mounted use
Zeltbahn mit Zeltleine   Shelter triangle with tent lines
Koppel   Belt
Brotbeutel   Breadbag
Feldflasche mit Trinkbecher   Water bottle with drinking cup
Portepee, Faustriemen (nur Kavallerie)   Portepee knot (for cavalry only)
Sporen   Spurs
Meldekartentasche mit Kartenschutzhülle   Reporting message pad with protective cover
Signalpfeife   Whistle
Fernglas   Binoculars
Gasmaske   Gas mask
Seitenwaffe   Side arm, usually the bayonet
Pistole   Pistol
Kleine Ordenschnalle   Small decorations (medal ribbons plus other badges)
Umhang für Radfahrer   Cloak for motorcycle riders
Bekleidungssack   Clothing sack, a form of kit bag
Patronentaschen, Trageriemen für Patronentaschen   Ammunition pouches plus 'Y' support straps
Schanzzeug   Entrenching tool

6.1(2). *Paradeanzug. The Parade Uniform worn with a Pack*

Stahlhelm   Steel helmet
Rock oder Feldbluse   Parade jacket or field tunic
Halsbinde, Kragenbinde   Neck band, collar band
Lange Tuchhose und Schnurstiefel (für Unberittene)   Long trousers and laced boots (for unmounted use and worn together)
Reithose und Schnurstiefel (für Berittene)   Riding breeches and laced boots (for mounted use and worn together)
Mantel   Greatcoat
Koppel   Belt
Portepee, Troddel, Faustriemen   Side arm knots
Sporen   Spurs
Seitenwaffe   Side arm
Graue Handschuhe (nur für Unteroffizier)   Grey gloves (only for NCOs)
Grosse Ordenschnalle   Full military decorations and orders
Patronentaschen   Ammunition pouches
Tragenriemen für Patronentaschen   'Y' support straps for ammunition pouches
Gepacker Tornister mit gerolltem Mantel für alle Schützenkompanien   Pack with rolled greatcoat for all rifle companies
Nach Befehl: Zeltbahn über gerolltem Mantel, Angezogener Mantel, Handschuhe. The tent shelter worn over the rolled up greatcoat or folded greatcoat. Gloves may be ordered to be worn or carried.

6.1(3). *Dienstanzug. The Service Uniform*

Mütze (*) (Stahlhelm)   Hat (steel helmet)
(*) Schirmmütze für die Portepeeunteroffiziere, Feldmütze für die übrigen Unteroffiziere und Mannschaften   The Uniform Peak Cap for senior NCOs, the Field Service Cap for the other junior NCOs and men
Feldbluse (Rock)   Field tunic (jacket)
Kragenbinde   Collar band
Lange Tuchhose und Schnurstiefel (für Berittene)   Long trousers and laced boots (for mounted use worn together)
Handschuhe   Gloves
Koppel   Belt
Portepee, Troddel, Faustriemen   Side arm knots
Sporen   Spurs
Seitenwaffe   Side arm
Pistole   Pistol
Kleine Ordenschnalle   Medal ribbons and badges only
Ausserdem je nach Tagesbefehl, Signalpfeife, Fernglas, Mantel, Tornister, Patronentaschen usw.   Plus, when ordered, wearing and carrying the following: whistle, binoculars, greatcoat, pack, ammunition pouches etc.

6.1(4). *Meldeanzug. The Reporting Uniform*

Schirmmütze   Uniform cap

Feldbluse (Rock)   Field jacket (tunic)
Lange Tuchhose und Schnurstiefel (für Unberittene)   Long trousers and laced top boots (for unmounted wear, worn together)
Reithose und Schnurstiefel (für Berittene)   Riding breeches and laced top boots (for mounted wear, worn together)
Kragenbinde   Collar band
Koppel   Belt
Portepee, Troddel, Faustriemen   Side arm knots
Sporen   Spurs
Seitenwaffe   Side arms
Kleine Ordenschnalle   Medal ribbons and badges only
Handschuhe (nur für Unteroffiziere)·   Gloves (only for NCOs)

6.1(5). *Ausgehnanzug. The Walking-out Uniform*

Schirmmütze   Uniform cap
Rock (Feldbluse)   Jacket (field tunic)
Lange Tuchhose   Long trousers
Mantel   Greatcoat
Halsbinde   Neck band, white side worn outermost
Handschuhe   Gloves
Schuhe (keine Knopf-oder Halbschuhe)   Shoes, but not buttoned, or half shoes
Koppel   Belt
Portepee, Troddel, Faustriemen   Side arm knots
Seitenwaffe   Side arm
Sporen   Spurs
Kleine Ordenschnalle   Medal ribbons and badges only
Berittenen Unteroffizieren und Mannschaften ist das Tragen eigener Reithosen u. Reitstiefel   For horse riding NCOs and men wear riding breeches and riding boots

6.1(6). *Sportanzug. The Sports 'uniform' or Sports kit*

Sporthemd   Sports shirt/vest
Sporthose   Sports shorts
Lauffschuhe   Running shoes
Badehose (nur zum Wassersport)   Swimming trunks (for water sports only)

6.2. **General Glossary : German/English**

German/English

Abzeichen   Insignia, badge, distinctive sign, decoration
Abzeichentuch   Badge cloth
Achselband   Aiguillette
Adjutant   Aide, Adjutant
Adjutantenschnur   Adjutants' cords
Adjutantenabzeichen   Adjutants' cords
Adler   Eagle
Allgemeines Heeresgerät   General Army equipment
Alter Art   Old type (as formerly in use), obsolete according to previously prescribed or customary manner
Aluminium   Aluminium
Amtsblatt   Official journal, register or gazette
Amtsverwaltungs-Departement   Army Administration Department
Anker   Anchor
Anlage   Arrangement, plan
Anwärter   Aspirant or candidate
Anzugordnung   Orders and regulations pertaining to uniform and dress (of the day, of a specific command, for a specific formation)
Arabisch   Arabic (figures)
Arbeitsanzug   Fatigue Dress
Archiv   Archive
Ärmelaufschlag   Cuff-facing pattern
Ärmelpatten   Arm patch
Ärmelstreiffen   Cuff-titles
Armspiegel   Arm badge
Armwinkel   Arm chevron

Artillerie   Artillery
Artillerie-Verbindungskommando   Artillery signals unit
Arzt   Physician, surgeon, doctor of medicine
Aufklärung   Reconnaissance
Ausbildungsvorschrift   Official regulations governing the training of a formation
Ausgabe   Issue, edition
Ausgehanzug   Walking-out dress
Ausladen, Ausladung   To unload, unloading, detraining
Ausladekommissar   Detraining or detrucking officer or commissioner
Ausrüstung   Equipment
Ausser Dienst (a.D.)   Literally retired, on the inactive list, out of service
Ausser Verwendung (a.V.)   Out of use, retired
Auszeichnung   Decoration, distinction
Bahnhof   Railway station
Band   Volume
Barracke   Barracks
Bataillon   Battalion
Bataillonstambourstock   Drum Major's mace or baton
Batterie   Battery
Befelshaber   Commander; generally a higher commander, chief of a larger unit, commander-in-chief
Befestigung   Fortification
Begleitbattallion   Escort battalion
Behörde   Authority, office, competent bureau
Beiheft   Supplement, annexe, additional leaflet or folder
Beinkleider   Trousers
Bekleidung   Pertaining to attire, uniforms or clothing
Befelshaber   Commander; general a higher commander, chief of a larger unit, commander-in-chief
Befestigung   Fortification
Begleitbattallion   Escort battalion
Behörde   Authority, office, competent bureau
Beiheft   Supplement, annexe, additional leaflet or folder
Beinkleider   Trousers
Bekleidung   Pertaining to attire, uniforms or clothing
Berg   Mountain
Beritten   Mounted on horseback
Besatzung   Garrison crew
Beschlag   Metal fittings, horse shoeing
Beschreibung   Description
Besondere Anordnungen   Special instructions
Bespannt   Horse drawn
Beurlaubstand   Reserve
Der Beurlaubtenstandes   One in the state of permanent leave; an officer on the reserve
Bezirkskommando   District command
Blatt   Paper
Blitz   Lightning
Blutorden   Blood Order, a decoration
Böhmen und Mähren   Bohemia and Moravia (the Protectorate)
Borte   Braid
Breecheshose   Breeches
Brotbeutel   Bread-bag (small 'haversack' carried hung from the belt)
Brustklappe   Lapel
Büro   Bureau, office, section
Charakterisiert   Holding honorary rank. Also holding a rank prior to confirmation and still receiving lower rank's pay. Being entitled to use the next higher rank previous to final orders of appointment
Chef   Chief
Chef des Generalstabes   Chief of the General Staff
Deckblatt   Supplementary sheet. Amendment to regulations
Deutsch(es)   German; used, for example, to designate a German national
Deutsches Reichspost   German postal service or system
Deutsches Rotes Kreuz   German Red Cross
Dienst   Service, duty
Dienstanweisung   Service directives
Dienstanzug   Service Dress
Dienstelle   Office, authority, duty station

Dienstgradabzeichen   Rank insignia—for men
Dienstgrade   Rank
Dienstmantel   Service overcoat
Dienstrock   Service Tunic
Dienstsiegel und Dienststampel   Official seal and stamp
Dienstvorschrift   Official Service Regulations
Division   Division
Dolch   Dagger
Dolmetscher   Interpreter
Doppelfernrohre   Binoculars
Dragoner   Dragoon
Drillich   Denim, strong ticking
Ehrenwache   Guard of Honour
Ehrenzeichen   Decoration
Eichel   Acorn
Eichenlaub   Oakleaves
Eichenlaubkranz   Oakleaf surround (to the Reichskokade)
Einheit   Unit
Einheitsfeldmütze   Replacement Field Cap
Einsatzgruppe   Formation for special tasks
Einsatzkommando   Special task detachment
Einsatztrupp   Task force
Eisenbahn   Railway
Eisenbahnoffizier   Railway officer
Eisernes Kreuz   Iron Cross
Elite   Elite
Ergänzung   Replacement
Ergängzungseinheiten   Replacement unit
Ergängzungsmannschaften   Supplementary reservists
Ergänzungsoffizier   Re-employed retired officer
Ergänzungsstelle   Recruiting offices and replacement centres
Erinnerungsabzeichen   Tradition badges (caps)
Erinnerungsband   Commemoration armlet
Erkennungsmarke   Identification disc
Ersatz   Reserve, replacement
Evangelisch   Evangelical or Protestant (generally Lutheran)
Exerzierplatz   Training ground, drill ground
Fabrik   Factory, works, plant
Fahnenjunker   A cadet normally on active duty. Non-commissioned officer aspirant from the ranks
Fahnen und Standarten   Flags and standards
Fahrer   Driver
Färbig   Coloured
Feind   Enemy
Feld   Field
Feldanzug   Field-dress
Feldausrüstung   Field equipment
Feldbinde   Field service belt
Feldbluse   Field blouse
Feldbluse mit Vorstossen   Field blouse with piping, Piped Field Service Tunic for officers
Feldgrau   Field-grey
Feldhose   Field trousers
Feldjacke (schutzjacke)   Field jacket (Panzer uniform)
Feldkommando   Field command post
Feldmütze   Field cap
Feldpfarrer   Chaplain (army)
Feldpost   Army post office
Feldstiefel   Field service boots
Feldzeug   Ordnance
Festung   Fortress
Firma   Firm, company
Flasche   Bottle, flask
Freiherr   Approximately Baron. A comparatively low-ranking title of nobility. Generally old military nobility, especially in Bavaria and Austria. Title was normally written between Christian and family names
Freiwilliger   Volunteer
Frontführung   Military leadership
Fronturlaubzüge   Front leave special train
Führer   Leader

Führer und Reichskanzler   The Leader and Chancellor of the Reich, Adolf Hitler
Führungshauptamt   Operational headquarters
Fuss   Foot
Fussbekleidung   Footwear
Gamaschen   Gaiters, leggings
Garnison   A garrison
Gas   Gas (poison)
Gasabwehrdienst   Chemical Warfare Defence Service
Gasmaske   Gas mask
Gasschutz   Poison gas defence
Gebirgs-Regiment   Mountain regiment
Gefangenschaft   Imprisonment, captivity
Gefolgschaftmitglied   Literally- armed forces followers
Geheime Feldpolizei   Secret Field Police. Officially units under Army control but, by infiltration and personnel supervision to a far reaching degree, was controlled by the S.D. and Gestapo
Gehobener Wetterdienst   Meteorological service
General Gouvernement   Government General of Poland
Genfer Konvention   Geneva Convention
Gericht   Court of Law, tribunal
Gerichtsrat   Literally, court councillor, a permanently appointed judge
Gesellschaftsanzug   Evening dress
Grenze   Border, frontier
Grenzaufsichstelle   Frontier control post or station (Customs guard)
Grenzschutz   Border security, frontier control
Grenzwacht   Frontier guard, reserve border patrol
Gross   Great, big, large
Grossdeutschland   Greater Germany. Name given to élite army formation
Grossergesellschaftsanzug   Full evening dress
Gruppe   Group
Gruppenkommando   Army group headquarters
Grussvorschrift   Regulations on saluting, military or para-military courtesy
Gummimantel   Waterproof overcoat
Gummistoff   Rubberized material
Güterbahnhof   Freight railway yard, goods station
Hafen   Harbour, port
Hakenkreuz   Swastika
Halbschuh   Shoe
Handbekleidung   Gloves, mittens
Handbuch   Hand book, manual
Handschrift   Signature, manuscript, handwriting
Handschriftlich   Written by hand 'in documentary form', autographed
Handschuhe   Gloves
Handwerker   Workman, artisan, craftsman
Hauptamt   Central department. One of the principal sub-divisions of a high administration or command headquarters
Hauptbahnhof   Main or central railway station
Hauptzeugamt   Central ordnance depot
Heer   Army
Heeres-Entlassungsstelle   Army demobilization depot
Heeresbergführer   Army mountain guide
Heeres-Ergänzungsbestimmungen   Army recruiting regulations
Heeresschule für Hunde und Brieftauben   Army School for dogs and carrier pigeons
Heeres-Standort-Verwaltung   Army local garrison administration
Heeresstreifendienst   Army patrol service
Heeresunterkunftsverwaltungs   Army quartering, bivouack-ing and billeting administration
Heeresverpflegungsdienstelle   Army rations and food supply office
Heeres-Waffenamt   Army Ordnance Department
Heimat   'Homeland' in Greater Germany
Heizer   Stoker
Hilfstelle   Auxiliary station
Hoheitsabzeichen   The National Emblem worn as a distinctive badge

Hoheitszeichen   The German National Emblem (the Eagle and Swastika)
Hornist   Bugler
Hose, lang   Long trousers
Husar   Hussar
Infanterie   Infantry
Infanteriegerät   Infantry equipment
Infanterist   Infantry soldier
Inhalt   Content(s)
Inspekteur   Inspector, normally a high ranking controlling executive
Institut   Institute
Intendant   Superintendant
Jäger   Forester, chasseur, rifleman
Jagdkommando   Pursuit or raiding detachment squad or command
Kadett   Cadet
Kameradschafts   Literally, a group or 'Comradeship'
Kammergericht   High tribunal
Kaserne   Barracks
Kaserniert   Permanently in barracks
Katholik   Catholic
Kavallerie   Cavalry
Kleiner Dienstanzug   Undress uniform, informal service dress
Knöpfe   Buttons
Kokarde   Cockade
Kommandant   Commandant
Kommandantur   Commandant's office. Command or commander's headquarters
Kommandeur   Commander, normally a higher commanding officer
Kommando   Detail, command, commando unit, special task detachment
Kommandostab   Operational command headquarters, command post
Kompagnie   Company
Kopfbedeckung   Head-dress
Koppel   Belt
Koppelschloss   Belt buckle
Kraftfahr   Motorized, motor
Kraftfahrer   Driver or operator of a motor vehicle
Kraftfahrschule   Motor transport or driving school
Kraftfahrzeug   Motor vehicle
Kraftrad   Motorcycle
Kraftradfahrer   Motorcyclist
Kraftwagenführer   Driver
Krank   Sick
Krankenhaus   Hospital
Krankenwagen   Ambulance
Kragen   Collar
Kragenpatten   Collar patches
Kriegs   War, duration
Kriegsakademie   Staff College, Military War College
Kriegs-Bekleidungsamt   Wartime clothing bureau
Kriegsberichter   Official war correspondent
Kriegsbetreuungsdienst   Welfare service to the members of the armed forces
Kriegsgefangener   Prisoner-of-war
Kriegsgericht   Court martial
Kriegsgliederung   Order of battle
Kriegsministerium   War Ministry
Kriegsoffiziersanwärter   Officer candidate for temporary wartime commission
Kriegspfarrer   Chaplain to the forces
Kriegsrecht   Martial law
Kriegssonderstrafrechtsverordnung   Special military penal code
Kriegsverwaltung   Military administration in occupied countries

Kriegsverwaltungsabteilung   Military or army Administration section or sub-district control headquarters in occupied countries
Kriegsverwaltungsrat   Official in military administration of occupied countries
Kriegswinterhilfswerk   Wartime winter help collection scheme
Lager   Camp, depot, centre
Landsturm   Secondary reserve (men over 45)
Landwehr   Reserve (men between 35 and 45)
Lang   Long
Lastwagen   Truck, lorry
Lazarett   Hospital, field hospital
Ledermantel   Leather greatcoat
Lederwaren   Leather wear
Legion   Legion
Lehr   Instruction, training
Lichtbild   Photograph
Litzen   Braid
Losungswort   Password
Magazin   Magazine, store, dump, depot
Mantel   Greatcoat
Maschinengewehr   Machinegun
Meister   Master
Meisterschütze   Marksman
Meldeanzug   Reporting uniform
Meldeblatt   Official gazette
Melder   Runner, messenger
Meldestelle   Message centre
Meldung   Message, report
Militär   Military
Militärbefehlshaber   Army commander-in-chief, in occupied country, territory
Militärverwaltungsbeamte   Army administrative official
Mit   With
Mitglied   Member
Mitte   Centre, middle
Motor   Motor
Motorisiert   Motorized
Motorradfahrer   Motorcyclist
Motorzug   Motorized platoon
Museum   Museum
Musikmeister   Band master
Musikzug   Band platoon
Mütze   Cap
Nachrichten   Signal communications (units)
Nachrichtendienst   Intelligence service
Nachschrift   Postscript
Nachschub   Supply service
Nachschubführer   Supply officer of a unit or establishment
Naht   Seam
Nationalsozialistisch   Pertaining to the official German Party, unit or organization which was an integral part *not* of the Reich Government but of the Party only
Nat.Soz.Führungs Offizier   National Socialist indoctrination officer
Nebel   Fog, mist
Nebeltruppen   Smoke troops
Neue Folge   New series; according to a new numbering system, revised sequence
Neuer Art   Of new type (style); as revised
Neue(r) Form   New pattern, in a newly adopted form
Oberkommando des Heeres   High Command of the Army
Oberkommando der Kriegsmarine   High Command of the Navy
Oberkommando der Luftwaffe   High Command of the Air Force
Oberkommando der Wehrmacht   High Command of the Armed Forces
Oberstbefehlshaber der Wehrmacht   Supreme Head of the Armed Forces
Offizier   Officer
Offizieranwärter   Aspirant officer, officer candidate
Originell, original   Original
Qst   East including the Baltic
Österreich   Austria, pre-Hitler designation
Östmark   Original Nazi term for Austria, term was no longer

permitted in official use and was outlawed owing to increased 'Anti-Prussianism' amongst Austrians

Ostpreussen   East Prussia, a province of Prussia
Panzerabwehr   Anti-tank defence
Panzerwagen   Armoured car, tank
Paradeanzug   Parade dress
Patronengürtel   Cartridge belt
Personal   Personnel
Pferd   Horse
Pionier   Engineer, army sapper
Platz   Place, square
Polizei   Police
Portepee   Side arm tassel
Propaganda Kompanie   Propaganda company, composed of uniformed (combatant) war correspondents
Protektorat   The 'Protectorate' of Bohemia and Moravia
Prozent   %, per cent
Prüfer   Examiner
Qualifikation   Qualification
Qualifiziert   Qualified
Radfahr. Radfahrer   Bicycle, bicyclist
Radio   Radio
Rangdienstalter   Rank and seniority, date of seniority or substantiation
Rangabzeichen   Badges of rank
Rathaus   Town or city hall
Regierung   Government, administrative régime
Regiment   Regiment
Reglement   Regulations, manual, text book
Reichskanzlei   Reich Chancellory or Chancery (not to be mistaken for Party Chancery or Chancery of the Führer)
Reichskokade   Cockade, colour emblem of the German Reich
Reichskriegsflagge   Reich War Flag
Reichskriegsgericht   Supreme court of justice of the Wehrmacht
Reichsluftfahrtsministerium   Air Ministry
Reichsparteitag   Yearly National Nazi Party meeting held at *Nürnberg*. Suspended for the duration of the war
Reichsverband Deutscher Offiziere   National Federation of German Officers
Reichsverordnung   A national decree
Reichswehr   Standing German Army of 100,000 troops; existed before 1935
Reiter   Horseman
Reiterabteilung   Cavalry unit
Reiter-Regiment   Cavalry regiment
Reiterstandarte   Cavalry regiment standard
Remonte   Remount
Der Reserve   In the reserve, reserve officer, etc.
Reserve Offizieranwärter   Candidate for reserve officers' commission
Res.Offiz.Anwärter Bewerber   Aspirant for a reserve officers' commission
Ringkragen   Gorget
Ritterkreuz   Knight's Cross to the Iron Cross
Röcke älterer Vorschrift   Old style (pattern) regulation uniform tunic
Rund   Round, circular
Rundbundhose   Belted trousers
Rüstung   Equipment
Säbel   Sabre
Säbelschlaufe   Attachment for carrying a sabre
Sanitäts   Medical (units) or first aid
Sanitäts Reserve Offizierbewerber   Aspirant for a reserve officers' commission in the medical corps
Schiesstand   Rifle range
Schirmmütze   Uniform peaked cap
Schlachtordnung   Battle order
Schmied   Smith
Schnalle   Buckle
Schnur   Cord

Schuh   Boot
Schulterklappe   Shoulder strap
Schulterklappen   Shoulder straps
Schulterklappenknöpfe   Shoulder strap buttons
Schulterstücke   Shoulder straps
Schützenabzeichen   Marksmanship lanyard
Schutzmantel für Kraftradfahrer   Protective overcoat for motorcycle riders
Schutzmütze   Crash helmet (Panzer Beret)
Schwadron   Squadron (cavalry)
Schwalbennester   'Swallows' nests', musicians' wings
Schwarzer Schlips   Black tie
Schwert   Sword
Seite   Page
Seitengewehre   Bayonets, side arm
Selbständig   Independent
Sicherung   Security
Ski   Ski
Socken   Socks
Soldat(en)   Soldier; member of the regular armed forces only
Soldatenkonzentrationslager or *Sonderkonzentrationslager*   Concentration camp for regular armed forces members
Sonder   Special (purpose)
Sonderaktion Wehrmacht   Disciplinary mass action against members of the armed forces. Also recruitment of former concentration camp inmates into the army
Sonderführer   Literally: special task officer. One temporarily holding rank or a higher rank for a special mission
Spaten   Spade
Sperrballon   Barrage balloon
Spielmann   Bandsman
Sporen   Spurs
Sportkleidung   Sports clothing
Sportplatz   Sports ground
Stab   Staff, headquarters administrative cadre
Stabsoffizier   Field officer
Stabsquartier   Headquarters
Stahlhelm   Steel helmet
Stahlhelm Tarnüberzug   Steel helmet camouflage cover
Stammtruppenteil   Tradition unit
Standarten und Fahnen   Standards and flags
Stempel   Stamp, rubber stamp
Stickereien   Embroidery
Stiefelhosen   Breeches
Stoffgamaschen   Gaiters
Stosstrupp   Shock or spear head troops, unit
Sturmpionier   Assault engineer
Sturmriemen   Chin-straps (cords)
S.w.u.—Siehe weiter unten   'see further down' or 'see below'
Tambour   Drummer
Tarnanzug   Camouflage uniform
Tarnjacke   Camouflage smock
Tarnung   Camouflage(-d), pretended
Technic, Technisch   Technic(-al), technique
Teil   Part
Titel   Title
Totenkopf   Death's head
Träger   Carrier
Trikothemd   Tricot shirt
Troddeln   Side arm tassel
Trommel   Side drum
Trompeter   Trumpeter
Trupp   Platoon
Truppen   Troops
Truppendienst   Service with a military unit, as distinct from interior or office duties
Truppenkennzeichen   Unit shoulder strap insignia
Truppenteil   Unit
Überwachung   Supervision, guarding, control
Übungslager   Training ground
Umhang   Cloak
Unter Umstäden   Circumstances permitting
Ungefähr   Approximately, about
Untauglich für Wehrdienst   Unfit for military service

Unter   Under, below
Unterkleidung   Underwear
Untersuchung   Examination, preliminary survey
Urlaub   Leave
Urschriftlich   Original
Verbandpackchentasche   Field dressing pack
Verfügung   Edict, decree, disposition, disposal
Verlag   Publishing house
Verordnungsblatt   Journal, official gazette of decrees
Versailler Vertag   Versailles Treaty
Versetzung   Transfer
Versuch   Attempt, experiment, trial
Verwaltung   Administration
Veterinär   Veterinary
Vor   Before, in front of, for, formerly
Vorgänger   Predecessor
Vorschrift   Regulation
Vortsösse   Piping
Wachanzug   Guard uniform
Wache   Guard, sentry
Wachefüher   Guard commander, NCO in charge of guard platoon or detachment
Wachregiment (Berlin)   (Berlin) Guard Regiment
Wachtdienst   Guard duty
Waffenfähig   Capable of bearing arms, able bodied
Waffengattung   Carrier of arms, arm of service
Waffen und Gerät   Ordnance and equipment
Waffenrock   Uniform tunic
Wappenschilder   Helmet and sun-helmet transfers or escutcheons
Wehrkreis   Military District
Wehrmacht   German armed forces
Wehrmacht Propaganda   Armed forces propaganda
Wehrmachtsauskuntstelle   Armed forces information bureau
Wehrmacht-Uniform-Bezugschein   Armed forces uniform clothing coupon
Wehrmacht Verwaltungs Vorschrift   Armed forces administrative regulations
Wehrsatzwesen   Armed forces depot or replacement and training system
Wehrunwürdig   'Deemed unworthy of the privilege to bear arms or to serve'
Weisser Rock   White tunic
Weisser Rock n/A.   White tunic new style (art)
Weisser Rock für Offiziere und Wehrmachtbeamte im Offizierrang   White tunic for officers and administrative officials with officers' rank
Werfer   Projector
Wetterschutz Umhang   Weather proof cape
Widrig   Illegal, against, contrary
Windjacke   Wind jacket
Winkel   NCO's rank chevron
Winterhilfswerk   Official German winter relief organization
Zug   A platoon
Zur Verwendung (Verfügung)   Special purpose, for special assignments, at disposal

6.3. General Glossary: English/German

Acorn'   Eichel
Adjutant, or aide   Adjutant
Adjutants' cords   Adjutantenabzeichen, Adjutantenschnur
Administration   Verwaltung
Aiguillette   Achselband
Air Ministry (German)   Reichsluftfahrtsministerium
Aluminium   Aluminium
Ambulance   Krankenwagen
Anchor   Anker

Anti-tank defence   Panzerabwehr
Approximately, about   Ungefähr
Arabic (figures)   Arabisch
Archive   Archiv
Arm badge   Armspiegel, Ärmelabzeichen
Arm chevron   Armwinkel
Armed forces administrative regulations   Wehrmacht Verwaltungs Vorschrift
Armed forces depot or replacement and training system   Wehrsatzwesen
Armed forces followers   Gefolgschaftmitglied
Armed forces information bureau   Wehrmachtsauskunftstelle
Armed forces propaganda   Wehrmacht Propaganda
Armed forces uniform clothing coupon   Wehrmacht-Uniform-Bezugschein
Arm pattern   Ärmelpatten
Army   Heer
Army administration department   Amtsverwaltungs-Department
Army administrative official   Militärverwaltungsbeamte
Army Commander-in-Chief, in occupied country or territory   Militärbefehlshaber
Army demobilization depot   Heeres-Entlassungsstelle
Army group headquarters   Gruppenkommando
Army local garrison administration   Heeres-Standort-Verwaltung
Army mountain guide   Heeresbergführer
Army ordnance department   Heeres-Waffenamt
Army patrol service   Heeres-Streifendienst
Army post office   Feldpost
Army quartering, bivouacking and billeting administration   Heeresunterkunftsverwaltungs
Army rations and food supply office   Heeres-Ergänzungsbestimmungen
Army School for Dogs and Carrier Pigeons   Heeresschule für Hunde und Brieftauben
Arrangement, plan   Anlage
Artillery   Artillerie
Aspirant or candidate   Anwärter
Aspirant officer, officer candidate   Offizieranwärter
Aspirant for a reserve officers' commission   Reserve Offizier Anwärter Bewerber
Aspirant for a reserve officers' commission in the medical corps   Sanitäts Reserve Offizierbewerber
Assault Engineer   Sturmpionier
Attachment for carrying a sabre   Säbelschlaufe
Austria   (a) Österreich, pre-Hitler designation (b) Östmark, the original National Socialist term for Austria
Authority, office, competent bureau   Behörde
Auxiliary station   Hilfstelle
Badge cloth   Abzeichentuch
Badge, distinctive sign, insignia or decoration   Abzeichen
Badges of rank   Rangabzeichen
Band master   Musikmeister
Band platoon   Musikzug
Bandsman   Spielmann
Baron   Freiherr
Barracks   Kaserne, Barracke
Barrage balloon   Sperrballon
Battalion   Bataillon
Battery   Batterie
Battle order   Schlachtordnung
Bayonets, side arms   Seitengewehre
Before, in front of, for, formerly   Vor
Belt   Koppel
Belt buckle   Koppelschloss
Belted trousers   Rundbundhose
Bicycle, bicyclist   Radfahr, Radfahrer
Binoculars   Doppelfernröhre
Black tie   Schwarzer Schlips
Blood Order, an NSDAP decoration   Blutorden

Bohemia and Moravia—the Protectorate   Böhmen und Mähren
Boot   Schuh
Border, frontier   Grenze
Border security, frontier control   Grenzschutz
Bottle, flask   Flasche
Braid   Litzen, Borte
Bread-bag   Brotbeutel
Breeches   Stiefelhosen, Breecheshose
Buckle   Schnalle
Bugler   Hornist
Bureau, office, section   Büro
Buttons   Knöpfe
Cadet   Kadett
Cadet normally on active duty. A non-commissioned officer. Aspirant from the ranks   Fahnenjunker
Camouflage   Tarnung
Camouflage smock   Tarnjacke
Camouflage uniform   Tarnanzug
Camp, depot, centre   Lager
Candidate for reserve officers' commission   Reserve Offizieranwärter
Cap   Mütze
Capable of bearing arms, able-bodied   Waffenfähig
Carrier   Träger
Carrier of arms, arm of service   Waffengattung
Cartridge belt   Patronengürtel
Catholic   Katholik
Cavalry   Kavallerie
Cavalry   Reiter
Cavalry regiment   Reiter Regiment
Cavalry unit   Reiter-Abteilung
Central department' One of the principal sub-divisions of a high administration or command headquarters   Hauptamt
Central ordnance depot   Hauptzeugamt
Centre, middle   Mitte
Chaplain   Feldpfarrer
Chemical Warfare Defence Service   Gasabwehrdienst
Chief   Chef
Chief of the General Staff   Chef des Generalstabes
Chin-straps (cords)   Sturmriemen
Circumstances permitting   Unter Umständen
Cloak   Umhang
Clothing, pertaining to uniforms or attire   Bekleidung
Cockade   Kokarde
Collar   Kragen
Collar patches   Kragenpatten
Commandant   Kommandant
Commandant's office. Command or commanders' headquarters   Kommandantur
Command, detail, commando unit, special task detachment   Kommando
Command post, operational command headquarters   Kommandostab
Commander. Normally a higher commanding officer   Kommandeur
Commander, generally a higher commander, chief of a larger unit, commander-in-chief   Befehlshaber
Commemoration armlet   Erinnerungsband
'Comradeship' or group   Kameradschafts
Company   Kompagnie
Concentration camp for regular armed forces members   Soldatenkonzentrationslager or Sonderkonzentrationslager
Content(s)   Inhalt
Cord   Schnur
Court councillor, a permanently appointed judge   Gerichtsrat
Court martial   Kriegsgericht
Court of law, tribunal   Gericht
Craftsman, workman, artisan   Handwerker
Cuff-facing pattern   Ärmelaufschlag
Cuff-titles   Ärmelstreifen

Dagger   Dolch
Death's Head   Totenkopf
Decoration, distinction   Auszeichnung, Ehrenzeichen
'Deemed unworthy of the privilege to bear arms or to serve'   Wehrunwürdig
Denim, strong ticking   Drillich
Description   Beschreibung
Detraining or detrucking officer or commissioner   Auslade-kommissar
Disciplinary mass action against members of the armed forces. Also recruitment of former concentration camp inmates into the army   Sonderaktion Wehrmacht
District command   Bezirkskommando
Division   Division
Dragoon   Dragoner
Driver   Fahrer
Driver or operator of a motor vehicle   Kraftfahrer
Drummer   Tambour
Eagle   Adler
East, including the Baltic   Ost
East Prussia, a province of Prussia   Ostpreussen
Edict, decree, disposition, disposal   Verfügung
Elite   Elite
Embroidery   Stickereien
Enemy   Feind
Engineer, army sapper   Pionier
Equipment   Ausrüstung, Rüstung
Escort battalion   Begleitbattallion
Evangelical or Protestant   Evangelisch
Examination, preliminary survey   Untersuchung
Examiner   Prüfer
Factory, works, plant   Fabrik
Fatigue dress   Arbeitsanzug
Field   Feld
Field blouse   Feldbluse
Field blouse with piping, Piped Field-Service Tunic for Officers   Feldbluse mit Vorstössen
Field cap   Feldmütze
Field command post   Feldkommando
Field dress   Feldanzug
Field dressing pack   Verbandpackchentasche
Field equipment   Feldausrüstung
Field-grey   Feldgrau
Field jacket (Panzer Uniform)   Feldjacke (Schutzjacke)
Field Officer   Stabsoffizier
Field service belt   Feldbinde
Field service boots   Feldstiefel
Field trousers   Feldhose
Firm, company   Firma
Flags and standards   Fahnen und Standarten
Fog, mist   Nebel
Foot   Fuss
Footwear   Fussbekleidung
Formation for special tasks   Einsatzgruppe
Fortification   Befestigung
Fortress   Festung
Frontier control post or station (customs guard)   Grenzauf-sichstelle
Frontier guard, reserve border patrol   Grenzwacht
Front leave special train   Fronturlaubzüge
Gaiters, leggings   Gamaschen, Stoffgamaschen
Garrison   Garnison
Garrison crew   Besatzung
Gas (poison)   Gas
Gas defence   Gasschutz
Gas mask   Gasmaske
General army equipment   Allgemeines Heeresgerät
Geneva Convention   Genfer Konvention
German (to designate a German National)   Deutsch(es)
German armed forces   Wehrmacht
German army of 100,000 troops which existed before 1935   Reichswehr
German postal service or system   Deutsche Reichspost
German Red Cross   Deutsches Rotes Kreuz
Gloves, mittens   Handbekleidung, Handschuhe

Goods station, freight railway yard   Güterbahnhof
Gorget   Ringkragen
Government adminstrative regime   Regierung
Government General of Poland   General Gouvernement
Great, big, large   Gross
Greatcoat   Mantel
Greater Germany, name given to élite army formation
    'Grossdeutschland'
Group   Gruppe
Guard commander, NCO in charge of guard platoon or
    detachment   Wacheführer
Guard duty   Wachtdienst
Guard of Honour   Ehrenwache
Guard Regiment (Berlin)   Wachregiment (Berlin)
Guard, sentry   Wache
Guard uniform   Wachanzug
Hand book, manual   Handbuch
Harbour, port   Hafen
Head-dress   Kopfbedeckung
Headquarters   Stabsquartier
High Command of the Armed Forces   Oberkommando der
    Wehrmacht
High Command of the Airforce   Oberkommando der Luft-
    waffe
High Command of the Army   Oberkommando des Heeres
High Command of the Navy   Oberkommando der Kriegs-
    marine
High tribunal   Kammergericht
'Homeland' in Greater Germany   Heimat
Honorary rank. A title given to a person holding a rank prior
    to confirmation and still receiving a lower rank's pay
    Charakterisiert
Horse   Pferd
Horse drawn   Bespannt
Hospital, field hospital   Lazarett, Krankenhaus
Hussar   Husar
Identification disc   Erkennungsmarke
Illegal, against, contrary   Widrig
Imprisonment, captivity   Gefangenschaft
Independent   Selbständig
Infantry   Infanterie
Infantry equipment   Infanteriegerät
Infantry soldier   Infanterist
Inspector, normally a high ranking controlling executive
    Inspekteur
Institute   Institut
Instruction, training   Lehr
Intelligence service   Nachrichtendienst
Interpreter   Dolmetscher
Iron Cross   Eisernes Kreuz
Issue, edition   Ausgabe
Journal, official gazette of decrees   Verordnungsblatt
Knight's Cross to the Iron Cross   Ritterkreuz
Lapel   Brustklappe
Leader   Führer
The Leader and Chancellor of the Reich (Adolf Hitler)
    Führer und Reichskanzler
Leather greatcoat   Ledermantel
Leather wear   Lederwaren
Leave   Urlaub
Legion   Legion
Lightning   Blitz
Long   Lang
Lorry, truck   Lastwagen
Mace or baton for Drum Major   Bataillonstambourstock
Machinegun   Maschinengewehr
Magazine, store, dump, depot   Magazin
Main or central railway station   Hauptbahnhof
Marksman   Meisterschütze
Marksmanship lanyard   Schützenabzeichen
Martial law   Kriegsrecht.
Master   Meister

Medical (units) or first aid   Sanitäts
Member   Mitglied
Message centre   Meldestelle
Message, report   Meldung
Messenger, runner   Melder
Metal fittings, horse shoeing   Beschlag
Meteorological service   Gehobener Wetterdienst
Military   Militär
Military administration in occupied countries   Kriegsver-
    waltung
Military or army administration section or sub-district control
    headquarters in occupied countries   Kriegsverwaltungs-
    abteilung
Military district   Wehrkreis
Military leadership   Frontführung
Motor   Motor
Motorcycle   Kraftrad
Motorcyclist   Kraftradfahrer
Motorized, motor   Kraftfahr
Motorized platoon   Motorzug
Motor transport or driving school   Kraftfahrschule
Motor vehicle   Kraftfahrzeug
Mountain   Berg
Mountain regiment   Gebirgs-Regiment
Mounted on horseback   Beritten
Museum   Museum
National decree   Reichsverordnung
National Emblem worn as a distinctive badge   Hoheits-
    abzeichen
National Emblem, the Eagle and Swastika   Hoheitszeichen
National Federation of German Officers   Reichsverband
    Deutscher Offiziere
National Socialist indoctrination officer   Nat.Soz. Führungs
    Offizier
NCO's rank chevron   Winkel
New pattern, in a newly adopted form   Neue(r) form
New series, according to a new numbering system, revised
    sequence   Neue Folge
New type (style), as revised   Neuer Art.
Oakleaf surround (to the Reichskokarde)   Eichenlaubkranz
Oakleaves   Eichenlaub
Office, authority, duty station   Dienststelle
Officer   Offizier
Officer candidate for temporary wartime commission   Kriegs-
    offizieranwärter
Official gazette   Meldeblatt
Official in military administration of occupied countries
    Kriegsverwaltungsrat
Official journal, register or gazette   Amtsblatt
Official Service Regulations   Dienstvorschrift
Official war correspondent   Kriegsberichter
Old style (pattern) regulation uniform tunic   Röcke älterer
    Vorschrift
Old type (as formerly in use), obsolete according to previously
    prescribed or customary manner   Alter Art.
Operational headquarters   Führungshauptamt
Order of Battle   Kriegsgliederung
Orders and regulations pertaining to uniform and dress (of
the day; of a specific command; for a specific formation)
    Anzugordnung
Ordnance   Feldzeug
Ordnance and equipment   Waffen und Gerät
Original   Originell, original, urschriftlich
Out of use, retired   Ausser Verwendung (a.V.)
Page   Seite
Panzer Beret, crash helmet   Schutzmütze
Paper, a   Blatt
Parade dress   Paradeanzug
Part   Teil
Password   Losungswort
Per cent, %   Prozent
Permanently in barracks   Kaserniert
Personnel   Personal
Photograph   Lichtbild
Physician, surgeon, doctor of medicine   Arzt

Piping   Vorstösse
Place, square   Platz
Platoon   Trupp, Zug
Police   Polizei
Postscript   Nachschrift
Predecessor   Vorgänger
Prisoner-of-war   Kriegsgefangener
Projector   Werfer
Propaganda company, composed of uniformed (combatant) war correspondents   Propaganda Kompanie
Protective overcoat for motorcycle riders   Schutzmantel für Kraftradfahrer
'Protectorate' of Bohemia and Moravia   Protektorat
Publishing house   Verlag
Pursuit or raiding detachment squad or command   Jagdkommando
Qualification   Qualifikation
Qualified   Qualifiziert
Radio   Radio
Railway   Eisenbahn
Railway officer   Eisenbahnoffizier
Railway station   Bahnhof
Rank   Dienstgrad
Rank and seniority, date of seniority or substantiation   Rangdienstälter
Rank insignia, for men   Dienstgradabzeichen
Reconnaissance   Aufklärung
Recruiting offices and replacement centres   Ergänzungstelle
Re-employed retired officer   Ergänzungsoffizier
Regiment   Regiment
Regulation   Vorschrift
Regulations governing the training of a formation   Ausbildungsvorschrift
Regulations, manual, text book   Reglement
Regulations on saluting, military or para-military courtesy   Grussvorschrift
Reich Chancellory or Chancery   Reichskanzlei
Reichs War Flag   Reichskriegsflagge
Remount   Remonte
Replacement   Ergänzung
Replacement Field Cap   Einheitsfeldmütze
Replacement unit   Ergänzungseinheiten
Reporting uniform   Meldeanzug
Reserve   Beurlaubstand
Reserve—men between 35 and 45   Landwehr
Reserve officer, in the reserve   Der Reserve Offizier
Reserve, one in the state of permanent leave, an officer in the reserve   Des Beurlaubtenstandes
Reserve, replacement   Ersatz
Reserve, secondary, men over 45   Landsturm
Retired, on the inactive list, out of service   Ausser Dienst (a.D.)
Rifleman, forester, chasseur   Jäger
Rifle range   Schiesstand
Round, circular   Rund
Rubberized material   Gummistoff
Sabre   Sabel
Salute, to the cap, military style   Militarische Gruss
Salute, National Socialist style   Deutscher Gruss
Seal and stamp, official   Dienstsiegel und Dienststempel
Seam   Naht
Secret Field Police   Geheime Feldpolizei
Security   Sicherung
'see further down' or 'see below'   s.w.u. Siehe weiter unten
Service directives   Dienstanweisung
Service dress   Dienstanzug
Service, duty   Dienst
Service Overcoat   Dienstmantel
Service Tunic   Dienstrock
Service with a military unit   Truppendienst
Shock or spear head troops, unit   Stosstrupp
Shoe   Halbschuh

Shoulder strap buttons   Schulterklappenknöpfe
Shoulder straps   Schulterklappen, Schulterstücke
Sick   Krank
Side arm tassel   Troddel, Portepee
Side drum   Trommel
Signal communications (units)   Nachrichten
Signature, manuscript, handwriting   Handschrift
Ski   Ski
Smith   Schmied
Smoke troops   Nebeltruppen
Socks   Socken
Soldier, member of the regular armed forces only   Soldat(en)
Spade   Spate
Special (purpose)   Sonder
Special purpose, for special assignments, at disposal   Zur Verwendung (Verfügung)
Special instructions   Besondere Anordnungen
Special military penal code   Kriegssonderstrafrechtverordnung
Special task detachment   Einsatzkommando
Special task officer, specialist officer   Sonderführer
Sports clothing   Sportkleidung
Sports ground   Sportplatz
Spurs   Sporen
Squadron, cavalry   Schwadron
Staff College, Military War College   Kriegsakademie
Staff, headquarters administrative cadre   Stab
Stamp, rubber stamp   Stempel
Standards and flags   Standarten und Fahnen
Steel helmet   Stahlhelm
Steel helmet camouflage cover   Stahlhelm Tarnüberzug
Stoker   Heizer
Superintendent   Intendant
Supervision, guarding, control   Überwachung
Supplement, annexe, additional leaflet or folder   Beiheft
Supplementary reservists   Ergänzungsmannschaften
Supplementary sheet, amendment to regulations   Deckblatt
Supply officer of a unit or establishment   Nachschubführer
Supply service   Nachschub
Supreme court of justice in the Wehrmacht   Reichskriegsgericht
Supreme Head of the Armed Forces   Obersterbefehlshaber der Wehrmacht
'Swallows' nests', musicians' wings   Schwalbennester
Swastika   Hakenkreuz
Sword   Schwert
Tank, armoured car   Panzerwagen
Task force   Einsatztruppe
Technic(al), technique   Technik, technisch
Title   Titel
Town or city hall   Rathaus
Tradition badges (caps)   Erinnerungsabzeichen
Tradition unit   Stammtruppenteil
Training ground   Übungslager
Training ground, drill ground   Exerzierplatz
Transfer   Versetzung
Transfers, escutcheons, on the steel helmet and sun-helmet   Wappenschilder
Trial, experiment, attempt   Versuch
Tricot shirt   Trikothemd
Troops   Truppen
Trousers   Bekleider
Trousers, long   Hose, lang
Trumpeter   Trompeter
Under, below   Unter
Underwear   Unterkleidung
Undress uniform, informal service dress   Kleiner Dienstanzug
Unfit for military service   Untauglich für Wehrdienst
Uniform peaked cap   Schirmmütze
Uniform tunic   Waffenrock
Unit   Truppenteil, Einheit
Unit shoulder strap insignia   Truppenkennzeichen
Unload, unloading, detraining   Ausladen, Ausladung
Versailles Treaty   Versailler Vertrag

Veterinary   Veterinär
Volume   Band
Volunteer   Freiwilliger
Walking-out dress   Ausgehanzug
War, duration   Kriegs
War Ministry   Kriegsministerium
Wartime clothing bureau   Kriegsbekleidungsamt
Wartime organization   Kriegsorganisation
Wartime winter help collection scheme   Kriegswinterhilfs-
   werk
Waterproof overcoat   Gummimantel
Weapons, ordnance   Waffen, Waffenwesen
Weatherproof cape   Wetterschutz Umhang
Welfare service to the members of the armed forces   Kriegs-
   betreungsdienst
White tunic   Weisser Rock
White tunic new style (art)   Weisser Rock n/A
Wind jacket   Windjacke
Winter relief organization, the official German   Winterhilfs-
   werk
With   Mit
Written by hand, 'in documentary form', autographed   Hand-
   schriftlich

7. Bibliography

7.1. Primary sources

The following are those books and periodicals that the author considers to be of importance, all having a direct bearing on the subjects discussed in this work.

EBERHARDT, Dr. Fritz; *Militärisches Wörterbuch*, Alfred Kröner Verlag, Stuttgart, 1940.

EHRLICH, Dr. Curt; *Uniformen und Soldaten—Ein Bilbericht vom Ehrenkleid unserer Wehrmacht.* Verlag Erich Klinghammer, Berlin, 1942.

ERLAM, Denys; *Ranks & Uniforms of the German Army—Navy—Air-Force. Collected from German semi-official sources and largely based upon 'Uniformen der Deutschen Wehrmacht' by Eberhard Hettler of the German Air Ministry.* Seeley Service & Co., Ltd., London, c. 1939.

HAID, Hauptmann Georg; *Ein Buch vom Neuen Heer.* Franckh'sche Verlagshandlung W. Keller & Co., Stuttgart, 1935.

HETTLER, Eberhard; *Uniformen der Deutschen Wehrmacht —Heer, Kriegsmarine, Luftwaffe, mit Zeichnungen von Herbert Knötel, Paul Pietsch, Egon Jantke.* Uniformen-Markt. Verlag Otto Dietrich, Berlin, c. 1938.

HETTLER, Eberhard; *Nachtrag 1939/1940 zu Uniformen der Deutschen Wehrmacht —Heer, Kriegsmarine, Luftwaffe, mit Zeichnungen Paul Pietsch. Das Hauptwerk enthält auch Zeichnungen von Herbert Knötel und Egon Jantke.* Uniformen-Markt Verlag Otto Dietrich, Berlin, c. 1940.

HIDDEMANN, Schneidermeister Fritz; *Uniform-Massschneidern für die Wehrmacht, —Eine Fachkunde auf der Grundlage der ämtlichen Bekleidungs Vorschriften.* Verlag und Druck von B. G. Teubner in Leipzig und Berlin, 1938.

KLEITMANN, Dr. K. G.; *Die Deutsche Wehrmacht, —Uniform und Ausrüstung 1934–1945. Band I und Band II.* Verlag Die Ordenssammlung, Berlin.

KLEITMANN, Dr. K. G.; *Feldgrau, —Zeitschrift für neuzeitliche Wehrgeschichte Organisation, Uniformierung, Bewaffnung und Ausrüstung.* Redaktion Dr. Kleitmann. Verlag Die Ordens-Sammlung, Berlin. January/February 1967 to date.

KROLLMANN, Friedrich; *Langenscheidts Fachwörterbuch Wehrwesen/Langenscheidt's Dictionary of Military Terms—English-German, German-English.* Langenscheidt, KG.Verlagbuchhandling Berlin-Schoneberg, 1957.

LITTLEJOHN, David M.A., A.L.A. and DODKINS, Colonel C.M., D.S.O., O.B.E.; *Orders, Decorations, Medals and Badges of the Third Reich (including the Free City of Danzig).* R. James Bender Publishing, Mountain View, California, 1968.

REIBERT, Oberstleutnant Dr. W.; *Der Dienst-Unterricht im Heere.* E. S. Mittler & Sohn, Berlin for years from 1935 to 1943.

ROEDER, Oberst von (OKW) und LEHMANN-HEINECKE, Major (OKW); *Der Soldatenfreund —Taschenjahrsbuch für die Wehrmacht mit Kalendarium für 1942. Ausgabe A: Heer.* Bearbeitet unter Verwendung ämtlichen Materials von Oberst v. Roeder (OKW) und Major Lehmann-Heinecke (OKW). Adolf Sponholz Verlag, Hannover, 1942.

SCHIRMER, Friedrich and WIENER, Dr. Fritz (editors); *Feldgrau —Mittleilungen einer Arbeitsgemeinschaft Feldgrau 1953–1966.*

TAYLOR, Telford; *Sword and Swastika, —Generals and Nazis in the Third Reich.* Simon & Schuster, New York, 1952.

TAYLOR, Telford; *The March of Conquest, —The German Victories in Western Europe, 1940.* Simon & Schuster, New York, 1958.

TRANSFELDT, Walter and BRAND, Karl Hermann Freiherr von; *Wort und Brauch im Deutschen Heer, —Geschichtliche und sprachkundliche Betrachtungen über Gebräuche, Begriffe und Bezeichnungen des deutschen Heeres in Vergangenheit und Gegenwart. Mit Bildern von Richard und Herbert Knötel, Alfred Gay, Joachim von Roebel, Klaus-Dieter Schack, Willy Schubert u.a.* Helmut Gerhard Schulz, Hamburg, 1967.

WARLIMONT, Walter; *Inside Hitler's Headquarters, 1939–1945. Translated from the German by R. H. Barry.* Weidenfeld and Nicholson, London, 1964.

WESTARP, E. J. Graf von; *Oertzenscher Taschenkalender für die Offiziere des Heeres.* Fruher-Farcks. E. J. Graf v.Westarp. 1.Okt.1940—Sept.30.1941.

WILLEMER, Wilhelm; *Camouflage* by Wilhelm Willemer, Oberst a.D. with a foreword by Franz Halder, Generaloberst a.D. 'Camouflage' Foreign Military Studies, Historical Division, Headquarters, U.S. Army Europe, 1954. MS No.P-130.

Allgemeine Heeresmitteilungen, —Herausgegeben vom Oberkommando des Heeres. Published by (Schriftleitung und Verlag:) Oberkommando des Heeres, Abt., für Allgemeine Truppenangelegenheiten/ Schriftleitung, Berlin. All years from 1935 to 1945.

Anzugordnung für das Reichsheer, (H.A.O.) H.Dv.122. Abschnitt A, von 14.Nov.1934. Verlag Offene Worte, Berlin 1934.

C. I. Handbook Germany, Published by the Office of Assistant Chief of Staff G.2. Counter-Intelligence, sub-division Evaluation and Dissemination Section, October 1944. SHAEF.

Das Geschicht des Deutschen Soldaten —Herausgegeben vom Oberkommando der Wehrmacht. Zeitgeschichte-Verlag Berlin, 1943.

Deutsches Soldatenjahrbuch, —Achtzehnter Deutscher Soldatenkalender. 1957 to 1970. Schild Verlag, München, West Germany.

Deutsche Uniformen-Zeitschrift, Combining *Schwert und Spaten* und *Uniformen-Markt.*

Die Wehrmacht —Herausgegeben vom Reichskriegsministerium. Verlag die Wehrmacht GmbH, Berlin, 1935(?)—1945.

Die Deutsche Wehrmacht, —Herausgegeben vom Cigaretten-Bilderdienst, Dresden, c. 1938.

Handbook on German Military Forces, U.S. War Department. War Department Technical Manual, TM-E 30-451, 15.March 1945, Washington, U.S.A.

Heeres-Kalender, Kohlers Illustrierter, Deutschland in Waffen 1943. Wilhelm Kohler Verlag, Minden (Westfalen) 1943.

Heeres-Verordnungsblatt, —Herausgegeben vom Oberkommando der Heeres. E. S. Mittler & Sohn, Berlin. All years from 1933 to 1945.

Heeresverwaltungs-Taschenbuch, —Hand-und Nachschlagerbuch über Verwaltungsangelegenheiten für den Deutschen Soldaten und Heeresbeamten 1940— 1941. Mit Genehmigung des Oberkommandos des Heeres. Herausgeben von M.Schreiber. Amtsrat beim Oberkommando des Heeres. 1.April 1940—31. März 1941. Verlag Alfred Waberg, Grimmen in Pommern.

Jahrbuch des Deutschen Heeres-1942 —Herausgegeben vom Oberkommando der Wehrmacht. Bearbeiter Major Judeich. Verlag von Breitkopf & Hartel in Leipzig. 1942. (Other years include 1936, 1937, 1938, 1939, 1940, 1941).

Joint Army and Navy Publication—Uniforms and Insignia (J.A.N.1), Assistant Chief of Staff, G-2, and Director of Naval Intelligence.

Schwert und Spaten, —Älteste deutsche Fachzeitschrift der gesamten Ausrüstungs-Industrie für Heer, Luftwaffe, Kriegsmarine, Reichsarbeitsdienst, Körperschaften, Organisationen und Verbände. 'Schwert und Spaten', Berlin.

Signal. Ministry of Propaganda/Deutscher Verlag, Berlin, 1939—1945.

Soldaten—Ein Bildbuch vom Neuen Heer by Max Burcharz, Hanseatische Verlaganstalt Hamburg, 1935.

Taschen-Brockhaus zum Zeitgeschehen, Verlag F.A. Brockhaus, Leipzig, 1942.

'Uniformen-Markt, —Fachzeitung der gesamten Uniformen—, Ausrüstungs—, Effekten—, Fahnen—, Paramenten—, Orden-und Abzeichenbranche. Mitteilungsblatt der Fachuntergruppen Uniform-Industrie, Uniform-Ausstattungs-Industrie, Mützen-Industrie, Fahnenhersteller und der Fachabteilung Mützen-Zutaten-Industrie. Verlag Otto Dietrich, Berlin.

Uniformen und Abzeichen des Heeres, Moritz Ruhl, Kunst— Verlag, Leipzig, various years.

7.2. Secondary sources

These consist almost entirely of illustrated publications and, as such, form a very useful source of photographic reference.

CARELL, Paul; *Invasion —They're Coming,* —The German account of the Allied Landings and the eighty days battle for France. Translated from the German by Ewald Osers. George G. Harrap & Co. Ltd. 1962.

CARELL, Paul; *Hitler's War on Russia,* —The Story of the German Defeat in the East. Translated from the German by Ewald Osers, George G. Harrap & Co. Ltd. 1964.

CARELL, Paul; *Scorched Earth,* —Hitler's War on Russia. Vol.2. Translated from the German by Ewald Osers. George G. Harrap & Co. Ltd, 1970.

CARELL, Paul; *Der Russlandkrieg,* —Fotografiert von Soldaten der Bildband zu 'Unternehmen Barbarossa' und 'Verbrannte Erde'. Verlag Ullstein GmbH. Berlin/ Frankfurt-am-Main/Wien, 1967.

HAUPT, Werner; *Der Kampf im Nordabschnitt der Ostfront,* —Heeresgruppe Nord 1941—1945. Eine Bilddokumentation. Podzun Verlag, Bad Nauheim 1967.

HOFFMANN, Professor Heinrich; *Mit Hitler in Polen.* Zeitgeschichte-Verlag, Wilhelm Andermann, Berlin, c. 1940.

HOFFMANN, Professor Heinrich; *Mit Hitler in Westen.* Zeitgeschichte-Verlag, Wilhelm Andermann, Berlin, c. 1941.

SCHEIBERT, Horst and WAGENER, Carl; *Die Deutsche Panzertruppe, 1939—1945 Eine Dokumentation in Bildern.* Podzun Verlag, Bad Nauheim, 1966.

SCHEIBERT, Horst; *Deutsche Panzergrenadiere, 1939—1945. Eine Dokumentation in Bildern.* Podzun Verlag Dorheim, 1968.